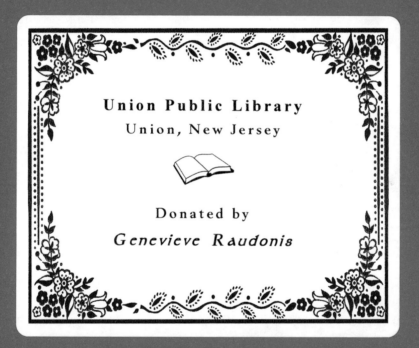

AMERICAN
HORTICULTURAL
SOCIETY

HOMEGROWN
HARVEST

AMERICAN
HORTICULTURAL
SOCIETY

HOMEGROWN
HARVEST

A season-by-season guide to a sustainable kitchen garden

RITA PELCZAR
EDITOR IN CHIEF

MITCHELL BEAZLEY

HOMEGROWN HARVEST
Editor-in-chief: Rita Pelczar
American Horticultural Society

First published in Great Britain in 2009 by Mitchell Beazley,
a division of Octopus Publishing Group Ltd,
189 Shaftesbury Avenue, London WC2H 8JY
An Hachette Livre UK Company
www.octopusbooks.co.uk

This revised American edition was published in 2010 in association
with the American Horticultural Society

American Horticultural Society
Project director: David J. Ellis
Coordinating art director: Mary Yee

Commissioning editor: Helen Griffin
Art director: Pene Parker
Senior art editor: Juliette Norsworthy
Designer: Lizzie Ballantyne
Copy editor: Joanna Chisholm
Production controller: Susan Meldrum
Proofreader: Caroline Bentley
Indexer: Michèle Clarke

A Cataloging-in-Publication record for this book is available
from the Library of Congress

ISBN 978-1-84533-560-1

Set in Caecilia, Frutiger, Glypha, and Interstate

Printed in China
Repro House Singapore

| contents

| Foreword

Not since the Victory Gardens of World War II has there been such a resurgence of interest in growing fruits, vegetables, and herbs as has occurred over the last few years in North America. The trend has manifested itself in a huge increase in people growing food at home, heightened interest in community gardens, and an upsurge in sales of vegetable seeds and cell packs of seedlings from mail-order retailers, garden centers, and farmer's markets.

According to a survey conducted by the Garden Writers Association, a national organization for garden communicators, in 2009 nearly eight million American households grew edible plants for the first time. In addition, one third of established gardeners reported growing more edibles in 2009 than in the previous year.

This exciting development appears to be the confluence of a number of different factors, including the locavore movement that encourages people to seek out local—and often organic—sources for their food, people growing their own food to help lower their grocery bills, and environmentally conscious younger adults who are looking to reestablish their connection to the natural world and become more self-reliant. Recent studies documenting the health benefits of eating fresh fruits and vegetables may also be influencing this trend.

Whatever the causes, this renaissance in vegetable and food gardening is very encouraging. As an organization whose primary mission is to connect people to plants and gardens, we at the American Horticultural Society (AHS) believe it is critical to both maintain the momentum and to get even more people involved in growing their own food. The best way to help new gardeners enjoy success, we feel, is by providing good basic information on growing food plants, from starting seeds to harvesting and preserving the garden's bounty.

That's what we have accomplished with this book, which offers authoritative, yet easy-to-use advice for people living in temperate regions throughout North America. The book is organized on a season-by-season format to make planning and implementing the garden as easy as possible. The sections walk you through the process of preparing the garden site, selecting edible plants appropriate to your site and region, starting seeds and taking care of young plants, planting and caring for the edibles (without reliance on toxic pesticides, of course), and then enjoying the bountiful harvest.

Of course the timing of gardening activities, particularly at the beginning and end of the growing season, depends on where you live. *Homegrown Harvest* therefore highlights major differences among cold-winter, mid-temperate, and mild-winter regions throughout the book and includes regional sowing and harvesting charts for vegetables.

In addition to the basic information on how to grow common crops are ideas for expanding your edible horizons—and your cuisine—such as trying tasty, native North American fruits; growing and using edible flowers; and planting a pesto garden. And to ensure that you can enjoy your harvest into the winter months, look for tips on extending the growing season and storing your crops. The more than 400 color photographs show step-by-step procedures for a number of garden tasks and offer inspirational views of different garden designs and delicious edibles.

We hope this book will awaken—or rekindle—your interest in growing vegetables, fruits, and herbs, and that it will provide an opportunity for parents and grandparents to share the joys of growing edible plants with the next generation of gardeners. Enjoy it and the connection with the earth that it will nurture, and pass your experience and knowledge along to family, friends, and neighbors.

Tom Underwood
Executive Director of the American Horticultural Society
(to learn more about the AHS, visit www.ahs.org)

FIGS ARE A LOW-MAINTENANCE—*not to mention delicious—fruit (above left) to try in your garden. The trees can grow large, so if you have a small garden keep them in check with seasonal pruning.*

COLORFUL YOUNG LETTUCE *(left) is attractive both in the garden and on the plate. Select among the many cultivars that differ in leaf shape, color, and texture to create tantalizing salads.*

| Introduction

We have become much more discriminating about our food in recent years. We want to know exactly how it has been produced; many people are concerned about the fact that fruit and vegetables in supermarkets and grocery stores may have been sprayed with pesticides, overfed with chemical fertilizers, and washed with chlorine before they land on our tables. We like to know where our food is from—is it local or has it been flown thousands of miles to give us an expensive, out-of-season treat? Flavor is also a matter of prime importance; no one wants to eat bland, tasteless fruit and vegetables just because the varieties chosen have a long shelf life and are easier for the commercial grower to pack and transport. It is shelf life rather than flavor that often determines the varieties grocers stock.

While the range of produce available has increased in response to consumer demands, prices have increased,

too. There may be lots of premium products on grocery shelves, but all of them carry a premium price tag. Organic produce, fresh herbs, unusual salad greens, potato varieties specially selected for their flavor… it's very easy to run up a large bill in no time. Even then, the produce we select has most likely spent a lot of time being transported over many miles and sitting around in warehouses or on the supermarket shelf—it is hardly at its peak of freshness.

Why grow your own?

Growing your own fruit and vegetables brings satisfaction on many levels. There is always something especially thrilling about harvesting a crop that you have raised from seed, no matter how many times you have done it before—it brings back a connection with the earth that too often tends to be lost in the busy modern world. Healthy living is a major concern to most of us, and growing your own wins on two counts: both in the gentle exercise of gardening itself and in the quality produce we grow and consume. It is easy to eat your 'five a day' (or more) when you have a range of delicious fruit and vegetables just waiting to be picked in your own garden. Growing crops means you know exactly what has happened to your food in its lifetime—what type of soil it has grown in, and what fertilizers, pesticides, or weed killers have been used. If you want to eat organic produce, you can be absolutely certain of its provenance. You can select varieties for their flavor and season, not just their appearance and shelf life, and you can have the fun of growing age-old 'heirloom' varieties that have been rejected by large-scale producers because they don't have sufficient commercial qualities, even though they might be exceptionally good to eat.

'Food miles' are another consideration. Is it really worth buying apples that have traveled from Australia or strawberries flown in from across the continent? Part of the pleasure of crops is their seasonality. The first new potatoes of summer, the eagerly anticipated short weeks of asparagus cutting. Parsnips sweetened by a touch of frost—they are all made more enjoyable when we have to wait for their proper time. When fresh strawberries and tomatoes are available year-round there is no doubt they lose something of their savor, often out-of-season crops are only a pale imitation of those that are grown locally to be enjoyed in season.

With many crops, freshness is vitally important. Crisp lettuce cut straight from the garden bears little resemblance to the limp offering on a supermarket shelf, and there is far less waste when faded outer leaves don't have to be thrown away. Corn is at its very sweetest when cooked within minutes of picking; freshly picked leaves of basil, cilantro, or dill add a gourmet touch to salads and sauces. And few of life's joys can beat the flavor of a juicy peach eaten straight from the tree.

Gardening where you live

While many aspects of gardening translate easily from one area of the country to the next, others must be adjusted for each region. For example, some fruit and vegetables, such as figs or globe artichoke, thrive in mild

RADISH *is an early vegetable that adds crunch and spiciness to salads. It is fast-growing, maturing in as little as four weeks, and will store for several days in the fridge once harvested and placed in a plastic bag.*

regions but do poorly or may not survive in colder climates. On the other hand, some crops such as rhubarb and lingonberry grow best in cooler climates and are not recommended for regions where winters are mild and summers very warm. Many tree fruits require a minimum number of 'chill days'—when daily temperatures are sufficiently cold to break winter dormancy—precluding the production of certain varieties in warm regions. Fruit and vegetable varieties are recommended by region depending on: soil type, days to maturity, prevalence of diseases or pests, and other factors. And the timing of many gardening activities, such as planting and harvesting, must be modified from one region to the next; while gardeners in warmer regions are tending their asparagus, spinach, and peas in early spring, cooler parts of the country may still be blanketed with snow.

Since many of our garden crops are annuals, that is, they are replanted from seed or young plants each year, the length of the growing season—the time between the last frost of spring and the first killing frost of fall—is very important. Timing of planting is often listed in terms of weeks before the last (or first) frost. Tender crops such as tomatoes, eggplants, melons, and cucumbers are generally planted in the garden only after all danger of frost has passed, unless extra protection against cold temperatures is provided. Average frost dates for every region of the country are available. To obtain these dates for your exact location, consult with your local extension service or garden center. Understanding these differences is important to your success in the garden. The regions covered by this book are those that experience some freezing winter weather; they have been divided into mild winter (roughly USDA Hardiness Zones 8–9), mid temperate (Zones 6–7), and cold winter (Zones 3–5). Of course, there will be variations within each region, but major regional differences are discussed.

General cultural information for growing different crops is also relevant to the warmest regions of the country—areas with a nearly frost-free to subtropical climate. In these warm regions, numerous crops can be grown year-round. Because planting and harvesting schedules as well as the scope of tender crops that thrive in these areas are radically different, they are not covered in this book.

ALTHOUGH THE TIMING *of gardening activities varies from region to region, the results are much the same—vegetable gardens (right) can produce a wide variety of crops that can be enjoyed at their peak.*

THE VIBRANT COLORS AND TEXTURES *of vegetables (below), both in their prime and when they are starting to go to seed, are demonstrated in this early summer kitchen garden.*

| Growing in a small space

If, like most people these days, you don't have a house with an extensive vegetable patch or an orchard, don't worry—there's plenty you can grow in even the smallest garden. A courtyard, patio, or balcony can house a range of containers.

Balconies

Many residents of apartments and condominiums have balconies as their only outdoor growing space. This area offers a variety of gardening options and a few advantages. Not only do balconies often provide a sheltered environment but they also, by their very nature, have plenty of vertical space for growing climbing plants such as peas, cucumbers, and pole beans. These can be trained to grow on freestanding or wall-supported trellises. Fruit trees can be cultivated using restricted forms, trained as espaliers, cordons, or fans. Growing climbers such as grape vines up balcony supports offers shade in summer and creates an ornamental feature, as well as providing fruit.

Balcony gardens are often more protected than those located on open ground. This may allow gardeners the option to cultivate some of the more tender crops, which would otherwise struggle outdoors in the region.

Protected balconies may permit gardeners to plant frost-sensitive crops a bit earlier in spring and harvest them later into fall than is otherwise typical for the area.

Before you get carried away, however, make sure your balcony is structurally sound and will hold the extra weight of your crops and the soil they grow in. Wet soil is surprisingly heavy, as you will know if you have ever tried to move a large tub around. Be extra careful with pots on walls or hanging baskets—they must be securely supported so there is no danger of them being knocked off and falling on some unfortunate person below.

Courtyards and patios

These usually provide gardeners with more space than balconies, allowing a wider range of crops to be grown. They are often sheltered and sunny (though there will always be some in the shade), and usually surrounded by plenty of vertical wall space. Many patios have beds for plants, but even if the area is completely paved there is enormous scope to grow fruit and vegetables in containers there.

Raised beds

If you have sufficient room, a raised bed will increase the range of plants that can be grown. Think of a raised bed as a large, specially constructed container with no base, so that the growing area is higher than the ground. Its sides are usually made of wood, stone, or brick; you can build it from scratch or buy a ready-to-assemble raised bed, which is an easier, if more expensive, option.

Ideally beds should be no wider than 4ft. so that they can be comfortably worked from both sides. If the bed is being positioned against a wall or fence, limit it to 2ft. wide. The maximum convenient length for a bed is probably about 10ft.; if any longer, it can be irritatingly long to walk around. Square or rectangular beds make the best use of a small space and are easier to construct.

Fill the bed with compost or with good-quality soil fortified with organic matter, and ensure there is good drainage at the base.

Containers

Growing in containers offers many benefits, particularly for fruit. You can control the size of a plant by restricting its roots in a pot, which also encourages the plant to produce a crop more quickly than a tree or shrub in the open ground whose roots have unlimited access to the soil. This is particularly useful if space is limited in your garden because it allows you to maximize your plants' cropping potential. Containerization also makes fruit and vegetables much more accessible for harvesting, and they are easier to protect from pests and diseases, too.

Containers are readily available in a huge range of materials, the most popular being plastic, terra-cotta, metal, and wood. Terra-cotta looks very attractive but tends to dry out more quickly than plastic, and it needs more regular watering. To combat this, line the inside walls of the container with thin plastic to reduce moisture loss. Look for frost-proof rather than frost-resistant pots unless protection can be given over winter.

PICK CONTAINER-GROWN STRAWBERRIES *as soon as they are ripe. Do this during the warmest time of day. Not only will they taste better but their beautiful fragrance will also be at its most intoxicating.*

TEN BENEFITS OF RAISED BEDS

❋ Raised beds allow easy access and require less bending.

❋ Soil in raised beds warms up more quickly in spring.

❋ You can plant closer and get higher yields.

❋ Well-constructed raised beds provide ample growing depth and excellent drainage.

❋ You can import new soil that is most appropriate to your crop.

❋ One raised bed is less daunting than a large vegetable garden and may be the best way to begin.

❋ Raised beds can be made in any shape, and from any material to match the style of your garden.

❋ Row covers, netting, and plant supports are easy to manage in a raised bed.

❋ Well-maintained raised beds provide an attractive landscape feature.

❋ Paths around raised beds allow the soil within the bed to remain uncompressed by treading, thereby protecting its structure.

Standing terra-cotta pots on 'feet' avoids waterlogging and therefore reduces the chance of frost damage and the pot splitting.

Plastic pots are lighter than terra-cotta (an important consideration when you are moving pots about), dry out less easily, and aren't as affected by frost. Imitation terra-cotta pots that look just like the real thing are now available in garden centers.

Metal containers have a smart, modern look. They are frost proof, can be heavy or lightweight, and won't dry out like terra-cotta. Their main potential problem is that they heat up (and conduct the cold) quickly.

Wooden planters, such as box planters, have a limited lifespan because the wood will rot, though this can be slowed down by lining the inside with plastic sheeting with drainage holes in the bottom.

Almost any shape and size of container can be used for growing plants—from old kettles, large tins, and wooden boxes to pails and wooden crates (lined with pierced plastic), depending on the look you want. Good drainage is important for all containers; check that there are enough drainage holes in the base of the container and make more if necessary. Cover its base with potsherds or stones, and raise it on feet to let the water drain freely. Use either a water-retentive, peat-, coconut fiber-, or bark-based potting mix or a soil- or loam-based medium to fill the containers; adding good-quality compost can make a positive difference to the health of a plant.

Ensure that the pot size is appropriate for what you want to grow. Root vegetables such as carrots need deep pots, while beets, which sit near to the top of the soil, and salad greens need less depth. Big plants such as tomatoes and summer squash, and fruit trees and bushes, require large pots to accommodate their roots. For tall plants that need a stable base, use a heavy pot and fill it with soil-based potting mix.

One of the advantages of containers is that they can be moved in or out of the sun as required, especially if they are on a base with wheels. In general, though, they are often too heavy to keep shifting about, so choose their position with care.

Regular watering will be necessary; do not rely on rainfall to keep your container plants moist, because it may not penetrate the leaf cover of the plants or be heavy enough to soak down to the roots. Water-retaining granules mixed with the growing mix when planting make the job of keeping plants moist much easier, and mulching the surface with gravel or other mulching material not only helps minimize evaporation but also looks attractive. If you have many pots, it might be worth installing an automatic irrigation system.

The relatively small amount of potting soil in a container will have limited nutrients for plants, so feeding will be necessary. Incorporate a controlled- or slow-release fertilizer when planting, or use a general-purpose, balanced liquid feed throughout the season.

Small gardens

For those lucky enough to have space for a garden, options for growing fruit and vegetables become more extensive. Where crops can be grown directly in the ground rather than in containers, maintenance is reduced because watering and feeding demands are much less rigorous, and obviously the more space you have, the greater the range of plants you can grow. Where gardens are small, fruit trees will need to be chosen with care, making use of the dwarfing rootstocks that are available to keep plants compact; restricted growth forms such as fans and cordons come into their own in small spaces.

Make use of vertical garden space, too; walls and fences make good supports for fan-trained fruit trees and climbing crops such as peas. Scrambling plants such as cucumber and squash can be trained to climb twine that has been attached to garden sheds and outbuildings.

Where space is limited, why not grow decorative varieties of vegetables and fruits in ornamental beds among the flowers. Lettuce and other leafy crops are available in red, green, and purple, with scalloped or frilly leaves, while basil can be dark red, and carrots have attractive, feathery foliage. Bushy tomatoes and tee-pees of peas or lima beans make interesting additions to a border, while strawberry plants, particularly alpine varieties, make a great edging. Fruit and vegetables certainly don't have to be dull.

EVEN IN A SMALL COURTYARD GARDEN (top right) it is surprising how careful use of a limited space can enable a good range of fresh produce to be grown and enjoyed.

CONTAINERS ARE A GOOD CHOICE (right) for growing vegetables and fruit where space is limited. Choose large containers for plants with extensive root systems, such as tomatoes and squash.

| Know your site

A good understanding of the geographical aspects of your site is essential if you want to grow food crops successfully. Planting moisture-loving crops in dry soils, acid-loving crops in alkaline soils, or sun-loving crops in shady locations will always result in disappointment. It is particularly important to get the conditions right for fruit crops, as most are perennials and therefore grow in the same piece of ground for years or even decades. Making sure they are in a suitable location initially is crucial, because moving them later could be both time-consuming and very difficult.

Assessing your soil

Healthy soil is essential for good crops, but fortunately if your soil isn't ideal you can amend it. Soils consist of minerals, clay, sand, and silt, which are coated in and bound by organic materials to produce small lumps called aggregates; these give structure to the soil and prevent it from becoming a solid mass impenetrable to roots. Aggregates have air spaces between them, which allow oxygen, water, and roots to enter the soil. Working or trampling on your soil, especially when it is wet, ruins the structure—and, remember, the better the soil structure, the better the crops you will be able to grow.

Take a really good look at your soil by digging a narrow, sharp-sided hole about 2ft. deep, and check the color of the sides. There should be a layer of dark topsoil at least 8in. deep above a base of paler subsoil. The topsoil should be open and friable, ideally with plant roots visible to their full depth. Hard, compacted soils block growing roots and drainage; incorporating generous amounts of organic matter such as compost helps to open up the soil.

After examining your soil profile, fill the hole with water, and leave it overnight. If the water is still there the next day, drainage is poor, so raised beds or a drainage

TESTING YOUR SOIL

A quick way to identify your soil type is to take a handful of soil, moisten it slightly and then try to mold it in your hands. You can then note its particular characteristics.

Sandy soils are made up of relatively large particles surrounded by air spaces. Water drains easily and there is plenty of air for plant roots.

Predominantly sandy soils warm up quickly in spring; drain very quickly and don't hold onto nutrients well; they are easy to dig and make into a seedbed; and they are well aerated and don't compact easily. To help improve their workability and texture, incorporate organic matter.

Silty soils are composed of medium-sized particles that can be sticky and heavy but are also quite nutrient rich.

Predominantly silty soils warm up relatively quickly in spring; hold onto nutrients well; drain quite slowly; can easily become compacted; are relatively easy to dig; and are generally sufficiently aerated.

Clay soils consist of very small particles that stick together so air is slow to penetrate and drainage is obstructed. They are therefore difficult to cultivate.

Predominantly clay soils warm up slowly in spring; hold on to nutrients very well; can easily become waterlogged; are very prone to becoming compacted; can be very heavy to dig; and can be poorly aerated.

__SANDY SOILS__ (top) feel gritty between your fingers and won't easily stick together to form a ball.
__SILTY SOILS__ (center) feel silky to the touch and can be rolled into a ball or cylinder relatively easily.
__CLAY SOILS__ (bottom) feel sticky and heavy, and can be rolled into a pencil-thick sausage and then bent into a ring.

system might be needed. Excess water excludes air from the soil and roots can't survive long without air. In effect, the plants drown.

Your soil's texture influences many physical and chemical characteristics of your garden such as nutrient availability, moisture-retention, drainage, fertility, and aeration. To determine whether your soil is made up of clay, sand, or silt particles, roll some of the topsoil between your hands. If it flakes and crumbles, it is low in clay. If it feels gritty between your finger and thumb, it is sandy. A soapy or silky feel suggests silty soil. And if it is easy to roll into a sausage shape, your topsoil is mostly clay.

Whatever your soil type, digging in well-rotted organic matter, such as garden compost or composted farmyard manure, and applying mulches of organic matter preserves and enhances its structure, as does working your soil only when it is reasonably dry.

TESTING YOUR SOIL'S pH LEVEL

TAKE A SOIL SAMPLE *from your garden following the directions in the box below, then carefully put a small amount of the soil sample into the pH kit's test tube.*

FOLLOW THE INSTRUCTIONS *carefully by adding testing chemicals to your soil sample. Give the tube a good shake, then allow the soil to settle.*

COMPARE THE COLOR *of the resulting mixture with those on the supplied color chart. The best match indicates your soil's pH from the area of your sample.*

HOW TO TAKE A SOIL SAMPLE

A typical soil test helps identify your soil's type, nutrient levels, and pH—its level of acidity or alkalinity. Testing can be done by a commercial lab or a lab associated with your local extension service. Inexpensive kits are also available for home use. However you test your soil, it is critical to obtain a representative sample for accurate results. Although soil can be tested at any time, early spring (prior to planting) or after harvest in fall are best, so that recommended amendments can be worked into the soil.

To gather your sample for a typical soil test, use a clean trowel, shovel, or soil corer and a clean plastic pail. Depending on your garden's size, select six to ten areas and remove the vegetation from the surface. Dig a small hole 7–8in. deep and slice a thin section of the soil profile and place it in the pail. Repeat this procedure at each of the areas you selected. Then thoroughly mix the soil in the pail. If the soil is wet, allow it to air dry for a day or two, but do not apply heat. A separate sample should be taken for each area of the yard where you plan to garden.

If you are sending your sample to a soil-testing lab, a pint is usually sufficient; most labs provide a container. Excess soil can be returned to the garden. Complete all forms for each sample and indicate the crops you intend to grow so that accurate recommendations can be made.

Weather and climate

One factor that will influence the positioning of specific crops is the site and orientation of your plot, with elements such as light, temperature, rainfall, and wind all having an important impact on what crops you can grow.

Light: Most vegetable crops will need as much sun as possible, and few are worth growing where buildings or trees limit the summer sun to less than six hours a day. Some fruits, such as alpine strawberries, sour cherries, red and white currants, and gooseberries, tolerate some shade, but others, such as grapes, figs, peaches, apples, nectarines, and apricots, love and need sun and warmth. Mapping out your yard to note key areas of shade and full sun is essential before you start planting.

Temperatures: The growing season gets shorter the further you go from the equator, limiting production of crops such as okra and globe artichoke that require a long growing season. Damage from frost is problematic for fruit gardeners; a badly timed late frost can destroy open blossoms as well as young fruit, reducing potential yield significantly. Frost can also damage the soft shoots and foliage of various crops, even reasonably hardy crops such as hardy kiwi and grapes. Some crops, such as kiwi, include species that tolerate considerable cold winter temperatures, while other species thrive only in warmer climates. For example, the hardy kiwi (*Actinidia arguta*) which produces clusters of small, smooth-skinned fruit, grows well in USDA Hardiness Zones 4–8, while the larger-fruited *Actinidia deliciosa* does best in Zones 7–9. Consult your local extension agent, garden center experts, and neighbors for details of annual temperature extremes and the length of the growing season for your area.

The length of the growing season will influence your selection of varieties. Gardeners living in areas with a short growing season should look for vegetable varieties that mature quickly. Seed packages usually include the number of 'days to maturity,' which indicates the average number of days from planting the seed until harvest. This number can vary significantly from one variety of the same vegetable to the next. For example, 'Racer' pumpkin requires an average of 85 days to mature, while 120 days are needed for the pumpkin variety 'Wolf'.

While some garden plants grow well in cool temperatures, others require warm, frost-free weather to thrive. Thus cool-season crops such as cabbage and potatoes are planted much earlier than tomatoes, cucumbers, and other heat-loving vegetables and herbs. The most reliable planting dates for annual crops are given in terms of their relationship to weather conditions, for example: 'plant two weeks before the last expected frost' or 'sow seed after all danger of frost has passed.' Some cool-season crops such as lettuce and peas can be planted 'as soon as the soil can be worked.' The charts on pages 278–283 provide schedules for planting vegetable crops based on the above factors.

Rainfall: Maintaining soil moisture is important for the healthy growth of all crops, and in areas with low rainfall frequent watering will be necessary. Plants near walls and fences are vulnerable to 'rain shadows', and so soil at the base of such vertical structures can become very dry, even in rainy weather. Mulching the soil surface helps prevent surface evaporation, reducing moisture loss.

High levels of rainfall will be a problem if soil drainage is poor—even moisture-loving species will fail to thrive in waterlogged soil. Fruit trees in particular, with their deeper root systems, need a well-drained soil. Improve drainage for vegetable crops by digging in plenty of bulky organic matter, such as composted bark to a depth of 6–8in. More permanent drainage problems, such as those caused by a sloping site or high water table, require more

---

AREAS WHERE COLD AIR COLLECTS

These are known as frost pockets. Cold air will naturally sink to and collect in the lowest point it can reach, so sloping sites are most at risk. If your garden is in a natural valley do not plant frost-sensitive vegetables or early-flowering fruit trees at the bottom of it, where there will be a natural frost pocket.

---

substantial treatment—digging diversion ditches or installing drainage pipes. In such cases it's often better to use raised beds or to grow crops in containers.

Wet soil in winter can cause overwintering root crops to rot or be difficult to harvest, while spring rains can delay working the soil. It's therefore often useful to turn an area of the garden in fall so that early spring crops can be planted with minimal soil preparation. If you need to walk in the garden when the soil is wet, it's a good practice to walk on planks to avoid compacting the soil.

Dry weather during the growing season can greatly reduce the quantity and quality of crops and supplementing natural rainfall is often necessary. For this reason, it is advisable to site your kitchen garden near a water spigot so you can run hose or irrigation lines, or else use it to fill watering cans to water plants when they are thirsty. Except for seedbeds, which require frequent, shallow watering to facilitate germination, most established plantings of vegetables and fruit benefit from a thorough soaking on a less frequent basis—once or twice a week—to encourage deep root growth.

Wind: The majority of tree fruits flower early in the year and require a sheltered site that attracts pollinating insects (predominantly bees) that are already on the wing. If these beneficial creatures are discouraged from visiting flowers by strong winds the fruits' flowers won't be pollinated and resulting fruit set will be very poor. Windy conditions also slow vegetable growth and make row covers difficult to keep in place.

Hedges make good windbreaks, are cost effective, and are good for wildlife; fences are an alternative in small gardens and where quick results are wanted. Porous fences (with 50 percent gaps) and hedges are better than solid barriers, which force the wind up, over, and down, creating turbulence that can damage plants and fences.

| Preparing the garden

Proper soil preparation is critical when starting a new fruit or vegetable garden from scratch, or when expanding an existing garden. Take the time and effort to create a nutrient-rich, well-aerated, and well-drained soil environment that encourages beneficial organisms. Such an environment will sustain healthy plant growth and reward you with bountiful harvests.

Tackling weeds

Getting rid of persistent weeds at the start could save hours of labor later on. In the vegetable garden there are opportunities to deal with weed growth as the crops are harvested each year. However, the more permanent nature of most fruit crops makes this much more difficult, so for a fruit garden and perennial vegetable crops it is even more important to tackle weeds right from the beginning of the preparation process.

Preliminary cultivation of the soil is worthwhile, even if you intend to follow a no-digging regime later. Young growth of annual weeds such as purslane, chickweed, and pigweed is easily removed with a hoe or skimmed off with a sharp spade. While you are cultivating the soil, remove as many weeds as possible, including those with deeper roots such as bindweed, dock, thistles, and dandelion. Take care that you do not leave roots behind to regenerate. Don't add perennial weeds to the compost heap. Instead lay them out where they are exposed to sun; they will soon dry out and die.

Some weeds are particularly deep rooted and troublesome and are more difficult to get rid of—bindweed, Japanese knotweed, and quackgrass being among some of the worst offenders. Make every attempt to dig out the entire root system or the weeds will return. Do not use a mechanical cultivator to clear areas covered with perennial weeds, because the blades chop up the roots into small pieces, each of which may grow into a new plant.

For areas with a lot of troublesome weeds, you may want to consider solarizing your soil, a process that traps the sun's heat beneath a plastic covering, raising the soil temperature to levels that kill many weeds. After the soil is cultivated, raked, and watered, clear plastic is spread over it and secured around all sides where it remains for 4–8 weeks. Solarization is most effective in warm weather, so it's best to solarize soil the year prior to planting.

TOOLS

Having the right tools for the job makes vegetable growing much easier and leaves more time for you to enjoy the end result. Good inexpensive tools are sold by hardware or garden stores and are widely available second hand, but buy the best you can afford. Handle the tools before buying to make sure they are well balanced and a suitable size, so that they are comfortable to handle. Clean your tools and store them carefully after every job. That way they will last longer and be a pleasure to use every time. Regularly sharpen the blades of tools like spades and hoes, and sand down wooden handles to avoid splinters. A typical starter-kit for growing your own vegetables includes:

* spade
* fork
* thrust and/or draw hoe
* trowel and hand fork
* rake
* pair of hand pruners
* hose and watering can
* gloves

Cultivation

A new vegetable plot will often benefit from 'double digging,' particularly if drainage is poor. This means digging the soil down to a spade's depth (known as a spit) and then thoroughly breaking up the soil at the base of the hole. Freely drained and reasonably fertile soils usually need only single digging—turning over the soil one spit deep. Single digging is generally sufficient for small and bush fruit crops.

To single dig a new bed, start by excavating a trench to a spade's depth and moving the soil to the far end of the bed. Then dig a second trench behind the first, placing its soil back in the first trench and breaking it up with a fork in the process. Repeat these steps until the whole bed has been dug. Incorporate soil amendments such as well-rotted garden compost or farmyard manure into the soil as you progress, and remove weeds, debris, and large stones. Finally, fill in the last trench with the soil excavated from the first one.

Rototillers are useful for cultivating larger gardens. Depending on its texture, you may need to make repeated passes to work the soil to the proper depth.

Fertilizers and cover crops

Fertile conditions boost the size, flavor, yield, and quality of your crops. Vegetables benefit from the annual addition of bulky, well-rotted organic matter, such as garden compost, leafmold, or farmyard manure. Fruit trees can be given an occasional mulch with these materials, taking care to keep them away from the trunk.

A soil test will help determine if you have any specific nutrient deficiencies, but, in general, most vegetable crops need the addition of a balanced fertilizer containing nitrogen, phosphorus, and potassium for optimal production. Fruiting vegetable crops such as peas, beans, and squash, as well as fruit trees and bushes, benefit from a fertilizer high in potassium, which promotes flowering and fruit formation.

IMPROVE YOUR SOIL *(top) by adding plenty of well-rotted organic matter such as farmyard manure or your own garden compost.*

WHEN DIGGING UP WEEDS *(center) use a fork to loosen the roots. Dig around perennial weeds such as dandelions carefully to ensure that no pieces of taproot remain in the ground, where they can regenerate.*

PLANT THROUGH BLACK PLASTIC SHEET MULCHES *(right) for low-maintenance weed control. They also warm the soil. The sheeting must be secured well at the sides of the bed so it does not blow away.*

Cover crops

In nature, the nutrients that plants take from the soil are returned to it when the plant dies and decomposes. When growing vegetables, the plant's topgrowth is generally removed so that the nutrients do not get a chance to be returned, which is why you need to supplement the soil.

Planting a cover crop (also called green manuring) is a more natural way of doing this than by adding chemical fertilizers, and is popular with organic gardeners. Vacant areas of soil are sown with a quick-growing crop that is dug in before it has matured. This adds bulky organic material to the soil, helping to improve its structure, as well as returning the nutrients from the plant. Cover crops sown in fall will take up nutrients left over by the crops, which would otherwise be washed away by rain. Growing a cover crop will also help to suppress weeds.

Plants with deep or spreading roots, such as ryegrass, are particularly useful as they search out nutrients in areas of soil not available to shallower-rooting plants. Leguminous (pea-family) cover crops are also helpful as they have the ability to enrich the soil by 'fixing' atmospheric nitrogen (converting it to a form that can be used by plants), and this will benefit following crops. Field peas, vetch, and crimson clover are types of leguminous green manure crops.

Seeds of various crops suitable for growing as cover crops are available from seed companies, either separately or as mixtures.

UNDERSTANDING SOIL FERTILITY

Soil fertility refers not only to the amount of nutrients a soil contains but also to the soil's general health. Just one teaspoon of healthy soil will contain thousands of fungi, bacteria, and other microorganisms, all of which are essential in maintaining a balanced and sustainable garden able to support healthy plant growth.

Many soils tend to be naturally fertile, but sandy and shallow chalky soils will benefit more from the addition of organic matter to enable them to hold on to nutrients. Also, a heavily cultivated piece of land could be devoid of certain nutrients so it's useful to research its history. An area previously used for corn production would be low in nitrogen, for example, because these plants have a heavy demand for this nutrient.

Composting

According to the Environmental Protection Agency, waste from our kitchens and gardens account for about 24 percent of the municipal solid waste stream. Composting can recycle much of this waste and put it to good use—improving soil structure and nourishing plants. Stick to plant waste rather than meat and dairy wastes, which tend to smell and attract more nuisance critters. And unless you're certain that the compost will heat up sufficiently to kill disease organisms, it's best to avoid adding diseased plants or plant parts from the garden.

To supply the organisms needed to turn wastes into compost, spread a thin layer of good topsoil or previously finished compost over each layer of organic material. The organisms require a certain ratio of carbon and nitrogen—about 25:1—for maximum efficiency. Most high-carbon material is brown and dry, such as straw, dry leaves, shredded newspaper, and sawdust, in contrast with the greener, wetter nature of nitrogenous matter. Good sources of nitrogen include grass clippings, coffee grounds, and vegetable scraps.

A good balance of water and air is also necessary for the aerobic decomposers to do their work. If the material becomes too wet and dense, there will be little air. If the material is too coarse, it may dry out quickly. Either extreme slows the process.

The main composting methods are as follows. **Hot composting** requires less time than other methods—usually less than eight weeks—but more labor. The entire pile should be assembled at once, watered, and covered. After a few days, the center reaches a temperature of 150–160°F, and the compost needs to be turned so that the bacteria can work on the rest of the pile. Every few days the temperatures will peak again, requiring further turning. When the compost cools it is ready to use.

Cold composting does not require turning, but it takes six months to more than a year for the composting to be complete. Since it never gets really hot, many disease organisms and weed seeds survive; on the other hand, beneficial organisms also survive. Although turning isn't necessary, it is a good idea to poke the pile occasionally with an aerating tool because over time it settles and air flow is reduced.

A THRIVING PLOT (right) is more likely if your plants are grown in soil that suits their particular requirements. Annual additions of organic matter help improve soil structure as well as fertility.

| All about growing

Obtaining strong, healthy plants is the first step in growing good crops, but they need regular care afterwards to fulfill their potential. This is a quick guide to some of the main techniques involved in growing good vegetables, herbs, and fruit.

Vegetables and herbs

Seed or plants: You can either raise your crops from seed, or you can buy young plants from a local nursery or by mail order. Growing plants from seed and purchasing young plants both have their advantages and disadvantages: you will have to weigh what is better for you and your garden's conditions. Buying young plants is particularly useful if you have a small garden and do not have the facilities for raising plants from seed. It is also a good idea if you want only a small number of plants.

If you want to grow from seed, there are two ways: either in containers or trays for later transplanting; or by sowing directly in the garden soil at the appropriate time. Which method you choose depends on the crop as well as the growing conditions at the time of sowing.

Sowing directly outdoors: The optimum daytime soil temperatures for germination of most vegetable seeds falls between 60°F and 80°F. These temperatures are achieved significantly sooner in southern parts of the country than in the North and Midwest. In cold areas, covering the soil with a sheet of plastic in late winter can help to advance spring sowing by keeping the soil dry and allowing it to warm up more quickly.

Rake the prepared ground for sowing until you have a smooth layer of fine particles over firm, but not too hard, underlying soil. If there are any clods of earth, break them down into fine crumbs by striking them firmly with the back of the rake to shatter them. Rake in a dressing of balanced fertilizer, if appropriate.

SPOT SOW PELLETED SEED *or larger ones such as beets or beans alongside a guideline of string. Press each gently into the soil and cover.*

MAKE A DRILL *with a corner edge of a hoe. In dry weather, water the bottom of the drill. Then space seed as directed on the seed packet.*

Make a drill (or groove) in the soil using the corner of a hoe or rake and sow the seed in the drill according to the depth and spacing indicated on the seed package. Alternatively, sow five or six seeds wherever you want a plant (such as lettuce or turnip), later thinning to one plant. Then draw back the soil with the hoe or rake to fill the drill and firm the soil gently.

Sowing in containers: Some crops such as tomatoes and peppers have to be sown in containers in a protected environment. They need to be sown early, long before it is warm enough to grow them outside. Other vegetables can be sown in trays or pots to get an early crop, or because it is a more convenient way of raising the plants. Use flats, pots, or cell trays filled with a moistened, fine-textured seed starter mix. Place the containers in a greenhouse, under grow lights, or outside in a cold-frame. Keep the soil moist and pot the seedlings up when they are large enough to handle. Gradually harden off before planting outside.

Transplanting: Seedlings in pots, or growing in a seedbed outside, can be transplanted to their final growing positions at the appropriate time and when they have reached a suitable size to handle. When doing this, hold them by a leaf, not by their stem. The stems of seedlings are very fragile, and it is easy to crush them and kill the plant. Leaves, on the other hand, can be replaced. Take care to damage the roots as little as possible.

Transplant seedlings on a cloudy, cool day, and water them thoroughly before and after transplanting to ensure a quick adjustment. Protect newly transplanted specimens from both sun and wind for several days.

Fruit

Planting: The ideal time to plant fruit trees and bush fruit is in early spring, before new growth starts, or in late fall, even though containerized plants are available to buy and plant year-round. Bareroot trees are available in the dormant season. Keep their roots moist until they are planted, which you should do as soon as possible after they arrive.

Dig out a planting hole that is about twice the width of the rootball and the same depth. If there is any compacted soil beneath the ground, break this up using

MANY SEEDLINGS CAN BE SOWN CLOSELY TOGETHER *as they are small in size, but they will soon need thinning or repotting if they are to develop properly.*

CROP ROTATION

Growing each group of crops on a different piece of land each year can help reduce the buildup of soil pests and diseases. Since many pests and diseases overwinter in the soil, moving a crop discourages reinfestation or reinfection. The further away from the previous year's crop placement, the more effective the rotation. Where possible, aim for a three-year rotation. Crops are grouped according to their likely pest and disease problems and their soil requirements. A common three-year rotation comprises one group of root vegetables (beet, carrot, parsnip, potato, etc.); another of legumes and fruiting crops (peas, beans, corn, squash, etc.); and a third group of brassicas (cabbage, cauliflower, broccoli, kale, etc.). Divide the vegetable garden into three sections and grow each group in a separate area, rotating the crops to a fresh area each year for three years. Such a rotation also allows you to tailor the soil preparation to the needs of the different groups of crops; for example, adding manure to the section for brassicas, but not the one for root crops (fresh manure causes roots to become misshapen).

a fork or mattock. Mix the soil from the hole with well-rotted organic matter and slow-release fertilizer at the rate that is recommended on the package.

Plant at the same depth as the bush or tree was grown previously in the nursery, using a planting stick placed across the hole to check the level against the soil mark on the stem. When correct, backfill the hole, firming down the soil around the roots as you go.

After planting, you should mulch a fruit tree with a generous amount of well-rotted compost or leafmold around the base of the plant, making sure that the mulch is kept away from the trunk to prevent rotting. Mulching helps to retain moisture and should suppress some weeds. Its gradual breakdown into the soil makes it a useful soil conditioner, too. Most fruit trees benefit from regular mulching each year in spring.

When buying a fruit tree such as an apple, make sure you choose an appropriate rootstock; this helps control the eventual size of the tree. Most gardeners prefer to grow trees on dwarfing or semidwarfing rootstocks, which keep trees compact and encourage early cropping. If you are short of space, choose trees suitable for growing as cordons, espaliers, or other restricted forms (see page 61).

Strawberries are one of the most popular fruits, and they can be cultivated in tiny spaces by using specialized planters or other containers. The trailing habit of a strawberry plant makes it a wonderful subject for a hanging basket outside a kitchen window. Alpine strawberries also make attractive border edgings.

Staking: Fruit trees planted in the open ground, as opposed to against a wall or fence, often require staking to ensure that they stay upright and are able to carry a crop of heavy fruit. Position the stake on the side from which the prevailing wind comes to prevent the tree from being blown against the stake.

Use tree ties with padding to protect the tree from rubbing against the stake. Panty hose are another useful alternatives because they are flexible and will also cushion the tree from the stake. Tree ties should never be overtight. Check them regularly—at least each winter—and loosen if necessary.

Trees in pots: Fruit trees can be grown in pots, so no matter how small your garden is you can be dazzled by a spectacular display of blooms in spring and later by tasty, homegrown fruit, fresh from your garden. Select a sunny, sheltered site for your container.

Because it will be very heavy once filled, move the container to its final position before potting up the tree. Place gravel, small stones, or potsherds in the bottom of the pot, and stand the pot on feet or bricks to allow it to drain freely. Use a loam-based potting soil mixed with some slow-release fertilizer to fill the pot.

A fruit tree in a pot will need daily watering during dry periods in the growing season, and once it starts to flower it will also benefit from a high-potassium liquid feed each week until the fruit begins to ripen. Some trees may require staking or another form of support to help them

PLANTING A BAREROOT FRUIT TREE

1 DIG OUT A HOLE *wide and deep enough to accommodate the root system. Hammer in a strong stake to support the tree when young.*

2 PLACE A STICK ACROSS THE HOLE *to ensure that the tree is at the depth at which it was previously planted.*

3 BACKFILL THE HOLE, *firming the soil around the roots using the tips of your fingers. Water the tree in well and secure to the stake.*

PLANTING STRAWBERRIES IN A GROWING BAG

1 MAKE SIX PLANTING HOLES *in the surface of the growing bag. Use a knife to cut a cross and then fold back the flaps.*

2 REDUCE A LARGE ROOT SYSTEM *by about half, using a pair of sharp hand pruners. This won't damage the plants.*

3 DIG OUT A HOLE *large enough to fit each plant, ensuring the crown is just above the soil surface. Firm each plant in well, then water.*

carry the fruit crop. Don't let the tree overcrop because this will stress it owing to its restricted root system. In regions with very cold winters you may need to provide winter protection.

For the first 3–4 years as it increases in height, replant the tree in a larger pot each year. The eventual size of the container can be as large as you want.

Soft fruit in containers: Soft fruit bushes and plants can also be grown in containers very successfully. Cane fruit, such as raspberries, gooseberries, and red, white, and black currants, will all grow well in a large pot of loam-based (or a mixture of loam-based and soilless) potting mix. Like trees, they need careful attention to watering in spring and summer.

Strawberries are particularly well suited to container growing. Special strawberry planters, towers, and barrels with holes in the sides can be used to pack lots of strawberries into a very small space—ideal for small, patio gardens. The trailing habit of strawberries makes them especially good for growing in a hanging basket, and they do very well in window boxes. If the growing container can be positioned on a raised surface it will take the backache out of weeding and picking, making it ideal for older or less mobile gardeners.

Pruning: Most fruit trees benefit from an annual removal of branches to encourage vigor and healthy fruit. The main reasons for pruning are: to remove dead, dying, and diseased parts of the tree or shrub; to allow air and

sunlight into the plant for the optimum development of fruit and to avoid disease; to develop a sturdy framework that will support a crop of fruit; and to improve the appearance of the tree or shrub and allow it to grow to the shape and size you want. Pruning is carried out in both winter and summer, depending on the effect you want to achieve. Pruning trees hard in winter tends to stimulate growth the following season, while pruning in summer will control growth. This is why summer pruning is such an important part of training restricted forms of trees such as cordons and espaliers. In most regions, winter pruning of fruit trees should be done at the end of the dormant season—in late winter or early spring—to avoid cold injury. In mild-winter regions, however, winter pruning can be done anytime during the dormant season.

Pollination: For almost all fruit varieties to produce fruit successfully, their flowers need pollinating. This process is usually carried out by flying insects such as honeybees and bumblebees. Many types of fruit are self-sterile and have to be pollinated by another variety of tree growing nearby. Some fruit trees such as 'Victoria' plums and 'Stella' cherries are self-fertile, meaning that they pollinate their own flowers; this is ideal in a small garden because only one tree is required to produce fruit. However, even self-fertile varieties tend to crop better when another tree is nearby for pollination. Ask a fruit specialist at your nursery or your local extension agent for advice on the best pollinators for the varieties you want to grow.

| Extending the season

Gardeners can lengthen the season for fruit and vegetables at both ends. In late winter and spring, raising plants under cover or giving them protection with cloches, row covers, and hot caps gives them a head start in the growing season. At the other end of the year, similar protection techniques can be used to extend the harvest period.

Spring

For vegetables, sowing can start indoors in late winter and very early spring for crops such as tomatoes and onions. This gets the plants growing early so that they are already a good size when it is warm enough to plant them outside, and it gives them a long growing season. A greenhouse is ideal for starting plants, heated at least sufficiently to remain frost free. However, a sunny windowsill supplemented with grow lights placed 2–4in. above the seedlings will provide sufficient light for sturdy plants. It is helpful to have an adjustable fixture so lights can be easily raised as the plants grow.

You can also gain some extra time by covering the soil outside with black plastic where you intend to sow early crops. Cover the soil at least six weeks before the anticipated sowing date; the plastic keeps off the rain and allows the soil to warm up and be ready for sowing up to four weeks earlier than if it was uncovered. After sowing, protection from wind and cold can be provided by floating or hoop-supported row covers. Made of spun polyester, polyethylene, or polypropylene, these coverings let in light, rain, and air, yet retain some warmth.

If the row cover is suspended over the soil on hoops, you can make sowings beneath it about two weeks before doing so in open ground. The young plants are protected from the worst frost and wind as well as flying pests, including birds. Unfortunately, slugs and weeds

A COLD-FRAME LID CAN BE PROPPED OPEN *on sunny spring days and closed at night when frosts are still possible. In this way the plants inside it will gradually become acclimatized and harden off, ready for planting out when appropriate.*

AN UNHEATED PROPAGATOR *acts like a mini-greenhouse and is perfect for germinating seeds of tender vegetables.*

Fall

As the weather starts to cool, tender plants such as outdoor tomatoes, peppers, and eggplants can be given protection with row covers and hoop tunnels to allow the fruits extra time to continue to develop and ripen. Frames can be constructed of wood, metal, or plastic pipe at any height, then covered with plastic sheeting or spun row covers. Alternatively, you can carefully take down plants from their supports, lay them on straw or similar material, and place row covers over the top of them.

Move tender container-grown fruit back under cover well before the first frosts arrive. A few vegetables, such as rhubarb and chicory, can be taken under cover in fall and 'forced' in the warmth of a greenhouse or basement into early growth. Such vegetables are usually grown in darkness. Trim chicory leaves to ½in. from the roots and then set the plant in moist peat or sand in a box deep enough for the roots to be covered but keeping ½in. of the crowns above the surface. Leave the pot in a warm, dark place while the chicons form.

Heap straw or dry leaves loosely over rows of vegetables such as carrots and rutabaga to help insulate them from intensely cold weather. Because such protection keeps the soil warmer, this makes it easier to lift the roots through the winter, as otherwise the vegetables can be frozen hard into the soil where they are impossible to dig up until the ground thaws.

appreciate protection as much as crops, so you will need to keep an eye out for both. In cold weather, use a double layer of the row cover, reducing it to a single layer as soon as possible. Be sure to secure your row covers with specially made ground staples, rocks, wood planks, or soil, to prevent their being dislodged by a strong wind.

Using floating row covers on crops for the early part of their life also encourages an early harvest. When transplants of cabbage, broccoli, or lettuce are covered they can be expected to mature about two weeks before uncovered crops. Strawberries may also have their flowers damaged by a late frost, so drape row covers over the plants when frost is forecast.

Cloches and hot caps can be used in the same way as row covers. These act like miniature greenhouses and are used to protect individual plants, although they can be prone to blowing over in windy weather. Some plastic hot caps include channels for water, which traps the sun's heat during the day to protect plants from cold night temperatures. Use them to cover tender plants such as eggplants, tomatoes, and peppers, in spring.

Fruit trees such as apricots and peaches flower very early in spring, and the flowers are often killed by frosts. Use row covers to protect these, too, covering the trees up on cold nights, but removing them as soon as possible to allow insects to pollinate the flowers. The easiest method of frost protection for container-grown fruit is moving vulnerable plants to a frost-free spot. This could be as luxurious as a heated greenhouse or as minimal as a sheltered porch.

ROW COVERS *are a versatile growing aid, easily moved from crop to crop, providing protection from the elements.*

| Coping with problems

Anyone who has grown vegetables or fruit will know that these crops can be affected by a whole range of problems. These may be cultural—caused by providing plants with less than ideal conditions—or by attacks from various pests and diseases.

Cultural problems

These may result from weather damage, incorrect soil conditions, and nutrient deficiencies. Exposed, windy sites are often difficult for plants: strong winds will scorch foliage and stunt growth. Pollinating insects are unable to work the flowers in windy conditions so that fruit crops may be poor.

A heavy clay soil is not suitable for plants that like well-drained conditions, such as many culinary herbs, while very light, free-draining soils will not satisfy hungry and thirsty plants, such as brassicas. Blueberries and lingonberries need an acidic soil and will never thrive in alkaline conditions. A shortage of soil nutrients, particularly on sandy soils, can cause a range of distress symptoms such as yellowing between the leaf veins and stunted growth.

A knowledge of the conditions that individual plants require is essential for successful cultivation. If the ideal conditions do not exist in your garden it is often possible to overcome the problem by, for example, providing windbreaks, enriching the soil with organic matter, or growing acid-lovers such as blueberries in containers of the correct acidic-soil mix.

Pests and diseases

The first line of defense is that well-grown plants in optimum growing conditions and with sufficient water and nutrients fend off pest and disease attacks much more readily than plants that are stressed. A certain level of attack can be tolerated, especially if the edible part of the crop is not directly affected, but if action needs to be taken there are various options (see pages 286–291).

Many gardeners do not like the idea of using chemical controls, particularly on edible crops. Safe biological,

BLOSSOM END ROT *on tomatoes can be identified by the dry, black or brown discoloration at the base of the fruit and a sunken, shriveled appearance. Control watering carefully to prevent the disorder.*

PHYSICAL BARRIERS, *such as this netting to prevent birds and squirrels from eating all your fruit, can be very effective. Be sure to apply the netting well before the fruit ripens.*

physical, and cultural controls can often be very effective against particular pests and diseases. When applied correctly, and at the right time, pesticides can work well, but in general they should be used as a last resort.

Pests: It is possible to boost natural countermeasures to do some of the control work for you. Encourage natural pest controllers, such as lacewings, ladybeetles, and preying mantises, into your garden by providing them with food and shelter. Beneficial insects, mites, nematodes, and microorganisms can be purchased and released to combat specific pests. Several varieties of the bacterium *Bacillus thuringiensis* (Bt), for example, are available to combat various leaf eating beetles and caterpillars.

Make life inhospitable for pests by removing hiding places and limiting access by getting rid of weeds, and raking the soil level to deter slugs. Prevent destructive pests from reaching the crop by erecting barriers and using row covers or netting. For example, use row covers on carrots to exclude carrot rust fly. Surround young transplants with cardboard cylinders, placing the bottoms just below the soil line to prevent cutworm damage.

Whenever possible, choose crop varieties that resist attack, such as fly-resistant carrots. Planting crops early or late is a good strategy for avoiding pests that arrive at a predictable time each year. Crop rotation and removal of crop debris at the end of the growing season are further methods of minimizing pest infestations.

When pests do attack, it may be possible to remove them by hand. For example, you can pick Colorado potato beetles or tomato hornworms off leaves under attack.

The last resort is to use a chemical control. So-called directed sprays with a physical action (such as oils, fatty acids, and insecticidal soaps) will do least harm to helpful insects. Of those that poison insects, the natural ones, such as pyrethrum and rotenone, are short-lived. Synthetic insecticides will normally persist for longer than natural materials and are often harmful to beneficial insects. All pesticides should be used strictly according to the package directions.

Diseases: These are caused by infections of bacteria, viruses, and especially fungi. There are many varieties that are resistant to specific diseases: for example, potatoes resistant to potato blight; peas that deter powdery mildew.

Many diseases are fungal in origin, and fungicides can be used as a preventive control, before disease strikes, as well as on plants already affected. Some diseases, particularly those caused by viruses, cannot be treated, and it is usually best to remove and destroy infected plants as soon as they are seen in an attempt to limit the spread of the disease.

BOTRYTIS *can be a problem on soft fruit crops, such as raspberries, particularly in wet or humid weather.*

BEER TRAPS *can be introduced to attract and kill slugs. Check them regularly to ensure they are well topped off.*

| Planning what to grow

It's easy to get carried away when you first start planning your fruit and vegetable garden. The temptation is to grow as many different plants and varieties as possible, but you soon realize that you have to be practical if you are to make optimum use of your space.

First of all, consider the resources you have available. Do you have a large yard, so that you can devote a good-sized area to fruit and vegetables? Or is space limited, so that your vegetable patch has to be kept small? Perhaps you have a limited growing area—you may need to make do with a bit of patio space or to include some vegetables and fruit plants among the flowerbeds. Obviously the space available will make a big difference to the type

and number of fruits and vegetables you decide to grow. Another resource that is often in short supply is time. Someone who has a full-time job or young children to look after is not likely to be able to devote as much time to gardening as, perhaps, a retired person who enjoys a daily session of gardening as their main hobby.

Think about how much time and effort your plants will need. Upright tomatoes, for example, require staking, training, and protecting from pests. As cucumbers and summer squash mature, they will need to be checked every day to harvest fruit before it becomes overripe. Monitoring for pests and diseases is an ongoing process, as is weed control—although mulching can help reduce this chore. During periods of dry weather, you will need to water the garden regularly.

Your gardening skills should also be taken into account—do you have the knowledge and confidence to grow some of the trickier crops, or would you prefer easy-to-grow, tried-and-true favorites? It is often better to start with a small, easily managed kitchen garden your first year and increase the garden size and number of crops in following years if time and space allow.

Then, consider your needs. There are some crops that are readily available at the grocery store or farmers' markets—is it worth spending the time and effort growing these crops, particularly if space is limited? It may be better to concentrate on more exotic varieties that are either very expensive to buy, such as asparagus and fresh herbs, or that are less commonly available, such as salsify or alpine strawberries. Some varieties of crops, including many heirloom tomatoes, do not hold up well on the grocer's shelf and are best enjoyed fresh from the garden. You may have favorite varieties of peppers, lettuce, or apples that are not reliably available, so these might be worth including in your kitchen garden.

Picking your own produce and getting it from garden to plate in a matter of minutes are some of the joys of growing your own. For some crops, absolute freshness is really important to quality and flavor. There's no comparison between freshly picked salad greens and wilted, store-bought lettuce that's been on the road and on the shelf for several days before you buy it. The sugars in corn start to turn to starch as soon as the cobs are picked, and corn that is in the pot within minutes of picking is often sweeter and juicier than any you can buy from a grocery store. Many soft fruits bruise very easily, and strawberries and raspberries that have been transported hundreds of miles are much more likely to be in poor condition than those that have traveled only a few yards between your garden and a plate.

When settling on which crops to grow, you should also take into account your family's likes and dislikes. There's little point in producing a huge crop of prizewinning parsnips if no one particularly enjoys eating them.

Once you have made a list of what you like, decide how much you require. Unless you have lots of grateful neighbors or a large freezer, it can be frustrating to experience the bounty and gluts of a garden's harvest. Careful planning at the outset and use of various storage methods can, however, keep these peaks and troughs to a minimum. Remember that many crops, such as lettuce and snap beans, can be planted in small quantities at intervals, so you can have a steady supply over a long period, rather than a glut all at once. The same space used for early maturing spring crops, such as spinach and radishes, can be replanted with warm-season vegetables, such as summer squash and eggplant. And planting a second crop of lettuce, spinach, cabbage, and other cool-season vegetables in late summer can provide a continuing supply of fresh produce well into the fall.

ORDERING SEEDS AND PLANTS *for the kitchen garden is exciting; seed catalogs and nurseries offer a wide range of varieties that are adapted to different regions and suitable to every garden size.*

| Kitchen garden design

A well-designed kitchen garden can be an attractive addition to your landscape. Whether you are planning a large garden that will include fruit trees and bushes as well as vegetables, or one that is limited to a few containers of tomatoes and herbs, plan to make it visually appealing and compatible with the style of your home and landscape. Regular maintenance, of course, is critical to both appearance and productivity.

Practical considerations

The garden must be sited where the plants will grow best, so you will need to place it in a sunny spot, and the soil must be well drained. If drainage is an issue, consider constructing raised beds. A series of raised beds can provide lots of growing space even on sloping sites or where the native soil is poor. It is also important to have ready access to a water spigot so you can water during dry spells. Ideally, the garden will be located close to the kitchen, for the convenience of harvesting exactly what you want as you need it. And since the garden will generate much of what goes into your compost pile, access to that part of your yard should be handy as well.

Walkways, both to the garden and within it, are an important style element. A mulched or paved path leading to the garden is inviting and reduces tracking mud from the garden into the house. Mulching between rows defines growing spaces, reduces weeds, and prevents moisture loss. Multiple raised beds can be kept neat and easily accessed when separated by turf, mulched, or gravel paths. Be sure the paths to the garden, between rows, and between raised beds are sized to accommodate any wheelbarrows or carts you plan to use.

A fence may be necessary to provide a windbreak or to prevent deer, rabbits, or other animal pests from eating your crops. Use fencing material that is in keeping with the rest of your landscape, if possible. Attaching chicken wire or other wire with small openings to the lower portion of your fence may be necessary to discourage rabbits. Fences can also serve as attractive supports for vining fruit such as kiwi or grapes, vegetables such as peas or cucumbers, or for ornamental flowering vines. Other vertical supports, including tee-pees, freestanding trellises, and cages, add visual interest to the garden and afford efficient use of garden space.

Adding style

The material you use for pathways, edging, fencing, containers, etc. will affect your garden's style. Brick pavers and glass cloches, for example, impart a classical style, whereas split-rail fencing and straw mulch invoke a more casual or cottage style. Arrangement of the crops in the garden also impacts its style, from the formal look of herbs planted in interlacing geometric patterns or apples espaliered against a wall to the practical appearance of single or wide rows of vegetables growing side by side.

Incorporating colorful flowers into the garden or along the garden's edge adds a great deal of visual appeal. A planting of mixed zinnias, cosmos, or marigolds provides season-long color in the garden and a source of cut flowers for indoors. Many flowers also attract beneficial insects and birds.

If you don't have space for a separate kitchen garden, edible plants can be stylish additions to ornamental beds. Low-growing herbs, such as parsley and creeping thyme, do double duty as ornamental edgings. Chives, dill, and other flowering herbs are well suited to flowering borders, and several varieties of Swiss chard, mustard, and kale contribute colorful foliage and interesting texture. Blueberries are a stunning addition to sunny shrub borders with their spring flowers and delicious blue fruit. And in fall their leaves sport deep red tones.

Containers of fruit trees and vegetables can be logistically placed to enhance a garden, deck, or patio. Grow individual plants in separate containers or combine several in a large container; a half whiskey barrel, for example, provides plenty of room for a well-stocked, mixed herb garden. Window boxes and hanging baskets of strawberries and herbs offer elevated growing space. Select containers that reflect other materials in the landscape for a coordinated look.

early spring

Early spring has many guises, depending on the region where you live. While fruit trees are beginning to bloom and vegetable gardens are being readied for planting in the South, northern gardeners must be patient—in many places the ground is still frozen. Yet, even in chilly climes, the beginnings of a new growing season are perceptible.

Regardless of the outdoor conditions, you can be busy indoors, planning the garden, ordering supplies, and starting seeds of vegetables and herbs for transplanting to the garden when temperatures rise. If you plan to grow plants indoors from seed, make sure you have a good supply of potting soil, containers, and trays as well as adequate light to produce sturdy seedlings; a sunny window is a good start, but supplementary fluorescent lights are usually necessary unless you have a greenhouse. Those in mild-winter regions should exercise some caution as they begin planting outdoors: night frosts and cold spells are still common, so care must be taken not to push ahead too quickly.

vegetables | GENERAL ADVICE

As winter retreats, the gardening season begins. How soon you can work your soil and plant your crops depends on the region where you live and local weather conditions. A late snowfall or heavy rains will often delay gardening activities.

ALL REGIONS

Prepare containers for sowing | Fill containers with potting mix and keep the mix moist, ready for sowing vegetables when conditions are right. If you are reusing old containers, be sure to wash and disinfect them, to avoid seedling diseases.

Set up an area for growing seeds indoors | Suspend lights so they can be adjusted to keep them 2–4in. from the tops of plants.

Sow crops indoors for transplanting | Sow eggplant, peppers, tomato, cabbage, broccoli, cauliflower, Brussels sprouts, and tender herbs (such as basil) in a greenhouse, or indoors under lights. Keep seedlings evenly moist. A heat mat is a useful tool for hastening germination.

Order seedling plants | If you have decided not to raise your own plants from seed, you can order plants from mail-order suppliers at this time. Alternatively, wait and buy them from a local garden center.

Turn your compost pile to get it cooking again | If the pile has been decomposing for several months, you may find that the material at the bottom is ready for use. And if you don't have a compost pile, now is a good time to start one.

Make a clean start | As soon as you can get out into the garden, double check that old crops and weeds have been removed and clean up where necessary.

MILD-WINTER AND MID-TEMPERATE REGIONS

Tackle weeds | Hoe young weeds the moment they appear. It is worth cultivating the seedbed to encourage weed seeds to germinate so that you can kill them before you sow your crops. Once the surface weed seeds have germinated and been removed, few others will sprout and you will have a clean bed.

Rake seedbeds | As soon as the soil is dry enough, rake it level and create a fine tilth. This means breaking up any clumps of soil until it is all an even consistency of fine crumbs.

Fertilize the soil | Most vegetable gardens need feeding. On a dry day, incorporate a layer of compost or composted manure and balanced fertilizer at the recommended rate on the package into the top several inches of soil.

Time sowing carefully | Although some cool-season crops can be sown outdoors, the soil in some areas is often still too cold to get good results. If in doubt, wait until weeds begin to emerge; when they germinate, the chances are your seed will too. It is better to wait a week or two than to sow in poor conditions.

Plant crowns, tubers, and sets | Plant asparagus crowns, tubers of early potatoes, and onion sets and shallots in the garden.

MILD-WINTER REGIONS ONLY

Sow vegetables outside | Sow early carrots, lettuce, onions, parsley, parsnips, peas, radishes, spinach, bunching onions, turnips, and herbs such as dill and chervil where they are to grow, after the danger of hard frost has passed. If frost and winds are a problem, cover the sown area with row covers.

Water dry seedbeds | With the soil still moist from winter, you seldom need to water in spring, but cold, dry winds can parch seedbeds, so check on their condition and give a light watering when necessary.

Protect carrots and cabbage | Cover carrot and cabbage-family crops with row covers to exclude cabbage root fly and carrot rust fly. The adults lay their eggs near the plants' roots and the larvae eat the roots when they hatch out. Covering the plants means the flies cannot get near to them to lay their eggs.

Apply slug controls | Seedlings are very vulnerable to slug damage, so use some form of slug control or preventative to keep them at bay.

HARVEST THE LAST OF WINTER CROPS *in early spring. Kale and parsnips may still be available where winters are mild.*

vegetables | WHAT TO DO NOW

Leek

Start leeks from seed

If you haven't done so already, sow leeks indoors in colder regions. In warmer regions, sow in a seedbed outside to mature in fall. Rake the soil to a fine tilth and sow thinly in drills 6in. apart and ½in. deep.

Onion and shallot

Sow onions and shallots

In colder regions, sow seed indoors. In warmer zones, sow seed outdoors as soon as the soil is workable to give a late summer crop. Sow seed thinly in rows 12in. apart in well-prepared soil.

Start onions from sets

Plant sets as soon as the soil is workable through mid spring for a summer crop. Sets are young onion or shallot bulbs that grow rapidly and are particularly useful when the growing season is short. Space rows 10–12in. apart, and push the sets into the soil with 3–4in. between each; place the pointed end up with the tip just visible.

General

In cold-winter and mid-temperate regions, sow seeds of Brussels sprouts, broccoli, cauliflower, and cabbage indoors under lights or in a greenhouse about six weeks prior to the last expected frost. Keep soil evenly moist. In milder regions, seed can be sown outdoors and young plants can be acclimatized to the outdoors (hardened off) in a cold-frame or other protected area for about two weeks and then be transplanted into the garden.

Broccoli

Sow broccoli seed indoors

Select Calabrese types for a single, large, domed head, Romanesco types for a conical, spiral head, or sprouting types for lots of small sideshoots.

SOWING CABBAGE SEED

EVENLY SPRINKLE *a good number of seeds across a whole tray of potting mix. Allow a finger width between each seed.*

COVER THE SEEDS *with a thin layer of potting mix and then gently firm this down by hand or using the bottom of another seed tray.*

WATER CAREFULLY *so that the potting mix is evenly soaked. Leave the seeds to germinate in a sunny place. Keep evenly moist.*

Brussels sprouts

Sow Brussels sprouts indoors

Sow seeds of Brussels sprouts indoors or outdoors, depending on your region; the seedlings should appear within 7–12 days.

Cabbage

Sow cabbage indoors

Red cabbage varieties tend to mature more slowly than green types, so sow them early. Cabbage can be transplanted into the garden once the danger of heavy frost has passed.

LEGUMES

Fava beans

Sow fava beans outdoors

Sow outside in mild- and mid-temperate regions. Unlike other beans, fava beans require cool temperatures to grow and may be planted as a substitute for lima beans where summers are short and cool.

Sow 4–6in. apart, in rows 24in. apart. They need a sunny, sheltered site because mature plants, when bushy and weighted with pods, are susceptible to wind damage.

Lima beans and snap beans

Prepare for summer beans

If you have not done so already, dig plenty of well-rotted organic matter into the soil where you intend to grow lima and snap beans. They need lots of moisture, particularly while flowering and setting pods, and organic matter will help hold on to soil moisture to keep it available to the roots. Dig a trench and work well-rotted compost or manure into the soil at the base.

Peas

Sow peas outdoors

Make a first sowing outside if the weather is now warm enough. Do not be tempted to sow into cold, wet ground, because germination will be poor. If spring is slow to arrive, warm the soil by covering it with black plastic before sowing the peas; then protect the seedlings with a row cover.

TYPES OF PEAS

There are three common types of peas grown for fresh eating. Garden or English peas are harvested for their fresh seeds, which are removed from their pods. Snow peas—also called edible podded peas—are eaten shell and all, before the seeds mature. Snap peas also produce edible pods, but the seeds are allowed to mature because both the seeds and pods remain sweet and crisp.

CLOCKWISE FROM TOP: 'Sugar Ann' (top) and 'Sugar Lord' (bottom left) are snap peas, while 'Oregon Sugarpod' (middle) and 'Delikata' (right) are snow pea varieties.

For shorter varieties, make a flat trench with a hoe, 2in. deep and about 10in. wide. Water the trench first, then sow the seeds 2–2¾in. apart in three rows along the bottom of the trench. Press each seed in a little to ensure it does not become displaced when the trench is backfilled with soil, then firm the ground lightly with the back of the hoe.

Sowing seed in a single row, or pair of rows, works best for taller varieties because it is easier to support them. It also gives increased air ventilation around the plants, helping to prevent powdery mildew and making weeding easier. Make a single, V-shaped drill, 2in. deep, and sow the peas 2–4in. apart. You can add a second row, 12in. away, and insert supports between the two. If you plan to use a tented trellis, space the rows about 30in. apart.

ROOT AND STEM CROPS

Beet

Sow beets outdoors

In mild regions, sow beets outdoors from now through to summer, sowing a short row every couple of weeks in order to have a regular supply of tender roots. Soak the seed overnight before sowing. Mark out straight rows using a string line, water the drill if the soil is dry, and sow the seed thinly, 1in. deep, in rows 12in. apart.

Seedlings should appear in 10–14 days. Thin to 4in. between seedlings as soon as possible. Light, free-draining soil produces the best early crops because it warms up more quickly than heavier ground. Wait another month to sow in cooler regions.

Carrot

Sow early carrots outdoors

In mild regions, sow a variety suitable for early crops such as 'Mokum' or 'Nelson'. Wait another month in cooler regions. Seeds will germinate more quickly if the soil is warm, having been covered with black plastic for several weeks.

All carrots require an open, sunny site and well-drained, fertile soil. To grow long-rooted carrots, such as 'Nectar' or 'Sugarsnax', you need a good loam or sandy soil that can be deeply cultivated to at least one spade's

depth. If your soil is shallow, stony, or heavy clay then opt for stump-rooted or round carrots such as 'Kinko 4' or 'Parmex', rather than long-rooted types that are likely to develop stunted or forked roots. If the soil is completely unsuitable or space is limited, try growing short-rooted types in containers or raised beds.

Use a string line to mark out rows, then with a draw hoe or trowel create drills ½in. deep with 6in. between the rows. If the soil is dry, water each drill and allow it to drain before sowing. Sprinkle the fine seed along the drill, cover with a thin layer of soil, and firm down.

Celeriac

Sow celeriac indoors

Sow the tiny seed thinly in pots or cell flats filled with equal parts of potting mix and fine vermiculite, mixed and moistened. Then cover the seed with vermiculite and keep moist. Transfer the pot-grown seedlings into individual biodegradable pots of potting mix once the first true leaves have formed. Make sure the plants have good light and that the temperature stays above 50°F. Sow early, as celeriac needs plenty of growing time for the roots to reach a good size.

Fennel

Sow fennel seed indoors

Sow in a warm greenhouse or indoors under lights. Fill pots or cell flats with potting mix, firm gently, water well, and allow to drain. In each pot, sow several seeds ½in. deep, spaced a little apart from each other, then cover with potting mix. Setting pots or flats on a heat mat will speed germination. Once the seed has germinated, thin to leave one seedling per pot.

Fennel tends to bolt to seed if the roots are disturbed, so it's important to keep root disturbance to a minimum when planting out. This is why seed should be sown in individual pots or cell packs. Keep plants evenly moist and plant out in 4–5 weeks—don't leave them in their pots for too long or they are more likely to bolt.

Parsnip

Sow parsnips outdoors when conditions are right

Parsnips need a long growing season so are traditionally

PARSNIP SEEDS *are notoriously slow to germinate, so try sowing fast-maturing vegetables, such as radishes, around them to make maximum use of the space. Parsnip seeds also store poorly, so use a fresh batch each year.*

sown very early. They like a sunny position and grow well in most well-drained soils, ideally one that is light and sandy. In colder areas, or on heavy clay soils, results will be better if you wait for a few weeks.

Choose a site improved with well-rotted compost or manure the previous year. A week before sowing, rake over the soil, adding a balanced fertilizer, then rake the surface to a fine crumbly texture to prepare a seedbed. Make a drill ½in. deep with a hoe. If the bottom of the drill is dry, dampen it before sowing. Sow the seeds in a 2in. band, spacing seeds about 1in. apart and lightly cover them with fine soil. Space the rows 12–18in. apart. Parsnip seed is notoriously slow to germinate, often taking several weeks before the first seedlings emerge; it is important keep the row moist until the seeds germinate. Thin the seedlings to 2–3in. apart.

Sow radishes next to the rows of parsnips. These will mark the row while you are waiting for the parsnips to appear. By that time the radishes will be ready for pulling, you will have made good use of your space.

Potato

Prepare for potato planting
Potatoes can be planted in early spring in mild-winter and mid-temperate regions. Cold-winter gardeners should wait a few more weeks. Just ahead of planting, dress the ground with an all-purpose fertilizer and rake well to break up any large clods. Avoid growing potatoes in waterlogged ground, in low-lying spots where frosty air could collect, and in very light, free-draining soil.

For early crops, increase the soil temperature by covering the site with black plastic several weeks before planting; this helps to accelerate growth. You can plant the tubers through holes made in the plastic.

Plant only certified disease-free seed potatoes
To avoid disease problems, be sure to purchase disease-free potatoes from seed companies or your local garden center. Don't use potatoes that were purchased at the grocery store, because these are often treated to prevent sprouting and they may not be the best variety for your region. The tubers can be planted whole or cut into pieces, each with at least two 'eyes.' You can start your seed potatoes into growth earlier by sprouting or chitting them (see page 269).

Radish

Sow radishes outdoors
In mild regions, sow radishes as soon as the soil can be worked. Use an early variety, such as 'French Breakfast', for an early spring sowing. Sow seed thinly, in drills ½in. deep. Thin the seedlings to at least 1in. apart; overcrowding makes them spindly and may delay or prevent the roots from developing fully.

Being fast growers, radishes are ideally suited to a number of small successional sowings. Where summers are hot, they can be sown until late spring and again in fall. Where summers are cool, they can be sown continuously until early fall. They can be grown among slower-maturing crops and to fill gaps where a couple of lettuce or a few beets have been harvested. They are best pulled when the roots are small and tender.

SOWING SMALL RADISH SEED *means you will inevitably end up with rows of tightly packed seedlings, but they can be easily thinned to avoid overcrowding and prevent spindly growth.*

Turnip

Sow turnip seeds outdoors

Sow seed as soon as the soil can be worked. Using a string line and draw hoe or trowel, make a drill about ½in. deep. Sow the seed thinly and cover with soil. Space rows 12–18in. apart. Once the seedlings are large enough to handle, thin to 2–3in. apart.

LEAFY GREENS

Chard

Sow chard seed outdoors

In mild-winter regions, sow chard seed in the garden as soon as the soil can be worked. Space seeds 2in. apart in rows 18–24in. apart and keep the seedbed moist. When the seedlings are large enough to handle, thin them to a spacing of 4–6in. apart; chard thinnings can be added to salads.

TYPES OF LETTUCE

Several types of lettuce can be grown in the kitchen garden. Plant different varieties to make your salads more interesting.

Leaf (loosehead) lettuce is easy to grow and forms a loose rosette of leaves rather than a tight head. Leaves may be green, red, purple, or speckled; crinkled, frilled, or deeply lobed. Some widely adapted varieties include: 'Simpson Elite', 'New Red Fire', and 'Salad Bowl'. Many seed companies offer their own mix of leaf lettuce varieties.

Bibb (Boston or butterhead) lettuce produces large, green outer leaves, which surround a very tender, blanched center; thus it is another type that does not form a tight head. It is fast maturing and has an exceptionally delicate flavor. Good varieties include: 'Nancy' and 'Buttercrunch'.

Crisphead (iceberg) lettuce requires a comparatively long growing season to develop its thin, crisp leaves that form a dense head. It does not tolerate much heat, so is best grown where summers are cool. Useful varieties include: 'Crispino' and 'Igloo'.

Romaine (cos) develops an elongated head of sweet, thick, crisp leaves, which may be green or red. It is more heat resistant than other types of lettuce. Among the many good varieties are: 'Green Towers' and 'Red Rosie'.

Chicory

Sow annual chicory seed outdoors

In warm regions, sow annual chicories, such as endive and escarole, outdoors as soon as the soil can be worked. Sow thinly in rows spaced 18in. apart. Thin seedlings to 6–12in. apart, depending on the variety.

Lettuce

Sow lettuce seed indoors

In colder regions, sow seed indoors six to eight weeks before the last expected frost in cell flats or pots. Read the directions on the seed package regarding covering seed; some varieties need light for germination, and seeds should not be covered. Once seeds germinate, thin or transplant to individual pots.

Sow seed or transplant seedlings outdoors

In mild climates, lettuce started indoors can be transplanted to the garden now after hardening off. Lettuce seed can also be sown directly in the garden now. Sow seed thinly in shallow drills, spacing rows 12–18in. apart. Alternatively, sow seed in 12in. wide bands. Press seed lightly into the soil and keep seed bed moist. Make successive plantings every 2–3 weeks until early summer.

Mustard

Sow mustard seed

Mustard is tolerant of cool conditions and adds zest to early spring salads. Sow outdoors as soon as the soil can be worked and the danger of hard frost has passed. Sow thinly in rows 18–24in. apart.

Spinach

Sow spinach seed

Sow spinach seed directly in the garden as soon as the soil can be worked. Sow seed thinly in rows 12–18in. apart or in blocks 12–18in. wide. Keep the seedbed moist. Thin the seedlings to stand 4–6in. apart, for full-sized leaves; for baby spinach use a closer spacing.

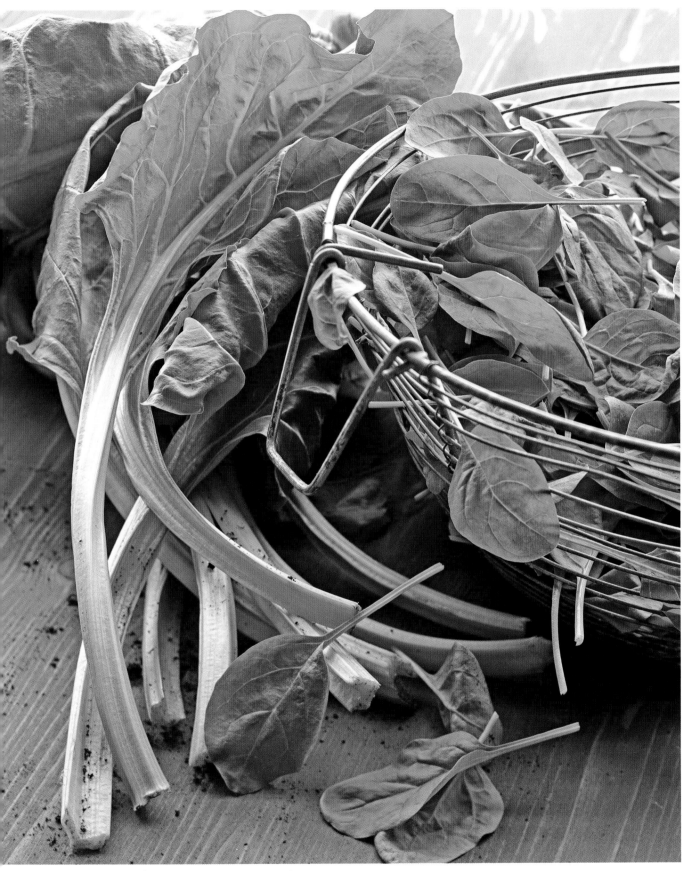

FRUITING CROPS AND CORN

General

When starting eggplant, peppers, okra, and tomatoes indoors from seed, it is helpful to use a heat mat to hasten germination. Unless you have a heated greenhouse, place seedlings under grow lights placed 2–4in. above the tops of plants, and keep them on 12–16 hours per day. Whether you start your own plants or purchase them from a garden center, do not plant them out too early—these crops will not begin to grow until the soil has warmed. Harden off plants before transplanting.

Eggplant

Sow eggplant seed indoors

Start indoors now at 70–86°F. Sow 8–10 seeds per 3½in. pot, then move to individual pots when the seedlings are large enough to handle.

Okra

Sow okra seed indoors

Okra is a half-hardy annual grown for its fleshy seedpods. Okra seed doesn't remain viable for long, so buy it fresh or save your own each year. Since okra seedlings will damp off and collapse in cold, wet soil below 65°F, sow in individual 3½in. pots of well-moistened growing mix and place on a heat mat. Don't let the seed dry out before germination occurs, and use tepid water when watering.

Peppers

Sow pepper seed indoors

Sow peppers indoors in a pot or tray of moist growing mix and cover lightly. If you don't have a heated greenhouse or heat mat, place the container in a plastic bag and put it in a warm place, such as on top of the refrigerator. Wait a few days and then check daily for signs of germination.

Once shoots emerge, move the container to a warm, well-lit spot and let the seedlings grow. Pot them up individually into 3in. pots as soon as they are large enough to handle. Keep the potting medium evenly moist. Sow peppers eight weeks before outdoor planting time.

Tomato

Sow tomato seed

Sow tomatoes indoors following the same procedure as for peppers. Tomatoes usually germinate easily and you are likely to have plenty of seedlings, so keep a few as spares and give away the rest to friends or family.

Since tomatoes are sensitive to frost, they can be planted outside only once all risk of frost has passed. Sow them indoors 6–8 weeks before planting time. If tomatoes are sown too early, the seedlings will become leggy before it is safe to plant them out.

SOME LIKE IT HOT

There are hundreds varieties of hot peppers that vary in color, shape, size, and most importantly how hot they are. Their heat comes from compounds called capsaicinoids, which tend to be concentrated in the membrane and seeds. The Scoville scale was developed to compare the heat of pepper varieties by measuring the amount of capsaicinoids in the mature fruit in 'Scoville units.' If you like your hot peppers on the mild side, try 'Anaheim', which boasts a modest 500–1,000 Scoville units. 'Mirasol' is a jalapeño type with a bit more heat —about 5,000 Scoville units. For those who seek really hot peppers, 'Caribbean Red' is a habanero variety that measures 445,000 Scoville units.

START TOMATO SEEDS OFF INDOORS *and move them to a warm, well-lit spot as soon as the shoots emerge. Keep grow lights 2–4in. from the tops of the seedlings as they grow.*

TO PLANT ONE-YEAR-OLD ASPARAGUS CROWNS, *dig a trench for each row, 6in. deep, and carefully spread out the fragile roots. Cover with 3in. of soil and water in well.*

Asparagus

Plant asparagus crowns

One-year-old asparagus crowns can be planted now. It is important that the ground is ready on delivery because the fleshy crowns must not dry out. If planting is delayed, wrap up the roots in wet newspaper. Soil should be particularly well prepared and enriched with organic matter since an asparagus patch can remain productive for 15 years or more.

The bed system produces high yields in a relatively small space, with one bed consisting of three rows of crowns, spaced 12in. apart in each direction. On heavy soil, make sure the bed is slightly raised and mounded up to improve drainage.

Dig a trench for each row, 6in. deep, and carefully spread out the fragile roots. Cover with 3in. of soil and water in well.

Sow asparagus seed outdoors

Asparagus seed can be sown in an outdoor nursery bed as soon as the soil can be worked. Sow seed 1½in. deep and 4–6in. apart. The seedlings should germinate in about three weeks. Allow them to grow in this bed throughout their first year. Next spring, the strongest one-year-old plants can be selected and moved to a permanent bed.

Fertilize and mulch established asparagus beds

Apply a balanced organic fertilizer and a 2in. thick mulch of organic matter before the spears emerge; this will help suppress weeds, retain moisture, and protect the early spears from frost. The mulch also assists in preventing the soil from forming a crust, which causes bent spears.

Globe artichoke

Locate planting site

Globe artichoke isn't fully hardy and needs a sunny, sheltered site with well-drained, moisture-retentive soil to which plenty of organic matter has been added. Avoid growing it in shade or in a frost pocket, or in heavy soil that gets waterlogged in winter. It can be grown as a perennial in mild-winter regions and as an annual in mid-temperate regions.

Always buy named varieties, which give more reliable crops than unnamed seed-raised plants.

Transplant outdoors

In mild regions, buy globe artichoke as small, pot-grown plants and space them 3ft. apart in the vegetable garden, or place them in a big flower border.

Move to cold-frame

In mid-temperate regions, move young seedlings with at least two leaves to a cold-frame, so they are exposed to the cold temperatures that are required to induce flowering. They need 2–6 weeks of temperatures between 34°F and 50°F.

Rhubarb

Plant rhubarb

Pot-grown rhubarb plants can be bought and planted now or as soon as the soil can be worked. One or two plants should be enough for most people, but if more are required space them 3½ft. apart. Provide a sunny position and well-drained, moisture-retentive, fertile soil. Before establishing a new bed, add plenty of organic matter and remove all perennial weeds. Avoid heavy soil, which can rot the fleshy crowns.

Fertilize established plants

For established plants, remove lasts season's growth. Rhubarb responds well to feeding. Apply a topdressing of pelleted poultry manure or well-rotted farmyard manure, but avoid direct contact with the crowns.

| Making a raised bed

Growing vegetables in a raised bed has several advantages over growing them in the ground. Think of a raised bed as a large, specially constructed container with no base. The sides are usually made of wood, brick, or stone blocks, the choice depending on cost, appearance, and available materials. Ready-to-assemble raised beds from garden supply stores are an easy option but tend to be more expensive.

Ideally, beds should be no wider than 4ft. so that they can be comfortably worked from both sides. If the bed is being positioned against a wall or fence, limit it to 2ft. wide. The maximum convenient length for a bed is

RAISED BEDS *can be built at a low level (above), ideal for small spaces, or up to 3ft. or table-top height depending on your needs.*

WATER RAISED BEDS *in dry weather (right) and mulch to prevent evaporation because they dry out more quickly than open-ground beds.*

probably 10ft.; any longer can be a nuisance to walk around. The bed can be any shape, but square or rectangular ones make the best use of a small space and are easy to build.

Planning a raised bed

In an area of 10 x 10ft., you can fit two square beds of 4 x 4ft. for vegetables and herbs. Separate them with a path 2ft. wide, to give easy access without having to step on and compact soil in the growing area. To prevent weeds from growing on the path, secure a permeable landscaping fabric to the soil using metal staples, then cover with a layer of ornamental bark or gravel at least 2in. deep.

To make the beds, use 1 x 6in. wooden boards for the sides, held together by 2 x 2in. stakes that are 12in. long. Long beds will need additional staking along the sides, to prevent the weight of soil from bending the boards. When a bed is

EDIBLE HERBS AND FLOWERS *can fit into small spaces to provide fresh ingredients for your table or can simply add a bit of color to raised beds.*

sited on a firm surface such as a patio, use corner brackets that are the same depth as the boards and just set the bed in place.

Cut the wood to the correct length, making two sides of each bed 2in. shorter than the other two sides, to allow for the width of the lumber they will butt up to. Screw the sides

onto the stakes to make the frame, predrilling holes to prevent the wood from splitting.

Prepare the soil by forking over the area to ensure good drainage, then place the frame on the soil and hammer the stakes into the ground. Fill the bed with good-quality topsoil fortified with organic matter.

MAKING A RAISED BED

ASSEMBLE THE FRAME *of the raised bed by attaching the wooden board edges to the stakes using galvanized screws.*

HAMMER THE CORNER STAKES *of the frame into the ground with a mallet. Use an old piece of wood to protect the frame.*

BREAK UP THE GROUND *in the bottom of the raised bed before filling it with soil. This will help drainage.*

fruit | GENERAL ADVICE

ALL REGIONS

Plant dormant fruit trees | If the tree is bare root, measure the spread of the roots so that you know what size hole to dig. Mark a circle a little wider than the diameter of the roots. Dig the hole out to the correct depth and thoroughly chop up the soil at the base of the hole. Mix the removed soil with well-rotted organic matter and a bit of balanced fertilizer. Set the tree in the hole, spreading out its roots. Be sure it is placed at the same depth that it was growing in the nursery—as indicated by a dark soil mark on the tree's trunk.

Refill the hole with the amended soil and gently jiggle the tree to allow the soil to trickle between the roots. Firm the soil as you go. Water thoroughly and stake the tree as necessary.

Last chance to apply a dormant oil spray | Dormant oil sprays are applied during the dormant season to destroy overwintering pests and their eggs. They cannot be sprayed when the plants are in growth, so this is a last chance to use them.

Before using a dormant spray, check that the growth buds on trees and bushes have not begun to break, or the new growth will be scorched. Protect plants that are growing nearby, and spray on a still day so that wind won't carry the spray where it's not wanted.

Mulch trees and bushes | Apply an organic mulch around fruit trees and bushes as long as the ground isn't frozen. This helps keep in soil moisture as well as helping prevent weed growth and supplying some nutrients as it gradually breaks down. Use well-rotted farmyard manure or compost, but make sure the mulch is kept away from the trunks and stems; otherwise it might cause rotting.

Protect early blossoms from frost | Plum, peach, apricot, cherry, and nectarine trees flower very early, and their blossoms (and, later, fruitlets) may need protection from frost if they are to survive. Drape a double layer of row covering fabric or a light sheet over the trees if a frost threatens. Erect a tent of canes around small plants to hold the fabric away from the blossom—if touching, it will allow the cold to penetrate through to the flowers.

It is much easier to protect blossoms from frost when the trees are grown as trained forms against a wall or fence than if they are freestanding. If the plants are growing in containers, they can be moved to a frost-free position (such as an enclosed porch) when frost is forecast. Strawberry plants are also subject to frost damage when flowering, causing the yellow centers of the flowers to turn black in the middle. They can be protected with a floating row cover.

It is important to remove the frost protection from fruit as soon as possible, as insects must have access to the flowers during the day in order to pollinate them.

Mulch acid-loving soft fruit | Give blueberries, cranberries, and lingonberries a mulch of well-rotted organic matter; avoid spent mushroom compost as this is too alkaline.

Keep on top of weeds | The key to good weed control is to act while the weeds are still young and never let their growth get out of hand. Keep weeding regularly right through the spring and summer.

Repot or topdress container-grown fruit | This is the time to move container-grown fruit trees and bushes on to the next size pot or, if you don't want to pot them up, to topdress them with fresh soil.

When repotting, remove the plant carefully from its pot by grasping the stem. Crumble away some of the old soil from around and on top of the rootball, being careful not to damage the roots. Make sure there is sufficient drainage material in the base of the larger pot, and a layer of fresh potting soil. Put the rootball on top of the new soil and fill in around the sides of it with more soil, using a piece of wood or a similar tool to push it firmly but carefully down the sides so there are no air gaps. Finish off with a thin layer of potting soil over the top of the rootball and water thoroughly.

If the plant is already in as large a pot as you want, scrape some of the surface soil away with a trowel, again making sure you don't damage the roots. Mix fresh potting soil with some slow-release fertilizer and use this to replace the soil you have removed.

MID-TEMPERATE AND MILD-WINTER REGIONS

Control aphids | Aphids can affect most fruits. Damage is particularly noticeable a little later in the spring and in early summer, but they often colonize new growth early in the growing season. By sucking sap they weaken the plant, distort growth, and, most importantly, spread harmful viruses for which there is no control. Do not spray plants with insecticides when they are in blossom because of the risk of killing beneficial pollinating insects.

When spotted, colonies can be squashed between finger and thumb, or dislodged with a powerful jet of water from a hose. When plants are not in flower, an insecticide can be used, following the manufacturer's instructions carefully.

Apply fungicide | Use this on peaches, plums, and nectarines, if needed. Follow the directions on the label for exact timing.

WHEN PLANTING A BAREROOT TREE, *be sure to set it at the same depth that it was growing in the nursery—as indicated by a dark line at the base of the trunk.*

fruit | WHAT TO DO NOW

General

Plant new container-grown or bareroot trees in well-prepared soil; water thoroughly and mulch. Fertilize and mulch established trees. Finish dormant pruning.

Apples and pears

Cut back newly planted apples and pears

Shorten the main stem of newly planted trees, or trees planted last fall, to 24–36in. and cut back lateral branches by one third.

Continue training trees

Use spreaders or ties to increase the crotch angle of lateral branches on established apples and European pears with a central-leader form. The wider angle gives greater strength, which is needed by branches to support heavy crops of fruit. Asian pears tend to be more wide spreading and are better trained to an open-center system (see page 61). Remove any branches lower than 18in.

Apricots

Train apricots

Apricots have a similar fruiting habit to plums and peaches and so are managed in much the same way. Open-center training helps prevent the canopy from becoming overly dense. Remove diseased, broken, or unproductive branches and any that cross through the center of the tree. The fan-trained form is also suitable for apricots (see peaches and nectarines).

COMPLETE DORMANT PRUNING of fruit trees before buds begin to swell. A significant advantage of dormant pruning is that, without leaves, you can clearly see the framework of the tree. Be sure to keep your pruning tools well sharpened, to ensure clean cuts.

Cherries

Water cherries when necessary
As well as providing frost protection for early blossoms, ensure trees are kept well watered during the early stages of fruit development, to avoid excessive blossom or fruit drop. This occurs in three main stages: when unpollinated flowers and blooms with immature embryos are shed; when pollination is incomplete; and when fruits swell but are then aborted because they have suffered a growth check through lack of moisture, inadequate food reserves, or excessively cool temperatures or frost.

Figs

Plant dormant trees
In mild-winter climates, plant nursery-grown trees before they break dormancy, setting trees 2–4in. deeper than they were growing in the nursery in well-drained soil that has been supplemented with organic matter. Do not apply fertilizer at planting time. Be sure to provide plenty of space—figs can grow 15–30ft. tall with an equal spread.

Peaches and nectarines

Open-center training
Prune standard peaches and nectarines so that the center of the tree remains open, to allow maximum light to

PEACHES, NECTARINES, AND APRICOTS *can be trained as fans against a wall, a technique that provides protection from wind and makes excellent use of limited space.*

penetrate the canopy. This will improve fruit color and encourage air circulation, which will reduce disease and pest problems.

First remove root suckers, water sprouts, and other vigorous upright growth. Then prune out unproductive, damaged, and crossing branches as well as any that grow toward the inside of the tree. Be sure to collect and remove all prunings, to reduce the potential spread of diseases and pests.

Fan-training a peach
A fan-trained peach is relatively easy to accomplish but it is important to train the fan when young to set a good branch framework. Select a one-year-old tree with several side branches (called a feathered maiden) and, once growth has started in spring, remove the central leader, cutting back to the lowest of two side branches, one on either side of the plant. They should ideally be about 16in. above the ground. If upright shoots are not removed, they will tend to hinder the development of the fan.

> **TRAIN AND PRUNE PEACHES AND NECTARINES**
>
> Peaches and nectarines can be treated in the same way because their flowering and fruiting habits are the same; both form fruits on the wood produced in the previous year. The pruning technique is sometimes called 'replacement' pruning, because it consists of replacing older branches with new growth from the current year. Pruning involves looking towards the future—one year in advance of the current year. If pruning more than one peach or nectarine tree, disinfect pruning tools between trees, to prevent passing on potential infections. Pruning late in the dormant season is best for peaches and nectarines, but avoid doing this just before predicted cold weather, in order to minimize injury to buds and flowers.

Train the side branches onto canes attached to wires, angling them to about 45 degrees. These two branches are sometimes referred to as 'ribs'. Remove any other sideshoots. Prune the ribs back by about one third to an upward-facing bud. This will stimulate buds to break along the pruned branch.

The following year, in early spring, cut back this new growth by about two thirds, to stimulate further growth. The basic structure of the fan will now be complete, with about eight ribs, or branches. Once the fan has been established, start pruning in early spring when the plant is in growth.

Remove any undesirable shoots, such as ones coming off the trunk and where they will cause congestion. It is important to leave all the swollen fat buds, which will become the current year's flowers and subsequently the fruit. Identify the vegetative buds or shoots, as these will bear the following year's crop.

Leave one new vegetative bud or shoot towards the base of the branch and another one half way up the branch. The shoot at the base will be used for next year's replacement, while the second one can be a backup in case the basal shoot fails. The terminal bud (in the tip of the branch) can also be left.

Train canes of established blackberries

Trailing and semitrailing types of blackberries should be trained to supports; upright types can be grown with or without supports. Train canes that will fruit later in the season onto arches or supports before the buds burst into growth. A simple and efficient training system includes sturdy 8ft. posts, spaced 12ft. apart, and set 30in. into the ground. Fix horizontal wires spanning the posts at 30in. and 60in. above the ground. Select the strongest second-year canes—these will produce this year's fruit; spread them out and tie them to the wires using soft twine or cloth strips. Allow the canes that develop this year to trail on the ground; they will bear next year's fruit.

An alternative training system is to grow the berries against a wall or fence. Provide a series of horizontal wires spaced 18in. apart, with the lowest wire 9in. from the ground. Spread the canes and tie them to the wires to provide good air circulation.

Black currants

Plant new bushes

Black currants are very good sources of vitamin C and a variety of antioxidants. They grow best in regions where

---

SOFT FRUIT

Blackberries

Plant new canes

Blackberries prefer moisture-retentive but free-draining soil, so dig plenty of bulky organic matter into chalky, sandy, or heavy clay soils before planting. While crops can tolerate some shade, they will be more productive in a sunny site.

Many varieties, especially the hybrid forms, are very vigorous and require at least 12ft. between plants when trained against a wall or fence. Thornless varieties of blackberry are very desirable—they make harvesting easy and painless. Some good thornless varieties are: 'Chester', 'Hull', 'Navaho', and 'Triple Crown'.

After planting, cut all canes down to a healthy bud. This may seem somewhat drastic but it will ensure your plant sends up lots of vigorous, healthy suckers once they begin growth.

BLACK CURRANTS AND WHITE PINE BLISTER RUST

Currants serve as an alternate host of a disease known as white pine blister rust. For the disease to complete its life cycle and spread, two different hosts must be present. Members of the Ribes genus (currants, gooseberries) serve as one of the hosts (black currants are the most susceptible species); five-needled pine species, including the eastern white pine, serve as the other host. While currants are minimally affected by the fungus, pines can be devastated. For this reason, many states banned growing black currants and gooseberries in the early 1900s.

Fortunately, varieties of black currant and other Ribes species have since been developed that are resistant to the fungus, and many states have lifted the ban on growing black currants. Be sure to select a resistant variety for your garden. Some recommended varieties are 'Consort', 'Coronet', 'Crandall', 'Polar', and 'Titania'.

PLANTING A BAREROOT BLACK CURRANT

1 ADD A BALANCED FERTILIZER *to the bottom of the planting hole if it wasn't added when the planting area was prepared. Work it into the soil at the bottom of the hole.*

2 LOOK FOR THE SOIL MARK *on the black currant plant; it should be planted at least 2¼in. deeper than previously. Place a board across the hole to assess the correct depth.*

3 BACKFILL WITH EXCAVATED SOIL *enriched with well-rotted farmyard manure, then firm the soil. Water thoroughly so the moisture reaches throughout the root zone.*

summers are relatively cool. In addition to being easy to grow, they begin producing their flavorful fruit the second year after planting, and often continue to bear heavy crops for 15 years. They tolerate a wide range of soil conditions but prefer a well-drained, moisture-retentive, slightly acidic soil. They produce best in full sun but will tolerate light shade. Avoid frost pockets—frosts can drastically reduce yields, even on later flowering varieties.

Plant black currants spacing the bushes 6ft. apart in all directions, unless you want to grow them as a hedge (then, space them 3–4ft. apart in a row). Prior to planting, clear the soil of all perennial weeds and enrich it with a generous amount of well-rotted farmyard manure and a balanced fertilizer. Allow the bed to settle before planting. Set each plant at least 2in. deeper than it was previously growing, so that it develops into a multistemmed bush. Deep planting encourages young, vigorous shoots to develop from the base. Mix the soil from the hole with well-rotted compost or manure and backfill the hole, firming well around the roots. Cut back all stems to 1–2in. above the ground to encourage strong roots. Water well after planting and during dry spells.

Blueberries

Plant new bushes

Blueberries need moist, well-drained, acidic soil in a sunny, sheltered spot. While they are tolerant of light shade, better crops (and fall color) are obtained if blueberries are planted in the sun. The pH should be at least as low as 5.5. If your garden soil is alkaline, add sulfur according to your soil-test results to decrease the pH; this should be done at least six months prior to planting the blueberry bushes. Alternatively, grow blueberries in containers of soil-based growing mix for acid-loving plants. For pot culture, use a container 12in. in diameter for a small plant, and a half-barrel or similarly larger pot for a bigger blueberry bush. Make sure the container is either glazed or lined with plastic sheeting (pierced at the base), in order to avoid excessive moisture loss.

When growing blueberries in your garden soil, add plenty of bulky, acidic organic matter such as pine needles or composted conifer clippings. Space plants at least 3ft. apart, to accommodate their spread—further, if more vigorous varieties are chosen.

PLANTING A BLUEBERRY

1 DIG A HOLE *twice the width of the rootball and to the depth of the pot, if the blueberry is container grown. Otherwise make the hole wide enough to plant it at its original depth.*

2 TEASE OUT THE ROOTS. *Then, using a planting stick or wooden board as a guide, ensure the top of the rootball or the old soil mark is level with the ground.*

3 BACKFILL THE HOLE, *working the soil around the rootball or roots. Firm the soil with the ball of your foot and water in well so that the soil can settle around the rootball.*

Blueberries can be grown as single plants, but they will carry a heavier crop if two or more different varieties are planted together for cross-pollination. Make sure you select varieties that flower at the same time and always purchase certified, disease-free plants.

BEDS FOR ACID-LOVING FRUIT

Blueberries and other acid-loving crops such as cranberries and lingonberries can also be grown in a raised or sunken bed filled with loam-based, acidic soil combined with composted bark. Sunken beds are extremely moisture retentive, while raised beds require constant irrigation throughout summer.

Make the bed, whether raised or sunk into the soil, at least 2ft. deep. Line the sides and base with plastic that has been pierced in several places with a garden fork. This piercing is important; while the aim of lining the bed is partly to conserve moisture in the soil, it is also necessary to ensure that there is sufficient drainage to prevent the bed from becoming waterlogged.

Feed established blueberries

Apply a topdressing of fertilizer for acid-loving plants to the soil at half the recommended rate and cover it with a mulch material of pine needles or composted conifer clippings. Keep plants well watered, especially during spring and summer, using rainwater whenever possible.

Cranberries and lingonberries

Plant new bushes

Cranberries and lingonberries can be planted in the same bed as blueberries, because the soil and moisture requirements of all three crops are very similar. While cranberries and lingonberries tolerate shade, a sunnier position is preferable.

Purchase young, bushy plants. If grown in the open ground, set them 12in. apart. Minimal initial training is required: on planting, just clip plants back to ensure they remain compact and bushy.

Both types of plants (cranberries in particular) have the ability to spread and will eventually knit together, to form a ground covering.

Gooseberries

Plant new bushes

Gooseberries prefer moisture-retentive yet well-drained soil. Avoid very shallow, dry soils because the roots will dry out quickly, causing problems with American gooseberry mildew. Gooseberries can tolerate some shade and will successfully fruit on a north-facing wall. Before planting, incorporate well-rotted manure and a balanced fertilizer into the soil. Plant single, vertical cordons 12in. apart and bushes 5ft. apart.

Gooseberries are shallow rooted, and will benefit from an organic mulch that will help moderate soil temperature and retain soil moisture.

Raspberries

Plant new canes

When ordering new raspberry canes, always buy from a supplier offering certified stock. This ensures that your canes will be free from virus infections, to which raspberries are particularly prone and which can severely deplete yields.

Raspberries prefer slightly acidic soil that retains moisture well, particularly in the summer when the fruits are swelling. Add plenty of bulky organic matter to the planting site, particularly to sandy soils. The plants will tolerate some shade, but will crop better in an open, sunny spot.

Summer raspberries require a sturdy support system: run two horizontal wires—one 2ft. high and the other 5ft. high—along the length of the row.

Clear the site of perennial weeds before planting, as these are difficult to control once raspberries are established. Plant bareroot canes now, spacing the new raspberry plants 2–3ft. apart. Then apply a mulch of organic matter such as garden compost. Avoid mushroom compost (which is too alkaline) or overly rich farmyard manure (which tends to burn off the new shoots as they push through the mulch layer).

Plant in containers

In small gardens, raspberries will grow surprisingly well in containers. Use a 12in. pot filled with a loam-based potting mix. Plant three canes to each pot. Keep plants well watered during the growing season and feed them with a high-potassium fertilizer.

Red and white currants

Plant new bushes

Red and white currant bushes are hardy plants that thrive in open, sunny positions. They grow best in cooler climates—Zones 5 and above—and may not perform well in warm regions. They are tolerant, however, of moderate shade and make attractive features when fruiting on a north-facing wall. Avoid frost pockets and exposed windy sites. Incorporate well-rotted organic matter into the soil before planting, and set the bushes 5ft. apart in each direction. Apply a heavy organic mulch to keep roots cool and moist.

Red and white currants, and the less commonly grown pink currants, are all cultivated in the same way.

PLANT BAREROOT RED CURRANTS NOW. *Having dug the planting hole, check its depth against the plant's old soil mark. To do this, hold the plant against a planting stick placed across the hole.*

However, while they are closely related to black currants, it is important to remember that black currants are pruned completely differently, so do not get the two groups of currants confused.

Strawberries

Plant new outdoor beds

In most regions, strawberries are best planted in early spring, as soon as the ground can be worked. They are very versatile; they can be planted in the fruit or vegetable garden, among ornamental plants or in separate beds—provided they have sun, shelter, and fertile, well-drained soil. Avoid areas prone to frost (because strawberries are low growing) as well as windy sites (which will prevent pollinating insects from reaching the flowers). Also do not use sites that have previously grown potatoes, chrysanthemums, or tomatoes, because they are all prone to the disease verticillium wilt. In poor soils, grow strawberries in raised beds, which improves drainage around their roots.

Prepare the planting site by digging to a depth of one spade blade. Remove perennial weeds, then add well-rotted manure. Level the soil and rake it to a fine tilth.

Dig a hole large enough to accommodate the strawberry plant. Trim the roots lightly to about 4in.

if necessary, then spread them out in the hole. Ensure that the base of the crown rests on the surface. Planting at the correct depth is important: if the crown is planted too deeply, it will rot; if it is planted too shallowly, the plants will dry out and die. Once the plant is at the correct depth, backfill the soil, keeping it off the crown and firming it around the plant, using finger tips. Set June-bearing varieties 18in. apart; space everbearing and day-neutral varieties 12in. apart. If planting another row, place it 30in. away—closer if in a raised bed. Water the plants well. To exclude weeds, plant through black plastic or landscaping fabric.

Keep strawberries weed free

Weed frequently between the rows of strawberry beds to keep the plants weed free and prevent any competition for water and nutrients. However, take care not to damage the plants, especially if you are using a hoe—it is very easy to sever a strawberry plant from its roots with a single push of the hoe.

Help strawberry pollination

If strawberry plants are covered by row covers to protect the flowers from frosts and encourage strong growth, roll up the sides when the plants are flowering, to allow pollinating insects access to them.

PLANTING STRAWBERRIES

STRAWBERRIES *can be planted now in prepared beds. Trim large root systems by about half their length, using sharp pruning shears before planting.*

MARK OUT A PLANTING LINE *across the bed using a taut string. Alongside it, set a board with the correct spacings (12–18in, depending on the variety) marked along its length and make the holes.*

DIG A HOLE *large enough to fit the plant roots along each line, then backfill and firm soil around the roots, ensuring that the crown of each plant is level with the soil surface. Water well.*

VINE FRUIT

Grapes

Plant new vines

Choose a sheltered, sunny location. A trellis or other support system should be constructed prior to planting. Space the vines about 8ft. apart. If planting a bareroot vine, soak the roots before planting.

For each vine, dig the soil to the depth of at least one spade and break up any clods. Add a bucketful of grit to the planting hole on heavy, clay soils and a small amount of balanced fertilizer. Trim the roots of bareroot plants to 6–12in. and spread them outwards and downwards in the hole. If planting a container-grown vine, place the rootball in the hole so that it will be at the same depth as it was in the container. Backfill the planting hole, firming the soil around the roots or rootball, and water thoroughly.

Prior to planting, construct a support system to provide the vine with maximum light penetration and air circulation. Several types of trellises work well for grapes; which you choose depends on your available space, the vigor of the vine, and how much effort you want to put into construction. Most systems establish an upright main trunk. One of the most efficient ones for supporting grapes is the four-arm Kniffen system (see page 277).

Remove unwanted shoots from established vines

Prune out surplus shoots that arise from the roots and trunk of an established grape vine.

THE INDIVIDUAL FLAVOR OF WINE is based very much on the unique soil characteristics of the place in which the grape vine is planted, derived from the natural nutrients in the soil.

PLANTING A CONTAINER-GROWN GRAPE VINE AGAINST A WALL

1 DIG A HOLE into prepared soil at least 12in. in front of a single, vertical cane attached to the horizontal wire support on the wall. Add grit if the soil is heavy.

2 PLACE THE ROOTBALL of the grapevine into the hole, angling the main stem toward the cane. Backfill the hole once the plant is at the same depth as previously growing.

3 TIE THE MAIN STEM to the vertical cane and lowest wire, using string or garden twine in a figure-eight loop. Then water thoroughly.

| Understanding fruit tree forms

Fruit trees can be grown in a variety of different forms to suit the size of your garden. Freestanding standard, semi-dwarf or dwarf trees are attractive additions to larger gardens. For small gardens, restricted forms such as cordons, fans, and espaliers are particularly ideal as they will make maximum use of the space they are in as well as adding ornamental appeal. Existing fences can also be employed as suitable supports for an espalier or fan, creating an attractive feature. Only spur-bearing (not tip-bearing) varieties can be trained in this way. If in doubt about whether a particular variety is suitable, ask your supplier for advice.

MATURE ESPALIERS *(above) make excellent ornamental screens and can be used to partition a garden in an eye-catching way.*

DWARF TREES, *like this open-center-trained 'Cox's Orange Pippin' apple (right) grown on a dwarfing rootstock, require less space than a standard tree and still bear a lot of fruit.*

Restricted tree forms

Cordon

This simple form is popular in a small garden as several varieties can be crammed into a small space. Each tree can be spaced as closely as 12–18in. apart. For proper training from the start, it's best to begin with a one-year-old tree. The tree is usually planted as an oblique cordon (shown) at an angle of 30–45 degrees, and it has fruiting spurs along the stem. A fruit tree can also be grown as a double-stemmed (or U-shaped)

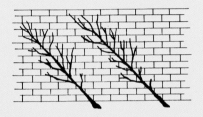

cordon. Consult your local nursery or extension service for appropriate varieties of apple and pear and suggested dwarf rootstocks.

Espalier

Probably the most intricate way to grow a fruit tree against a wall or fence. A central stem is trained upwards with pairs of opposite branches trained horizontally along a system of wires. There are usually three or four tiers. Fruit spurs are encouraged along these horizontal

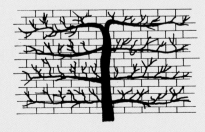

branches. Check with your nursery for appropriate varieties and rootstocks for your region.

Fan

Perhaps one of the most attractive and popular tree form shapes, a fan has a short trunk in the center of the plant and then branches radiating out on either side into a fan shape, usually to cover a wall or fence. Check with your nursery for appropriate varieties and rootstocks.

Unsupported tree forms

Central leader

The tapering shape of a central-leader-trained tree lets sunlight reach most parts of the tree. A main branch (leader) is selected followed by sets of three or four lower branches (scaffold branches) at intervals about 2ft. apart, to create

a pyramid that is widest toward the bottom of the tree. Scaffold branches are cut back by about a third during the dormant season, to encourage branching. Other branches arising from the leader should be removed. Spreaders may be used to promote

wide angles where the lateral branches meet the main trunk. This is usually the best form for an open-grown apple or pear tree. The central-leader form can be used for a dwarf tree that grows to only 25–50 percent of the height of a standard tree, for a semidwarf that grows to approximately 50–85 percent of the height of a standard tree, or for a standard or full-sized tree. Although the rootstock is significant when deciding the size of tree you want to grow, pruning to maintain the tree's size and form is as important, if not more so. Check with your nursery or extension service for appropriate varieties and rootstocks.

Open center

Open-center training is a good choice for stone fruit such as peach, plum, nectarine, apricot, and cherry, although apples can be trained to an open center as well. Three or four main scaffold branches that grow in different directions are selected to form an open framework. Lateral branching is encouraged by heading back scaffold branches during the dormant season. The open-center form allows sunlight to penetrate an otherwise dense canopy. It also encourages good circulation, which helps reduce disease and pest problems. Open-center forms work well for dwarf, semidwarf, and standard-sized trees.

mid spring

This is a busy time in the garden wherever you live. In mild-winter regions, the first harvests of early crops are being enjoyed, while other crops are growing fast. In mid-temperate regions, vegetable plants are continuing their move from indoors or the protection of cold-frames to the vegetable patch, while seeds of other crops are being sown directly in the garden. In cold-winter regions, it's time to sow seeds of a few early crops in the garden, as soon as the soil can be worked, while later crops can be started indoors.

Crops are growing—but so are the weeds. From now on, right through the end of the growing season, you have to be vigilant, or weeds will quickly take over. As plants put on more growth, pests, too, are increasing. Watch out for aphids in particular colonizing the tender young growing tips of plants.

This is the time to enjoy the magnificent blossoming of fruit trees, with their promise of heavy crops to come.

vegetables | GENERAL ADVICE

ALL REGIONS

Water seedbeds | Cold, dry winds can soon parch seedbeds, and frequent light watering is helpful. In general, the soil is still moist from winter, so deep watering is seldom necessary.

Thin seedlings | Start thinning seedlings as soon as they are large enough to be handled. In some cases, thinnings can be used to fill gaps further along the rows, but this technique is not suitable for root crops such as parsnips and carrots, as it will result in stunted or misshapen roots.

Guard against slugs and snails | Tender young seedlings are very attractive to slugs. Protect them with slug controls or deterrents.

Protect carrots and cabbage | If you have not already done so, place row covers over crops of young cabbage and carrots to exclude cabbage root maggot and carrot rust fly.

Make successional sowings | Make further sowings of crops such as lettuce, peas, beets, radishes, carrots, and turnips to ensure a continuous supply.

Avoid working in the garden when it's wet | Walking in the garden when soil is wet can cause it to compact, compromising its structure. If you need to get into the garden when the soil is wet, set out planks of wood to walk on, to better distribute the weight.

Harden off seedlings | Before transplanting young vegetable plants to the garden, be sure they have been properly acclimated to the outdoors. Whether you purchase young seedlings from a local garden center or a mail order supplier, or grow them yourself, it is critical to introduce them to outdoor conditions gradually, otherwise they become stressed, stunted, and may even die after a sudden move outdoors.

Hardening off is best accomplished by taking indoor- or greenhouse-grown seedlings outside for a couple of hours a day, placing them in a partly shaded area that is protected from wind, and bringing them indoors at night. Each day, increase the time the plants are left outside as well as the amount of sun they receive. After about two weeks they should be ready to transplant into the garden. Alternatively, a cold-frame provides a sheltered location for hardening-off seedlings. If temperatures are likely to drop below 50°F at night, close the lid, but be sure to vent the top on sunny days or your seedlings will burn. After about two weeks in the cold-frame, your seedlings should be ready for the garden.

To further reduce stress to the seedlings, transplant them on a mild, overcast day.

MILD-WINTER REGIONS ONLY

Sow heat-loving crops | Seeds of corn, squash, melons, okra, beans, and cucumber can be planted directly in the garden once the soil has warmed and all danger of frost has passed.

Transplant tender crops | Tomato, pepper, and eggplant plants can be moved from indoors (or purchased from a local garden center) for planting in the garden after proper hardening off.

Resow failed seed | Early-sown crops are always more subject to failure, particularly if there has been an unexpected cold spell after sowing. Where necessary, resow crops, but ensure you have allowed enough time for slow-germinating seeds (such as parsnip) to emerge.

YOUNG LETTUCE, CARROT, AND CORIANDER PLANTS
make an attractive feature in the spring vegetable garden. Close spacing helps to keep down weeds.

vegetables | WHAT TO DO NOW

Garlic

Water during dry weather

An occasional thorough watering during dry spells will improve the yield. Don't water once the bulbs are large and well formed, because this could encourage rotting.

Leek

Sow outside

Leeks can be sown now to mature in fall. The growing instructions are the same as for leeks sown in early spring (see page 40).

Onion and shallot

Sowing outside

Continue sowing onion and shallot seed thinly in rows spaced 12in. apart. After seeds germinate, thin onions to 2–4in. apart, depending on variety.

Broccoli

Transplant young plants

Broccoli grows best in cool weather and needs a relatively early start in the garden. Finish transplanting broccoli to the garden in mid-temperate regions, and begin transplanting in cold-winter regions. If you did not start plants indoors from seed, young plants are usually readily available from garden centers now.

Harvest heads and shoots

In mild-winter regions, begin harvesting before buds open to reveal yellow flowers. Sprouting varieties will continue producing sideshoots for several weeks. After cutting, large-head types will usually produce a few smaller sideshoots as well.

Cabbage

Transplant young plants

Finish hardening off and transplanting cabbage to the garden in mid-temperate regions, and begin transplanting in cold-winter regions. Space plants 12–18in. apart.

Water regularly

Cabbage grows quickly given a steady supply of water and nutrients. If less than 1in. of rain occurs in a week, supplement with additional water.

Cut heads as they are ready

In mild-winter regions, harvest early cabbage as soon as their heads are firm.

Cauliflower

Transplant young plants

In cold-winter and mid-temperate regions, transplant hardened-off seedlings to the garden after all danger of hard frost has passed. Space plants 24in. apart.

Blanch heads and harvest

In mild-winter regions, loosely tie leaves over the forming head to blanch. Harvest when curds are tight and heads reach the size appropriate for the variety.

Kohlrabi

Sow outside

Sow seed outside in drills ½in. deep, after any danger of hard frost has passed. Space seeds 1in. apart, and allow 12–18in. between rows. After seeds germinate, thin seedlings to 4in. apart.

Harvest the bulb

In mild-winter regions, early plantings may be ready to harvest. Cut when the bulb reaches the appropriate size for the variety, usually 3–4in. in diameter, but before it becomes tough. Young leaves can also be harvested for use in stir-fries or salads.

LEGUMES

Fava beans

Plant seed outdoors

In cooler regions, where fava beans are a useful substitute for lima beans, sow fava beans now, spacing seed 4–6in. apart in rows 24in. apart.

Lima beans

Sow seed outdoors

In mild-winter regions, sow seed in the garden after all danger of frost has passed and the soil has warmed. Plant seeds 1in. deep and 3in. apart; allow 2–3ft. between rows. Provide support for pole varieties.

Peas

Support seedlings

Put supports in place before the young plants become top-heavy and flop over. For dwarf and shorter varieties, twiggy peasticks, chicken wire attached to stakes, or string and stakes are fine. For taller varieties, a trellis or bamboo canes and netting are more appropriate. To help them get started to climb, gently guide the stems toward the support until their tendrils take hold.

It is easy to underestimate just how sturdy such supports need to be, especially in windy weather. The foliage of fully grown plants acts like a sail, catching the wind and causing vines to topple, so make sure that the supports are well secured.

Snap beans

Sow seed outdoors

In mild-winter regions, sow beans after all danger of frost has passed and the soil has warmed. Plant seeds 1in. deep and 2in. apart for bush varieties, 3–4in. apart for pole varieties; allow 2–3ft. between rows. Make successive sowings every two weeks for a continuous supply. Provide support for pole varieties.

BOTH RED AND GREEN VARIETIES *of kohlrabi are available. They should be harvested before the bulbs become tough. Young leaves make a delicious addition to a stir-fry.*

USE TALLER VARIETIES OF CLIMBING PEAS *to edge the kitchen garden or to create attractive divisions between sections of a bed. Be sure that supports are sufficiently sturdy to stand up to strong winds.*

ROOT AND STEM CROPS

Beet

Sow seed outdoors

In mid-temperate regions, sow seed in the garden following directions from early spring (see page 42). Make small, successive sowings, for an extended harvest.

Parsnip

Sow outside

If the weather was too cold or wet for sowing parsnips in early spring, seed can be sown now.

Thin seedlings

When the seedlings appear, thin them so that they are 2–3in. apart. Hoe them regularly to keep weeds down. Large, easy-to-peel roots are obtained by wide spacing of plants and the absence of weeds. Parsnips are highly drought-resistant plants that need watering only once every 10–14 days if the foliage starts to wilt.

Potato

Continue planting tubers

The two methods are to dig a trench or to plant in individual holes. Handle each sprouted potato carefully so you don't knock off any of the shoots, and plant 6in. deep. Space 12in. apart, with 24–30in. between rows.

Closer planting often results in smaller potatoes at harvest time.

You can also plant potatoes through black plastic mulch by simply cutting holes in it. Doing this means you won't need to mound soil around the plants.

Mound soil around plants

As soon as the first shoots emerge from potatoes planted earlier, start to mound soil up and over them to produce a rounded ridge. This will prevent the shoots from being damaged by a late frost.

Continue mounding soil at one- to two-week intervals until the ridge is 8–12in. high; this not only inhibits weeds but also helps reduce disease and prevents the tubers from being exposed to light and turning green. You do not need to mound soil around potatoes growing under black plastic as they are already protected from light and the plastic prevents weed growth. During dry spells, give potatoes an occasional but thorough watering. Plenty of water early on in the plants' development will lead to initiation of tubers and a heavy crop later.

DIG A TRENCH *6in. deep, then space your potatoes 12in. apart. Leave a gap of about three years before growing potatoes in the same spot to avoid the accumulation of soil-borne pests and diseases.*

SPROUTING SEED POTATOES *before planting helps to produce an earlier crop, but the tubers need to be handled carefully to avoid knocking off the fragile sprouts.*

Radish

Keep roots growing steadily

Water regularly in dry weather to prevent plants from bolting or becoming woody. Irregular watering can result in splitting of the roots, while lush, leafy growth instead of root development may be caused by overwatering.

Sweet potato

Plant slips

In mild-winter regions, it is time to transplant the rooted cuttings of sweet potatoes, called slips. Plant them in ridged rows of mounded soil after all danger of frost has passed, spacing slips 12–18in. apart. Allow 3–4ft. between rows because the vines require lots of space.

THERE ARE SCORES OF LETTUCE VARIETIES *to choose from, each with its own flavor, texture, and color. Growing instructions will vary slightly depending on the variety, so always read the seed packet.*

LEAFY GREENS

Chard

Sow seed outside

Chard (also called Swiss chard) is a good alternative for spinach for warmer weather and on dry soils where spinach quickly bolts. The leaves have prominent midribs, which can be cooked as well; these can be creamy white, pink, yellow, or red according to the variety. Although the leaves of chard taste similar to spinach, it is a member of the beet family.

Sow chard now for summer and fall picking, spacing seed 2in. apart in rows 18–24in. apart. Thin seedlings to 4–6in. apart after they are large enough to handle.

Lettuce

Continue sowing outside

Sow lettuce in full sun on moisture-retentive, reasonably fertile soil. Sow seed thinly in drills ½in. deep. Final spacing in the row will be 4–12in., depending on the variety of lettuce; see the seed packet for individual instructions. Water well. Alternatively, sow rows of lettuce seeds at a similar density to a leafy cut-and-come-again crop (see page 74).

Thin earlier-sown seedlings

Thin lettuce seedlings as soon as they can be handled comfortably. First thin them to half their final spacing, with a further thinning later on to leave them at the correct distance. With care, the thinned seedlings can be transplanted, provided this is done in cool weather and plants are well watered afterwards. Replanting them among slow-maturing crops such as brassicas is an effective use of space. Thinnings can also be eaten.

Mustard

Continue to sow outside

Continue to sow mustard seed in the garden. Plant small patches of seed, 2–3 weeks apart until late summer for a continuous supply. Follow spacings on page 44.

Spinach

Sow outside

In cold-winter and mid-temperate regions, sow spinach seed directly where it is to grow in drills ½in. deep in rows 12in. apart. Spinach needs plenty of moisture and lots of nutrients, so apply a general fertilizer and do not attempt to grow it in dry soil with low fertility. Add plenty of well-rotted manure or compost to the soil before sowing.

If you like spinach, be generous with your sowing so that you can gather lots for the steamer or wok—it cooks down to almost nothing. Since spinach will not easily

SPINACH SEEDLINGS *won't germinate easily in hot weather, so where temperatures are still cool, sow now and again in early fall. Thin seedlings to 4–6in. apart, for full-sized leaves, closer for baby spinach.*

germinate in hot weather and tends to bolt if sown too early, make sowings now and again in early fall.

Baby spinach leaves also make great additions to salads. To grow small salad leaves, make an 8–12in. wide band and scatter the seed thinly across it. You should not need to thin the seedlings.

CUCURBITS

General

Summer squash, winter squash, and pumpkin are all closely related members of the same family—Cucurbitaceae—and there is often confusion over exactly what is meant by each term.

Summer squash includes the long, narrow zucchini, scalloped pattypan, and the bulbous-shaped, yellow crookneck or straightneck. All are fast growing and are harvested when the fruit is immature. Some popular varieties include: 'Raven', 'Bush Baby', and 'Meteor' (zucchini); 'Sunburst', 'Flying Saucer', and 'Starship' (pattypan); and 'Gentry' and 'Sunray' (yellow crookneck).

Winter squash and pumpkins require a longer growing season and are harvested when the fruit is mature; they will keep for much of the winter. Their flesh is drier, sweeter, and nuttier than summer varieties, and they

are available in a wide range of shapes. Good varieties of winter squash include: 'Honey Bear' and 'Table Ace' (acorn); 'Waltham' (butternut); and 'Red Kuri' and 'Blue Ballet' (hubbard).

Pumpkins are a type of winter squash and, although typically orange, come in shades of white, tan, green, and blue. Varieties range from the very small 'Wee-B-Little' and 'Baby Bear' to the enormous 'Wolf', 'Big Rock', and 'Howden Biggie'.

Cucumber

Sow seed indoors

In cold-winter and mid-temperate regions, sow seed in pots indoors about one month before the last predicted frost in your area. Sow two seeds per pot and remove the weakest seedling if both germinate.

Sow seed outdoors

In mild-winter regions, after the soil has warmed, sow seed directly in the garden, ½in. deep and 4in. apart, in rows spaced 3–4ft. apart. Thin to a final distance of 12in. apart. Alternatively, plant in hills with three seeds each. Space hills 2–3ft. apart. Cucumbers can also be planted in containers, but select short vine or bush varieties.

Melons

Sow seed indoors

In cold-winter and mid-temperate regions, sow seeds in individual pots indoors 3–4 weeks before the last predicted frost. Keep seedlings warm.

Sow seed outdoors

In mild-winter regions, sow seed outdoors after the soil has warmed, planting seeds 1in. deep, 4in. apart, in rows spaced 4ft. apart. Thin seedlings to 12–18in. apart. Or sow 2–3 seeds per hill, spacing hills 3–4ft. apart.

Summer squash

Sow seed indoors

Follow the same procedure as for sowing cucumbers indoors (above). Some varieties produce very vigorous vines, so refer to the seed package for the appropriate spacing for these.

Sow seed outdoors

Follow the same procedure as for sowing cucumbers outdoors (see page 71).

Winter squash and pumpkin

Sow seed indoors

Follow the same procedure as for sowing cucumbers indoors (see page 71). Winter squash and pumpkins need a long, hot growing season to ripen fully, so choose early ripening varieties if your season is short.

FRUITING CROPS AND CORN

General

In mild-winter regions, these heat-loving crops can be sown or transplanted outdoors after all danger of frost has passed and the soil has warmed.

In other regions, thin seeds sown indoors or transplant them to larger pots as needed.

Corn

Sow seed outdoors

In mild-winter regions, begin sowing corn after the soil has warmed (to 60–65°F). Sow in blocks of at least four rows, 30–36in. apart, for optimum pollination. (These are wind- not insect-pollinated plants.) Sow seed 6in. apart in 1in. deep drills. Make successive sowings through mid summer for an extended harvest.

Eggplant

Transplant outdoors

In mild-winter regions, harden off seedlings, then transplant into the garden, spacing them 12–18in. apart in rows 30in. apart. Use row covers to accelerate growth and protect plants from pests.

Peppers

Transplant outdoors

In mild-winter regions, peppers can be transplanted outdoors after they have been hardened off, following the same procedure and spacing as for transplanting eggplant (above).

Tomato

Space out seedlings

Like eggplants and peppers, tomatoes are very sensitive to frost, so plants that are raised indoors can be planted outside only after all risk of frost has passed. Space plants 18–24in. apart. If you plan to stake your tomatoes, place stakes at planting time to avoid injuring roots later. Tomatoes can also be grown within circular wire cages that help keep the plants from sprawling on the ground. Set cages in place immediately after planting. For added protection and earlier harvest, use row covers.

TOMATOES IN A SMALL SPACE

Where space is limited, tomatoes can be grown successfully in hanging baskets or large window boxes. Most seed catalogs have a range of trailing varieties specially bred for growing in containers. Fill the container with good-quality potting mix supplemented with good garden compost and slow-release fertilizer. Plant three trailing tomatoes to each medium- to large-sized basket or window box. Suitable tomato varieties include 'Patio Princess', 'Tumbler', and 'Tumbling Tom'.

Asparagus

Continue planting crowns
Finish planting crowns (roots) following the same procedure as in early spring (see page 47).

Fill in trenches
Add soil to trenches gradually over the next few weeks until you form a slight mound along the planting row.

Water and weed seed beds
If you planted asparagus from seed in early spring, keep the seedbeds moist and weed free as the seedlings develop.

Harvest spears from established beds
Gathering root-planted asparagus can begin the second spring after planting. For the initial harvest year, cut stalks for only two weeks, to encourage further root development. The following year (the third year after planting) harvest for three weeks; the fourth year after planting, harvest for four weeks. Beginning the fifth year after planting, stalks can be harvested for 4–6 weeks, until they become thin.

Harvest spears that are thicker than a pencil, snapping them off or cutting them 1in. below ground.

BEGINNING THE SECOND YEAR AFTER PLANTING, *harvest asparagus stalks that are thicker than a pencil. Check the bed every day, because new stalks grow rapidly.*

Rhubarb

Plant new stock
In cold-winter and mid-temperate regions, where rhubarb thrives, continue planting dormant crowns or pot-grown plants. Be sure to work plenty of organic matter, such as well-rotted manure or garden compost, into the soil prior to planting.

Rhubarb plants have an attractive appearance with their large, wrinkled leaves and thick, often red stalks, and can be planted in a perennial border to provide a bold accent. Be sure to allow plenty of space—about 3ft. in each direction—for each plant. Good varieties include: 'Victoria', 'Valentine', and 'Cherry Red'. Rhubarb does not perform well in warmer regions.

Begin to harvest stalks
On established plants, cut or pull stalks as they become large enough to use. Grab the stem at its base, close to the crown of the plant, and pull it down with a slight twist. Discard the leaves; they contain harmful amounts of oxalic acid and are poisonous.

PLANT RHUBARB CROWNS NOW *positioning each one so that the dormant buds are just above soil level. One or two plants should supply sufficient stems for most people's needs during the growing season.*

| Grow your own salad leaves

The days when lettuce was the only leafy salad vegetable are long gone—now you can enjoy a whole mix of different colors, tastes, and textures in your salads. For some time, supermarkets have been selling bags of mixed salad leaves at a premium price, but growing your own could hardly be easier.

Salad leaves can be grown in the open ground, in window boxes, or in patio planters. They are very fast growing and are ready to harvest within a few weeks of sowing. Because they are eaten so young, they hardly have time to fall prey to pests or diseases. Sow short rows of seeds in well-prepared soil and keep them moist. Make several sowings for a long succession of baby leaves.

When the plants have made sufficient growth, harvest them by either picking a few leaves at a time or simply cut the entire crop, leaving a short stump from each plant in the ground. Keep the soil moist and these stumps will resprout and new leaves can be harvested. The process can often be repeated for a further cut.

Because salad leaves are so quick to mature, they are perfect for intercropping— sowing in the spaces between slower-maturing crops. When sowing a very slow-germinating crop such as parsnip, sow seed of salad leaves down the row between the parsnips; not only will they make good use of the space, but they will also germinate quickly to mark out the row for you, making weeding between the rows easier.

To enjoy fresh salad in very early spring and again in late fall and into the winter, leaves can be grown in a cold-frame.

LETTUCE AND OTHER SALAD GREENS *offer different colors and textures, which look as good in the garden as they do on the plate.*

Recommended salad crops

Seed companies sell a range of leafy greens for salads, either separately or as preselected mixes, often with a spicy, Oriental, or gourmet theme. Colorful, interestingly shaped lettuce varieties feature strongly, but there are plenty of other types of leaves to try as well.

Amaranth
Similar to spinach, with a sharp bite to the leaves and attractive, red-veined foliage.

Beet
A mild, earthy, sweet-flavored leaf. 'Bull's Blood' (below) has burgundy-red foliage for impact on the plate. The color deepens as plants mature.

Buckler-leaved sorrel
Bright green, shield-shaped leaves (below) with a sharp lemony flavor. Also known as French sorrel, it has a variegated form called 'Silver Shield'.

Claytonia
Also called miner's lettuce. Very cold tolerant with pairs of small, heart-shaped leaves that surround a stem bearing a delicate, white flower. Can be grown all winter in mild regions.

Corn salad
Also known as mâche (above). Forms rosettes of small, bright green, succulent leaves; very hardy, so useful in winter and in early spring.

Cress
Quick-growing cress with a lovely, peppery tang. For a less spicy taste, cut the leaves young, as they get hotter with age.

Kale
Full-flavored and full of vitamins (above). Try dark-leaved 'Nero di Toscana' or deep purple 'Redbor'.

Mustard
Spicy leaves that become hotter as they get larger. 'Red Giant' has purple-tinged, rough-textured leaves.

Red orach
Arrowhead-shaped leaves that are harvested when young (below). Some varieties are deep maroon-red. Make several successive sowings because the young leaves are the most tender.

Rocket/Arugula
Distinctive, peppery-tasting leaves (below). In the height of summer it will bolt rapidly, becoming tough. Turkish and wild rocket are more bolt-resistant than leaf rocket, with a different flavor but still delicious.

Spinach
Deep green, soft-textured foliage with a subtle flavor (below). Keep the soil moist to avoid bolting.

fruit | GENERAL ADVICE

Plant fruit trees | Bareroot trees can still be planted in cold-winter regions, but container-grown trees should be planted now in mid-temperate and mild-winter regions. Although container-grown trees can be planted year-round, they will establish more quickly and be easier to care for if they are not in full leaf at planting time.

Feed fruit in pots | Apply a balanced liquid feed to fruit trees growing in containers.

Check on fruit pests | Fruit trees and bushes can be attacked by a number of pests including aphids, apple maggots, codling moths, pear psyllas, and plum curculios. Watch out for any problems and take action early –early insecticide spraying must be done before the blossoms open because of the risk of harming beneficial pollinating insects. Always read the instructions carefully before using a pesticide.

Apply protective fungicide sprays | If any of your fruit suffered from fungus diseases last year, this is a good time to give a protective spraying with an appropriate fungicide. Consult with your local extension service for advice on the best material to use and timing of its application. As with all garden chemicals, follow the package instructions carefully.

Remove galls from red cedars | Brown, golf-ball-size galls that form on red cedars or junipers should be removed and destroyed. These are fruiting bodies of a fungus that causes cedar-apple rust. If galls are allowed to release their spores, apples will be infected with the fungus, reducing yields and causing yellow or orange spots on leaves and fruit.

CHERRY TREES *flower early in the year, so in colder regions it is important to continue covering them at night throughout mid spring, where practical, to protect against frosts if a good crop is to be expected.*

fruit | WHAT TO DO NOW

TREE FRUIT

Apples and pears

Protect against scab
If scab has occurred in previous years, start preventive sprays beginning as soon as buds show signs of growth. Consult your local extension service for recommended fungicides and spray at intervals as recommended on the package. Scab causes dark patches on the leaves followed by brown or black corky scabs on the surface of the fruit.

Watch out for mildew
Developing shoots on apples are often affected by powdery mildew, which forms a white coating on the leaves and distorts and stunts growth. Control with the appropriate fungicide as recommended by your local extension service, and always follow the package directions carefully.

Continue formative training of espaliers
The unbranched whip you plan to use to form an espalier should have been cut back to 18in. above ground after planting to encourage buds to break just beneath the cut. Two of the shoots that should have developed just below

TRAIN AN ESPALIER'S TIERS OF HORIZONTAL BRANCHES *along supporting wires. Patience is required to create an espalier, but it is very effective once established.*

GRAFT FRUIT TREES

Fruit trees can be propagated by whip-and-tongue grafting now. This involves taking a shoot from the tree you want to propagate (called the scion) and grafting it onto a rootstock. It's not a common procedure for gardeners but is useful if, for example, you have an existing tree of an unknown or commercially unavailable variety that you want to increase.

Scion wood should have been collected in mid winter when it was fully dormant and stored in a refrigerator (see page 262). The scion is prepared by making a long sloping cut below a healthy bud. The rootstock is cut down to about 12in. from ground level and a similar but opposite sloping cut made at the top of the stem. A tongue is then made by cutting into the exposed surface of the cuts on both the scion and the rootstock so that the two lock snugly together. It is important to get the sloping surfaces at exactly the same angle so they fit without any gaps. Use a very sharp grafting knife and practice making cuts on spare pieces of stem until you have perfected the technique.

Bind the scion and stock firmly using grafting tape and cover any exposed surfaces with grafting wax. The graft should callous over after a couple of months and the tape should then be removed.

THE SLOPING SURFACES *on both the scion and the rootstock need to be at exactly the same angle (left) so they lock together without any gaps. Bind them together using grafting tape (right).*

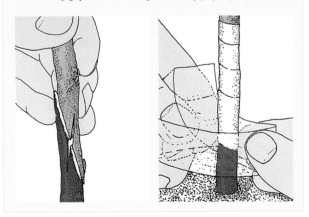

the initial cut will now become the first horizontal tier. Train the top shoot up the vertical cane attached to the wire, so the stem grows upward.

To form the next tier, select a vigorous shoot from either side of the main trunk and tie each to a cane placed at 45 degrees to the main stem. Remove other shoots growing from the main stem. The following year, the shoots of the new tier can be repositioned at 90 degrees. Repeat this process each year until the desired amount of tiers has been created.

Cherries

Continue to protect flowers

In colder regions, continue to cover cherry trees when frost is predicted, to protect blossoms. If late frosts are a problem, select a northfacing site for your cherry; this will help delay flowering.

Feed and train trees

Cherries are vigorous growers and will benefit from a topdressing of balanced fertilizer now.

Sweet cherries can be trained to an open-center form (see page 61).

To form a fan, train a branched whip to strong, horizontal wires spaced 15in. apart. At bud-burst, cut the central leader back to two healthy sideshoots. On each side of the leader, secure a sturdy bamboo cane tightly to the wire supports at an angle; tie the sideshoots to form the framework of the fan.

Figs

Plant outside or in containers

Figs need a warm, sunny site. They grow well as freestanding trees in Hardiness Zones 8 and 9 and can be planted now. Good warm-region varieties include 'Brown Turkey', 'Celeste', 'Alma', and 'Hunt'.

In mid-temperate regions, figs can be grown with a bit of added protection. 'Brown Turkey' and 'Celeste' are the most hardy varieties. They can be planted against a south- or southwest-facing wall, trained as a fan, which can be covered if cold weather threatens, or in containers.

To encourage figs to bear good crops of fruit, it is advisable to limit their root system; by restricting its vegetative growth, the plant will channel its energy into

reproduction and should bear more fruit. Growing a fig in a container will restrict its roots effectively. Another advantage is that it can be moved before winter arrives into an unheated greenhouse, enclosed porch, or basement. The container can also be plunged into the ground if you want the fig as a permanent feature in one place in your garden.

Start the plant off in a 10in. container, and as the

TIE WALL-TRAINED FIGS *to a sturdy support (top) to form a strong framework. New shoots may attempt to grow away from the support; tie these in or remove them.*

FAN-TRAIN OUTDOOR FIGS *against a sunny wall (above). Train two side branches, one for each side of the fan, and as they grow, tie in the sideshoots so they are evenly spaced.*

plant grows repot it each year, until it is eventually in an 18in. container. Use a pot with plenty of drainage holes and lots of gravel or broken potsherds at the bottom. Standing the container on bricks helps excess water to drain away. If you intend to plunge a containerized fig into open ground, fill a 12–16in. pot with a soil-based potting mix and plant the fig, then position the container well into the ground.

Another method of root restriction for figs is by creating a planting pit. Dig a hole 2 x 2 x 2ft. Line the sides of the hole with paving slabs, setting them 1in. above the ground to prevent the roots from spreading over the top of the soil. Leave the bottom unlined; instead fill the hole with broken bricks and gravel to 4–6in. deep, which will prevent roots penetrating the soil underneath. After planting, backfill the hole using ordinary garden soil or a soil-based potting mix.

Peaches and nectarines

Finish planting

Plant new peach and nectarine trees in well-drained soil in full sun. Allow 15–20ft. between full-sized trees and 8–12ft. between dwarf trees. Genetic dwarf trees can be planted just 3ft. apart; they are also good in a container.

Mulch and feed trees

Mulch established and newly planted peach and nectarine trees with well-rotted farmyard manure or garden compost to help retain soil moisture, keep down weeds, and provide nitrogen. This can be supplemented with a topdressing of dried poultry pellets or a slow-release fertilizer high in potassium.

FIGS NEED A WARM, SUNNY SITE *with well-drained soil. In cooler regions, they require some winter protection or they can be grown in containers, which are carried indoors for winter.*

Plums

Finish planting
Allow 20–25ft. between full-sized plum trees and 8–12ft. between dwarf varieties.

Mulch and feed trees
Follow the procedure for peaches (see page 79).

SOFT FRUIT

General

Topdress blackberries and raspberries with a balanced fertilizer. For blueberries, use a fertilizer for acid-loving plants. Apply a thick layer of thoroughly rotted organic mulch such as pine needles, garden compost, or farmyard manure, keeping the mulch away from the crowns and emerging stems.

Blackberries

Cut back sideshoots
Shorten lateral stems on this year's fruiting canes to 12in.

Cranberries and lingonberries

Feed with fertilizer for acid-loving plants
These fruit require a relatively cool climate and will not perform well in warm regions. Apply a liquid ericaceous fertilizer at half the recommended rate, especially if yields have been low. Water plants with rainwater whenever possible, keeping the soil moist at all times. To encourage plants to spread, maintain a layer, 1in. deep, of sharp sand on the surface of the bed or pot.

Strawberries

Finish planting
In colder regions, finish establishing new beds, following the same procedure as for early spring (see page 58).

De-blossom spring runners
In their first year, remove the blossoms from spring-planted strawberry runners so they put all their energy into establishing their root systems.

RASPBERRIES AND BLUEBERRIES *are rich in vitamins and antioxidants and are well suited for growing in backyard gardens. Feed them now so they will bear an abundance of fruit later in the season.*

VINE FRUIT

Grapes

Finish planting vines
Plant new vines in cooler regions following the procedures outlined for early spring (see page 59).

Train new vines and prune established vines
A year after planting, begin to train vines using a T-shaped trellis or the Kniffen system (see page 277). For established vines, remove unwanted shoots arising from the roots and thin branches along the main arms so that they are about 4in. apart.

Kiwi

Mulch with bulky organic matter
Once the ground has warmed slightly and the soil is moist, mulch kiwi with bulky, well-rotted organic matter to a depth of at least 3in. This will help suppress weeds, retain soil moisture, and keep the root system cool.

late spring

Even in the coldest regions, the kitchen garden should be well underway by now. Cool-season crops are in and may need thinning. As soon as the soil warms, tender young tomatoes, peppers, and eggplants raised indoors can be planted out safely; be sure to gradually harden them off first. Heat-loving vegetables such as snap beans and corn can be sown outside as soon as all danger of frost has passed.

In warmer regions, successive plantings of warm-season crops will provide an extended harvest season. Keep the hoe close at hand to deal with weeds and water plants in dry spells.

Bees and other insects should have been busy among the fruit blossoms, and swelling fruitlets will be visible as the petals fall.

Best of all in late spring, harvest of the new season's crops begins in earnest—it is time to enjoy the flavors of fresh lettuce and other salad greens, radishes, baby carrots, and succulent asparagus spears.

vegetables | GENERAL ADVICE

ALL REGIONS

Buy young plants | If you have not raised your own plants, garden centers should be well stocked with vegetables and herbs in small pots or cell packs. Be sure to harden off purchased seedlings just as you would those you grow yourself.

Avoid seedling diseases | Seedlings are vulnerable to fungal diseases such as damping off, which can often be avoided by sowing at the optimum time when the soil is warm and not too wet.

Seedlings sown directly outside should be thinned to a suitable spacing as this will increase air circulation around them. Avoid the humid conditions that many fungal diseases thrive on.

Protect against pests | By now, many crops sown from seed are up and growing, and transplanted crops have become established. Since carrots, parsnips, and cabbage-related crops are particularly vulnerable to pests, keep them protected with floating row covers for as long as possible. Cutworms feed on young stems at ground level, causing newly transplanted seedlings to topple and die. If cutworms are a problem, place a cardboard or plastic collar around the plants, sinking it slightly into the soil to create a physical barrier to the pest.

Thin seedlings | Crops will now be growing very fast, so thinning is a priority. Overcrowding increases the competition for nutrients and water, leading to a reduction in crop quality, and poor air circulation can increase the risk of disease.

Seedlings can be thinned in stages rather than being thinned to their final spacing all at once. For example, if the final spacing is 12in. between plants, thin them first to 6in. apart, and then a little while later to 12in. This gives you more leeway in case some seedlings die or are damaged by pests or diseases, and the larger seedlings

from the second thinning can often be transplanted to make another row.

Keep things tidy | Remove weeds and debris and maintain edges and paths to keep the kitchen garden looking good, as well as being productive. Tidiness also helps prevent accidents in the garden (leaving less around for you to trip over) and deprives slugs and other pests of shelter.

Plant flowers | Consider including some easy-to-care-for flowers in or around your kitchen garden, both to add appeal to the garden and as a source of cut flowers for indoors. Zinnias, celosia, calendula, marigold, cosmos, and gaillardia are good choices. These can be sown directly in the garden after the soil has warmed or they can be started indoors for earlier blooms. Garden centers will also have a good selection of young flowering plants at this time.

COLD-WINTER REGIONS ONLY

Start late tender crops indoors | Plant cucumbers, winter squash, pumpkins, melons, and okra in peat pots or other plantable containers so that roots will be minimally disturbed when transplanted to the garden.

Sow cool-season crops outdoors | Sow beets, carrots, kohrabi, lettuce, spinach, radishes, and peas outdoors where they will grow.

Plant cabbage family crops outdoors | Cabbage, broccoli, Brussels sprouts, and cauliflower that were grown indoors can be planted in the garden after they have been hardened off. Harden plants off by gradually acclimatizing them to the cooler outdoor conditions. Start by putting them outside in a sheltered spot for a few hours on a mild day and returning them under cover in the evening. Gradually increase their outdoor exposure, then leave them out day and night, and finally move them to a more open position near to where they are to grow. After planting, use a temporary row cover if the weather turns cold.

MID-TEMPERATE REGIONS ONLY

Continue sowing | There are still important crops to be sown. Beets, carrots, lettuce, parsnips, radishes, arugula, rutabaga, turnips, snap and lima beans, corn, and herbs (such as parsley, basil, dill, and cilantro) can all be sown in the ground where they are to grow.

Transplant or sow cucurbits | The soil should have warmed sufficiently to plant heat-loving crops such as cucumbers, squash, and pumpkins. If you started plants indoors from seed, transplant them into the garden after hardening off. Alternatively, sow seed directly where they are to grow. Although these crops, with their trailing habits, tend to be hogs for space, there are short-stemmed or bush varieties available. Trailing varieties can also be trained to grow vertically, on a fence, tee-pee, or trellis. This technique makes efficient use of garden space.

MILD-WINTER REGIONS ONLY

Continue weeding | Weed growth is at its peak. Hoeing between crops on dry days reduces hand weeding to a minimum. Use a well-sharpened hoe, slide it flat along the ground, and sever weeds from their roots. On a dry, bright, breezy day, the topgrowth of chopped-off weeds will soon wilt and die; weeds that have been dug up and left lying on the soil surface with a little soil around their roots may regrow.

Make successional sowings | Continue to make regular small sowings of various vegetables for a steady supply to harvest, but remember that by the time plants sown now mature later in the summer, tender crops such as snap beans, summer squash, and tomatoes will also be ready.

GIVE YOUNG PLANTS *the best possible chance by weeding regularly, thinning seedlings, watering well in dry spells, and keeping pests and diseases at bay. A tidy kitchen garden is a productive one!*

vegetables | WHAT TO DO NOW

Leek

Transplant young plants

Transplant young leeks after any danger of heavy frost has passed. Water thoroughly the day before transplanting and loosen the soil using a fork.

Make wide, deep holes—6in. deep and 2in. across—and drop a single seedling in each. Don't backfill with soil, but simply fill each hole with water to settle the soil around the roots.

Onion and shallot

Plant sets

In cold-winter regions, plant onion and shallot sets, spacing them 3–4in. apart in rows that are 10–12in. apart.

Sow seeds of bunching onions

Seeds of bunching onions (scallions) can be sown now for use as green onions in summer. Sow seed thinly in ½in. deep drills or in 2–3in. bands. Mound soil around plants as they grow to blanch the bottoms of stems.

General

These crops should be well established by now in mild-winter regions; keep plants weeded and watered and harvest them as they mature. In cooler regions, continue to transplant indoor-grown or purchased plants to the garden. Protect young cabbage family plants from cutworms by placing a cardboard or plastic collar around each seedling as you transplant it to the garden. A paper or plastic cup with the bottom removed, and its base slightly pushed into the soil, works well.

WATER LEEKS THOROUGHLY *after transplanting (top). Repeat as necessary during long dry spells.*

PROTECTIVE COVERINGS *of fine netting (above) or floating row covers are very useful when it comes to growing brassicas, because they keep many of the common pests at bay—such as cabbage worms and loopers.*

Broccoli

Transplant young plants

In cooler regions, set young plants from cold-frames or pots in their final positions when they are 4–6in. tall and after they have hardened off, watering them well before and after transplanting.

Make sure plants never go completely dry as they develop, which will stunt growth and prevent the formation of good heads. Reduce competition for moisture and nutrients by carefully hoeing weeds around the plants the moment they appear. Mulching between rows will help suppress weeds.

Brussels sprouts

Transplant young plants

In cooler regions, transplant Brussels sprouts when they are 4–6in. tall. If the seedlings have been grown in cell packs, transplant them when the roots begin to show through the bottom. Allow 30in. between the plants and the rows. Resist the temptation to squeeze in more plants, because the distance makes picking easier and the improved air circulation will help to prevent fungal diseases. Plant the seedlings so that the soil is level with the first set of true leaves, and keep them well watered. Continue to water the crop regularly while it is establishing, and during dry spells.

TRANSPLANT BRUSSELS SPROUT SEEDLINGS, *making sure that you allow enough space around them for air to circulate over the leaves as this will help to prevent fungal diseases.*

Cabbage

Transplant young plants

In cooler regions, transplant young plants into the garden after hardening off. Space plants 12–18in. apart in rows 2ft. apart.

Cauliflower

Transplant young plants

In cooler regions, set young plants from seedbeds or pots as for Brussels sprouts (left). Adjust spacing to 24in. between plants and 30in. between rows.

Kohlrabi

Sow seed outdoors

In cold-winter regions, sow seed outside in drills ½in deep, after any danger of hard frost has passed. Space seeds 1in. apart, and allow 12–18in. between rows. After seeds germinate, thin to 4in. apart.

LEGUMES

Fava beans

Provide sturdy supports

Use stakes or strong bamboo canes to provide strong support for plants; in exposed sites, they will fall over in the wind or stems will break off under the weight of the swelling pods unless they are well staked. When young beans appear, pinch out the growing tips in order to concentrate the plant's energy on pod formation.

Lima beans

Sow outdoors

Once soil has thoroughly warmed, sow lima bean seeds where they will grow, spacing seed 3in. apart in 1in. deep drills. Thin pole varieties to 6–10in. apart. Pole limas, such as 'Big Mama' and 'Burpee's Best', develop heavy vines that reach 10–12ft. long, requiring sturdy supports. Bush varieties, such as 'Fordhook 242' and 'Baby Fordhook' are somewhat less vigorous. Lima beans require a long, hot season to produce their crop, and they may not perform well in cool regions.

Peas

Support growing plants

Provide peas with twiggy sticks, a wire or string trellis, or netting stretched between sturdy posts to climb. Some varieties, such as the garden pea 'Caselode', the snow pea 'Oregon Giant', or the snap pea 'Sugar Ann', produce short vines and can be grown with or without supports, but most will be easier to pick and be more productive when trained up supports.

Snap beans

Sow outdoors

Sow snap beans outdoors now where they will grow. Plant bush varieties in 1in. deep drills, spacing seed 2in. apart in rows 2–3ft. apart. Good bush varieties of snap bean include 'Jade', 'Royal Burgundy', 'Rocdor' (wax bean), and 'Tavera' (filet bean).

Plant pole varieties, which produce greater yields but require sturdy supports, 3–4in. apart. If growing pole beans on a tee-pee, sow 5–7 seeds at the base of each pole. Good varieties of pole beans include 'Garden of Eden' and 'Fortex'.

Sow for succession

To maintain a steady supply of snap beans through the season, make successive sowings of bush beans at intervals of 2–3 weeks through mid summer.

SURROUND CARROTS *with a 20in. barrier of row-covering material or plastic to exclude carrot rust fly, which flies close to the ground and leaves its destructive larvae next to the plants.*

CULTIVATE THE SOIL *between rows of beets, being very careful to keep the hoe blade well away from the roots so they don't get damaged and bleed. Regularly hand weed close to the plants.*

ROOT AND STEM CROPS

Beet

Sow seed outdoors

In cold-winter regions, sow seed in the garden following directions from early spring (see page 42).

Weed and water young plants

Water beets thoroughly every 10–14 days during dry spells. A lack of water causes woody roots, while a fluctuation in water supply can cause splitting, and an excess of water will result in the production of leaves at the expense of roots. Regularly hand weed close to the plants and hoe the soil between the rows, but keep the blade well away from the roots because they will 'bleed' if they are damaged.

Carrot

Thin seedlings

In warmer regions, thin carrot seedlings leaving about 2in. between plants; the thinnings may be large enough by this time to use in salads as baby carrots. Water the crop several hours before thinning to make the job easier.

Protect seedlings from weeds and pests

Weed the rows every couple of weeks by hoeing between them, but hand weed close to the plants to avoid damaging the roots. From late spring to summer, cover or surround the crop with a barrier of row-covering material to help prevent an attack of carrot rust fly. The low-flying insects lay their eggs next to the plants and the larvae tunnel into the carrots, leaving holes that may then rot.

Sow for succession

Switch to sowing main-crop carrot varieties, such as 'Hercules' and 'Bolero', for the rest of spring and summer. For a regular supply of vegetables for your kitchen, make sowings every 3–4 weeks from now until late summer. Carrots are generally ready for harvesting about 12–16 weeks after sowing.

Celeriac

Harden off and plant out seedlings

Acclimatize celeriac seedlings raised indoors to outdoor conditions before they are planted out over the next couple of weeks. Space the seedlings 12in. apart in rows 18in. apart, and water in well. Protect the young seedlings from slugs and snails.

MOUND SOIL AROUND POTATOES *by drawing soil up around the crops, to stop weeds, help prevent blight, and keep the tubers from being exposed to the light, which turns them green.*

Fennel

Sow outside

Fennel can be sown in the garden once all danger of frost has passed, from now until mid summer. Plants should mature about 14–16 weeks after sowing, so a direct-sown crop will be later than one started off earlier indoors (see page 42).

Mark out straight lines and make a shallow drill ½in. deep. Water if dry and allow to drain before sowing the seed thinly. Space rows 18in. apart. It is a good idea to make several sowings over a period of several weeks as insurance against poor germination or bolting caused by low or fluctuating temperatures. The direct-sown seedlings need to be thinned once they have germinated and are growing strongly, leaving about 8in. between each young plant.

Fennel can be fussy. It thrives in a sunny, sheltered site with rich, moisture-retentive soil, ideally free draining and with lots of organic matter. Avoid heavy clay, stony, or poorly drained soil. It is probably best not to bother growing it if you can't meet its exacting requirements because the plants will bolt if they become stressed.

Plant out earlier sown seedlings

Container-grown plants from an earlier, indoor sowing can be planted out from now until very early summer, depending on whether you live in a mild or cold area. Before doing so, acclimatize plants to outdoor conditions for a couple of weeks, then plant out at 8in. spacings and water in well.

Potato

Plant potato tubers

Plant potatoes in cold-winter regions, following the procedure for planting tubers in mid spring (see page 68).

Continue to mound soil

As shoots emerge, continue to mound soil around potato plants. In many gardens the risk of frosts will be over now, though in some areas late frosts may still occur; if frost is forecast, remember to cover the shoots completely to protect them. Mounding soil is also important to prevent the tubers from being exposed to the light and turning green—green patches on potatoes are bitter and poisonous.

HARVEST RADISHES *by taking hold of their topgrowth and easing them out with a fork, trowel, or even a sturdy plant label. Don't leave them in the ground for too long when mature.*

Radish

Sow seed outdoors

In cooler regions, continue sowing radish seeds outside until early summer. Keep plants well watered and weeded.

Harvest regularly

Pull up radishes as soon as they are large enough to eat. They do not last well in the ground but will store for several days in the refrigerator if they are first rinsed, patted dry, and placed in a plastic bag.

Sweet potato

Plant slips

Plant slips (rooted cuttings) in mid-temperate regions now, following the procedure on page 70.

Turnip

Harvest young roots

Start pulling turnips when they reach the size of a golf ball. Do not let them develop any larger than a small orange, because they become woody and much less tasty—check the size of the roots first by pulling back the foliage. Tender young roots can be thinly sliced or grated for eating raw in salads, or cooked.

The roots will be ready about 6–10 weeks after sowing, depending on the variety grown.

General

Lettuce, arugula, and spinach should be planted now only in the coolest regions. Gardeners in warmer climates should continue to harvest these cool-season crops as they mature; summer's heat will soon cause them to go to seed. They can be sown again in late summer or early fall for a late fall crop.

Chard

Continue sowing outdoors

Continue sowing chard until mid summer for summer and fall harvest. Follow the spacings provided for mid spring (see page 70).

Spinach

Harvest leaves

Cut spinach leaves frequently for use fresh or cooked and to encourage new leaves to develop. Keep plants well watered to help delay their bolting.

THE SHINY, CRINKLY LEAVES *of fresh spinach are rich in iron and folic acid, but as warm weather advances, spinach goes to seed, so enjoy it while you can.*

CUCURBITS

Cucumber

Harden off and plant out seedlings
Once the soil has warmed and all danger of frost has passed, transplant hardened off seedlings to the garden, spacing plants 12in. apart with 3–4ft. between rows. Take care not to disturb roots and water well.

Sow seeds outdoors
Sow cucumber seed in the garden only after the soil temperature has reached at least 70°F. Sow seeds ½in. deep and 2in. apart, in rows 3–4ft. apart. Thin seedlings to 12in. apart.

Melons

Harden off and plant out seedlings
After the soil has warmed and the weather has settled, transplant hardened off seedlings to the garden, spacing plants 18in. apart in rows 4ft. apart. Disturb the roots as little as possible. Water well.

Sow seeds outside
About two weeks after the last expected frost, sow seeds directly in the garden. Plant seeds ½in. deep, setting 2–3 seeds per hill and spacing hills 3–4ft. apart. Once seedlings have developed, select the strongest from each group and remove the others.

Protect young plants with row covers
Use floating row covers to protect young plants from cool temperatures and pests. Use of row covers will also encourage an earlier crop. Be sure to remove the covers as soon as plants begin to bloom so that insects can pollinate the flowers.

Summer squash

Harden off and plant out seedlings
Harden off and set out plants raised in pots after the weather settles and the soil warms. If the soil is poor, dig a deep planting hole and mix lots of well-rotted manure or compost into the soil before planting; this helps to retain the soil moisture that the plants need.

Prior to planting, a plastic mulch can be laid over the soil and planting holes can be cut to allow planting through the plastic. This will help retain moisture and suppress weeds. However, plastic is a breeding ground for slugs so be vigilant if you use this method, particularly when the plants are small and vulnerable to attack. Alternatively, water the plants in well, then place a mulch of well-rotted organic matter over the surface.

Seed can also be sown outdoors now, directly where the crop will grow. Amend the soil as above, then spot sow 2–3 seeds per hill, thinning as soon as possible to one seedling. Outdoor sowings will often overtake plants that have been raised indoors. Many summer squash plants tend to be compact and bushy, and should be spaced about 3ft apart. Trailing types, however, can require much more room, needing spacings of up to 6ft. apart.

All summer squash thrive in hot summers and need the sunniest position available.

Winter squash and pumpkin

Plant out after frosts
Once the risk of frost has passed, plant out winter squash and pumpkins. These plants require fertile, moist soil and the sunniest spot available; they need a long hot summer to do really well.

Improve the soil before planting with well-rotted compost and a balanced fertilizer. Water the plants in thoroughly and mulch the soil around them. Protect with a floating row cover if the weather turns really chilly; it will also minimize pest attacks. Remove the row cover when flowering begins.

WINTER SQUASH SEEDS *can be started indoors for transplanting outside after all danger of frost has passed. Alternatively, sow seed directly in the garden—seedlings will grow quickly in warm soil.*

FRUITING CROPS AND CORN

General

Transplant hardened off seedlings when conditions are appropriate. Plant tender crops such as eggplants, peppers, and tomatoes outdoors after all danger of frost has passed and the soil has warmed (follow spacings recommended on page 72). Those living in cool regions may need to wait a few more weeks.

Corn

Sow corn outdoors

Once the weather settles, gardeners in mid-temperate regions can begin sowing corn in the garden, making successive plantings every two weeks through mid summer for an extended harvest (follow the planting directions on page 72). In mild-winter regions, continue sowing successive plantings.

Tomato

Set stakes and cages

Tomatoes can be grown on stakes or in circular wire cages to prevent them from sprawling on the ground and improve air circulation around plants. Install stakes and/or cages at planting time.

PERENNIAL VEGETABLES

Asparagus

Harvest spears

The short harvest season for asparagus has begun in most regions. In established beds, cut off each spear just below soil level when it's 6–8in. tall. It is essential to cut every spear, even those that are thin or bent, because this stimulates the dormant buds in the crown to grow. Spears grow quickly as the weather warms, and the beds need checking daily once they start to emerge.

It is essential not to overcrop asparagus in its early years; if you do, future yields will be severely reduced. If you planted two-year-old roots, their spears can be harvested a year after planting; harvest spears from seed-raised 'F1 hybrids' two years after planting. The first year that you harvest, cut the spears for 2–3 weeks and then allow the fernlike stalks to form; these will feed the roots for the next year's crop. In following years, gradually extend the harvest season; eventually you should be able to harvest for about six weeks.

BEFORE TRANSPLANTING FRUITING CROPS, *prepare soil by incorporating generous amounts of organic matter. Be sure the soil is in good tilth, that is, it crumbles easily when rubbed between your fingers.*

TRANSPLANT TOMATOES *and other fruiting crops such as eggplant and peppers to the garden only after all danger of frost has passed, the soil has warmed, and plants have been properly hardened off.*

| How to grow vegetables in containers

Even if you have room for only a few pots, tubs, and window boxes in your garden, you can still grow a range of produce, from herbs to leafy greens and tomatoes. To enhance their visual impact and convenience, arrange the containers in groups near the kitchen. A huge range of pots and planters in different shapes, sizes, and materials is now available from mail order suppliers and garden centers, so you should be able to find some that suit your style and needs. There are a few key points to container gardening that you need to follow, and lots of opportunity for creative combinations; with a little effort, you will soon be enjoying a productive patio.

CHARD *(above) is an attractive plant for containers. It produces an abundance of nutritious leaves throughout the growing season.*
COMMON SAGE *(right), like many herbs, thrives in the restricted environment of a pot and adds a decorative touch to a patio or deck.*

The key points

Size
Ensure that the container size is appropriate for what you're growing. Root vegetables such as carrots need deep pots, while beets sit near to the top of the soil so requires less depth. Shallower pots are also fine for herbs or leafy greens. Big plants such as tomatoes and cucumbers need large pots to accommodate their roots.

Drainage
Good drainage is vital. Check that there are enough holes in the base of the pot; drill more if necessary. Cover the base with potsherds or stones and raise the pot on bricks or pot feet. Use a free-draining but water-retentive, soilless potting mix or a soil-based growing medium.

Watering
Do not rely on rainfall as it may not penetrate the leaf cover or be heavy enough to soak to the roots. Water-retaining crystals can be mixed in with the potting soil when planting. Mulching the surface with gravel or shredded bark looks good and minimizes evaporation.

Self-watering containers are also available and may be a practical option for busy gardeners. These are equipped with water reservoirs that supply moisture to the plants as needed. Of course, the reservoirs must be refilled regularly.

Feeding
Pots hold a relatively small amount of growing mix and so nutrients are limited. Add a controlled-release fertilizer at planting time, or apply a diluted, liquid, all-purpose fertilizer each week. Nitrogen-rich fertilizers encourage leafy growth so are good for crops such as spinach, chard, and lettuce; phosphorus-rich fertilizers help root growth so use for root crops; potassium-rich fertilizers aid fruit and flower formation and are good for crops such as tomatoes and squash. In practice, most balanced liquid fertilizers are satisfactory.

Placement
The advantage of pots is they can be moved around as needed, especially when on a base with wheels. But in general they are too heavy to keep shifting about, so choose their placement with care. Avoid windy areas when growing vines. An open, windy site can dry out potting soil as quickly as if it were in a hot, sunny site. Vegetables dislike shade.

TOMATOES (top left) require large containers to accommodate their extensive root system.

PEPPERS (above) are both productive and attractive when grown in containers.

fruit | GENERAL ADVICE

Take care of pollinating insects | Without pollinating insects such as bees, there would be very little fruit. While crops are in blossom, do not spray trees with insecticides because of the risk of killing pollinators. Give bees and other insects a helping hand by growing plants that provide food for them out of season. Dogwoods, goldenrod, and rudbeckia are just a few of the many flowering plants that will attract pollinating insects to your yard.

Water fruit when necessary | In a dry spell, fruit trees can become stressed through drought. Take particular care with the water requirements of newly planted trees and those in containers or growing against a wall.

Feed fruit trees in pots | Use a balanced liquid fertilizer to give containerized fruit a boost. Follow the instructions on the package.

Give pollinators access to flowers | Ensure that plants growing under protective covers (such as strawberries) remain accessible to pollinating insects. Remove the covers during the day.

Watch out for frosts | Listen for forecasts of late frosts and protect blossoms as necessary. Generally, the later the frost, the more harm it does, as trees are further along in growth and therefore more vulnerable to damage. However, in most areas frost-protection covers can soon be completely removed from peaches, nectarines, and apricots.

AN APPLE IN BLOOM *presents a stunning spring display, enticing bees and other insects to pollinate the flowers. Do not spray with insecticides while fruit trees are in flower to ensure these beneficial insects are not harmed.*

fruit | WHAT TO DO NOW

General

Fruit trees that are growing too strongly will not only outgrow their space but will also produce leafy growth at the expense of fruit. Winter pruning stimulates growth further, so prune strong-growing trees only in summer. Overfertilizing, particularly with high-nitrogen fertilizers, can also cause excessive vegetative growth and a reduction in fruit set. Avoid high-nitrogen fertilizers on all fruit trees; a better option is to use a slow-release or organic fertilizer, which provides a slow, steady supply of nutrients over time.

Water trees, especially those that are newly planted, and apply fresh mulch of well-rotted compost or leafmold as needed to reduce evaporation and inhibit weed growth.

Remove wayward shoots on fan-trained trees and tie in better-placed ones to help trees develop and maintain the proper shape and provide for adequate air circulation.

Poor fruit set can be caused by frost damage to flowers, poor flowering, or inadequate pollination. The appearance of only a few flowers might be a result of heavy pruning, inadequate nutrition, or the buildup of old, unproductive wood. Prune trees correctly and apply high-potassium fertilizer early next spring to promote better flowering. Many fruit crops require cross-pollination by another variety to set a crop; fruit catalogs have details of suitable pollinators.

Apples and pears

Limit nitrogen application
When feeding apple and pear trees, avoid fertilizers high in nitrogen. Nitrogen encourages rapid leafy growth that is particularly susceptible to fireblight infection.

Check trees for infection
Fireblight is a bacterial disease that causes twigs, leaves, and branches to appear as if they were scorched by fire. Advanced infections result in bark cankers. Be alert for symptoms of fireblight, and if they appear, prune out and destroy infected branches, taking care to disinfect pruning shears or loppers between cuts to avoid spreading the infection.

Obtain codling moth traps
Codling moths will soon be on the wing, laying their eggs on apple fruitlets. The larvae tunnel into the fruit, and can cause a great deal of damage to your crop.

A good way to control them is to use glue traps baited with a pheromone lure, which can be hung in apple trees to attract and trap the male moths. Originally they were designed simply to indicate when the moths were active so that chemical controls could be applied more effectively, but trapping the males reduces mating activity significantly and cuts down the number of caterpillars. They are a useful organic control for home orchards. A single trap may be sufficient for a dwarf tree (under 8ft.), but as many as eight traps may be required for standard size apple trees (20–25ft.).

A GOOD SHOW OF FLOWERS *on apple (above) and pear trees should indicate a good fruit set. Apples and pears make beautiful trees, with their blossoms in spring and their colorful fruit in fall.*

Capture plum curculios

These long-nosed beetles scar fruit and severe infestations will cause fruit to drop prematurely. The beetles can be dislodged from trees by gently tapping or shaking the branches several times during the two weeks following petal drop. Spread a light-colored sheet beneath the tree to collect the insects and destroy them.

Cherries

Keep trees watered

Developing fruits of cherries can turn yellow and fall off if they receive a check to growth at this time of year, either through lack of moisture or excessively cool temperatures. There is little you can do about the temperatures, but you can make sure the tree's roots are kept moist in dry spells. Maintaining an organic mulch around trees helps reduce water loss.

Prune young trees

Carry out pruning of cherry trees to a restricted form, such as a fan.

Trees being trained as fans (see page 61) should have a strong sideshoot tied loosely to each angled bamboo cane. To avoid snapping the stems, untie and lower the canes as the season progresses until the desired angle is reached. As the tree's framework develops, tie new main stems onto canes already secured to the wires, the aim being to develop a framework of well-spaced branches radiating from the center of the tree. Rub off or prune unwanted shoots as they appear.

CHERRY TREES *naturally shed some of their immature fruits, pictured above, but this can be overly excessive if there is a check in growth or inadequate pollination.*

Figs

Bring plants outside

Move container-grown figs that were put into an unheated greenhouse, garage, or porch in fall back into the open garden now. As the weather warms, remove insulation from fan-trained trees that were protected with straw and floating row covers over winter.

Repot figs in containers

Repot figs every couple of years even when they have reached their established size. Remove them from their container, gently tease out their roots from the rootball, and replant them into fresh, soil-based potting mix and water well.

Peaches and nectarines

Feed and water trees

Give peach and nectarine trees an occasional application of a high-potassium liquid fertilizer such as tomato fertilizer, and keep the area around their root zone free of weeds.

Regularly water the trees as the fruits start to swell. This is particularly important for trees planted near walls, as the soil there can be very dry from now right through the summer. Water container-grown trees almost every day during the growing season and apply a high-potassium liquid fertilizer every couple of weeks.

A SPRING CROP OF FIGS *forms on last year's growth in mild climates, but the buds usually do not survive winter in cold regions; a second crop of figs develops on new growth, maturing in the fall.*

Plums

Capture plum curculio

Plum curculios cut crescent-shaped wounds in the fruit, often causing it to drop before it ripens. To prevent damage from this pest, follow the same procedure for removing it as for apples (see page 98).

Festoon trees for good fruiting

Festooning is a useful technique to encourage plums to fruit more heavily and to restrict the size of the tree. When trained to grow horizontally, branches tend to produce more fruit. Loop string gently over the ends of the branches and tie them downwards to the stake base. Remove the strings or weights a few weeks later.

SOFT FRUIT

General

Bird protection is often vital if you don't want to lose a lot of your crop. A fruit cage is the best answer, but covering vulnerable crops with bird netting also helps. Some birds such as blackbirds don't wait for fruits to ripen and will strip a bush in minutes, so get protection in place early— before plants come into flower.

Blackberries

Water regularly and mulch

Water blackberries during periods of dry weather and mulch with well-rotted compost or wood chips, to prevent surface evaporation and to reduce weeds.

Continue to train

Tie the current season's fruiting canes to the trellis wires using strips of fabric or soft twine. Spread canes to allow good air circulation.

Blueberries

Remove flowers from new plantings

Pinch off flowers as they form on newly planted blueberries to channel growth into establishing a healthy root system. Cropping can begin next year.

Apply mulch and water

For highest quality, keep the plants evenly moist from now until fruit matures. Mulch with well-rotted compost or pine needles to protect the shallow roots from drying out or from fluctuating temperatures.

MAINTAINING AN ORGANIC MULCH *around fruit trees not only discourages weeds but also helps moderate soil temperatures and reduces moisture loss through evaporation.*

THIS YEAR'S FRUITING CANES *of trailing and semitrailing varieties of blackberry should be tied to the trellis wires to keep them off the ground and to provide adequate air circulation.*

Gooseberries

Thin for larger fruits

Remove one quarter to a half of the gooseberry fruits to leave well-spaced berries to swell and provide large fruits.

Raspberries

Check canes for disease

Anthracnose is a fungal disease that causes oval, purple or brownish spots with silvery centers to develop on the canes of raspberries and blackberries. The spots enlarge, weakening the canes, which may then die. Prune out and burn infected canes as soon as you see them.

Thin raspberries

If raspberry rows are crowded, thin out the canes to leave 6–8 strong canes per plant. This will give a better crop than allowing them to remain crowded, and it enables you to keep the pathways clear to access the plants and control weeds.

RASPBERRY BLOSSOMS *are pretty and are backed by lush green foliage, which the plants will need to sustain during summer when the fruits are swelling. Thin out crowded canes now to produce a better crop.*

Strawberries

Pick forced fruit

Strawberries growing under floating row covers should be ready for picking now.

De-blossom young plants

Remove the flowers from strawberry runners planted this spring so they put their energy into establishing a strong root system.

FRUIT NETTING IS ESSENTIAL *if birds are a problem, but if your fruit garden suffers from troublesome squirrels, a sturdy wire netting may be necessary to stop them from getting in and ruining your crops.*

TUCK A LAYER OF STRAW *under strawberry plants to help keep the strawberries clean and free from rot. Pull it back it after cropping because it can encourage slugs and botrytis.*

Plant out alpine strawberries

Seedlings sown in early spring should be planted out now. Space them in rows 30in. apart with 12in. between plants in the row. They make a pleasing decorative edging for a border, spaced about 2ft. apart, or they can be grown in a stone wall or as a ground cover.

Maintain even moisture

Keep beds evenly moist until the berries are nearly ripe. A lack of moisture as fruit develops will reduce crop quality.

ALL ABOUT KIWIS

Kiwis are vining plants that produce sweet, tart fruit on female plants. Although a few varieties are self fertile, most require a male plant for fruit production. The hardy kiwi (*Actinidia arguta*) bears small, smooth skinned fruit as far north as Zone 4. The large-fruited, fuzzy kiwi (*A. deliciosa*), can only be grown outdoors in mild-winter regions.

Mulch beds with clean straw

Tuck clean straw around and under strawberry plants in beds; this gives the developing fruits a clean surface to rest on and protects them from soil splashes, gray mold (botrytis), and (to some extent) attack from slugs. For even better weed control, place a layer of newspaper beneath the straw. This will prevent most weed seeds from emerging. Bails of straw can be bought from garden centers or pet supply shops.

VINE FRUIT

Grapes

Feed and water vines

Apply high-potassium liquid fertilizer, such as tomato fertilizer, and ensure they are watered frequently.

Continue training newly planted vines

Once the main stem reaches the bottom wire of a Kniffen system trellis (see page 277), select two lateral branches that will become the first set of arms and secure them to the wires with twine.

Kiwi

Tie up shoots

Tie the fast-growing shoots onto the support framework regularly, to keep the plants tidy.

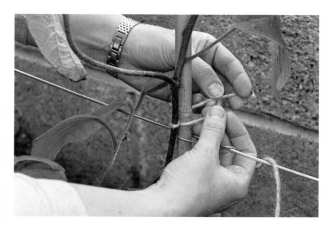

TIE IN NEW KIWI SHOOTS *as they appear using a figure-eight knot if a productive plant is desired. Left to its own devices, a newly planted kiwi will quickly become unruly.*

| How to grow fruit in small spaces

Most kitchen gardens have limited space. Fortunately, there are several techniques that can be employed to help you get the most from the available plot.

Maximizing your fruit

Naturally compact fruits

Plant breeders have developed many naturally compact varieties and dwarfing rootstocks, because commercial growers can harvest a greater fruit yield per acre. However, gardeners can also enjoy their benefits by growing these varieties and rootstocks. Many are suitable for growing in containers, including 'Sunshine Blue' or 'Top Hat' blueberry, 'Necta Zee' nectarine, 'Bonanza' peach, and 'Golden Sentinel' and Northpole™ apples, which produce spur systems around a main vertical stem.

Restricted forms

Fruit trees can be trained to develop a framework of compact growth on which fruiting spurs develop, which adds ornamental value as well as saving space. Cordons, fans, and espaliers (see page 61) and festooned trees (see page 99) all make maximum use of the space available, and keep the crop within easy reach.

Easy pollination

Some varieties need to be pollinated by a different variety of the same plant in order to develop fruit, which means growing two plants instead of one. Where space is limited, it's a good idea to choose self-fertile crops, such as

APPLES ARE IDEAL TREES FOR TRAINING *as an espalier. They are not only productive but also decorative, especially when grown against a wall with bricks that complement the color of the fruit.*

currants and gooseberries, which do not need a pollinating partner. However, you can have more than one variety of apple, pear, plum, peach, or nectarine on a small plot by growing what's known as a 'family tree.' This is a rootstock onto which a number of compatible varieties have been grafted, giving the gardener maximum crop variability from minimum space.

Long-season crops

Extend the fresh harvest period by weeks if not months by growing varieties of fruit that crop far longer than others. For example, by growing everbearing strawberries, such as 'Ozark Beauty' and 'Tribute', you will be provided with a supply of fresh fruits from early summer until mid fall, rather than a sudden peak in early or mid summer, as is often the case with conventional summer-fruiting varieties. Everbearing raspberry varieties, such as 'Encore' and 'Heritage' can be grown to produce both summer and fall crops.

Storage potential

Fruits that store well enable you to continue enjoying them for an extended period. By choosing varieties that have a long storage life you can continue to eat them raw, which also allows you to benefit from their maximum vitamin content. Many fruits also freeze well or can be dried or made into preserves.

Dual-purpose varieties

The more uses you can get out of a particular fruit the better, especially if space is an issue. Some fruits—notably apples, pears, plums, blueberries, and cherries—have dual-

THESE ESPALIERED APPLE TREES *growing at the American Horticultural Society's headquarters at River Farm in Alexandria, Virginia, provide an attractive landscape feature.*

purpose varieties that are suitable for both cooking and eating raw. By focusing on growing these more versatile types, you can maximize the use of your space.

Plant protection

The fresh harvest period of some fruit can be extended at either end of the growing season by the use of floating row covers and hoop houses. This is particularly useful for lower-growing crops, such as strawberries and blueberries, which are more easily be covered, and for fruit planted in containers that can be moved into a protected environment. Extra protection in spring can allow fruits to be harvested 3–4 weeks earlier than those left uncovered, and a protective covering at the end of the season will shield later-maturing varieties right up until the first hard frosts, ensuring successful yields from all your fruit.

FRUIT TREES *such as apples can be grown in pots to restrict growth and encourage fruiting.*

early summer

Now there is real warmth in the sun and garden plants are responding with accelerated growth. Sowing and transplanting continues as the weather has now settled and it's safe to move tender crops outdoors—even in cooler climates. Many sowings will need thinning to provide space for a healthy crop to develop. Weeds are also growing with gusto, and it is important to remove them as they appear or they may overtake your crops.

Dry spells are not uncommon at this time of year, so have a watering can or garden hose ready to supplement rainfall, especially on newly planted crops. It is well worth the effort to mulch both vegetable and fruit plantings since this helps control weed growth and retain soil moisture.

In the fruit garden, strawberries are ripening and early raspberries will be coming into season—the advance guard of the delicious fruit crops you can look forward to over the coming season.

vegetables | GENERAL ADVICE

ALL REGIONS

Keep planting | As space becomes available, cultivate the ground, add fertilizer, and sow or plant suitable varieties to keep crops producing throughout the season.

Thin earlier sowings | Start thinning out seedlings early before they get overcrowded, as overcrowding makes them weaker and more prone to disease.

Harvest cool-season crops as they mature | Continue regular harvesting of lettuce, spinach, radishes, and other cool-season crops. As these crops begin to bolt, remove them to make room for warm-season crops.

COLD-WINTER REGIONS

Transplant tender crops | Tomatoes, peppers, eggplants, cucumbers, melons, pumpkins, and squash that were started indoors can be transplanted to the garden after hardening off.

Sow outdoors | Snap beans, corn, cucumbers, squash, pumpkins, and melons can now be sown outdoors where they are to grow.

MID-TEMPERATE AND MILD-WINTER REGIONS

Make successive sowings | Make successive sowings of crops such as beans, cucumbers, corn, summer squash, and carrots to provide an extended harvest season.

SOW CROPS DIRECTLY *if you can. It saves time repotting, but beware of pests. Crops that need a long season, such as tomatoes and eggplant, benefit instead from an earlier, indoor sowing and should be transplanted.*

vegetables | WHAT TO DO NOW

Garlic

Harvest early bulbs

The earliest varieties should be maturing now; most mature around mid summer. Plants are ready to harvest when the stems begin to yellow and bend over. Use a fork to loosen the bulbs from the soil, then spread them out in the sun to dry, ideally on wire mesh or netting so that the air can circulate around them. Keep them dry.

To store garlic bulbs once they have dried, knock off the dry soil, place the bulbs in a net bag and hang it up in a cool, dry shed or garage. Alternatively, the stems can be braided together to form a traditional garlic rope.

ONION BULBS *begin to swell during early summer. It is essential to keep them well watered and free from weeds at this stage in each plant's development.*

Leek

Mound soil around plants

Draw soil up around the base of leek plants as they develop to extend the length of the tender, white-blanched stems.

Onion and shallot

Start to lift fall-sown varieties

In mild-winter regions, overwintered onion varieties that were sown last fall will soon be large enough for use. Lift bulbs as you require them, using a garden fork to pry them out of the soil, but leave the rest in the ground to develop and ripen fully.

ALL ABOUT GARLIC

There are two main types of garlic: hardneck and softneck. The one you most often see at the grocery store is the softneck type; it has a white, papery skin and forms many cloves. It is popular with commercial growers because of its long-keeping qualities.

Hardneck garlic produces a hard, woody flowering stalk in early summer known as a scape, which is removed in order to encourage the formation of larger bulbs. The scapes are edible and considered a delicacy. There are fewer but larger cloves to each hardneck bulb than softneck varieties, and they have a thinner outer covering. Their flavor is generally held to be superior to softneck varieties.

When using garlic in dishes such as stir-fries, be careful not to let it burn in hot oil because it becomes bitter in taste. The characteristic smell is caused by an organic compound called allicin, which also gives garlic the antibacterial properties that have made it one of the most valued plants for centuries. It is easy to grow, and its juicy bulbs will transform your cooking—you'll never want to go back to store-bought garlic once you've grown your own.

CABBAGE FAMILY

General

Protect cabbage, broccoli, Brussels sprouts, and cauliflower from flea beetles as well as cabbage worms and loopers by growing them beneath floating row covers. Flea beetles cause numerous tiny holes in the leaves of these and other crops. Cabbage worms and loopers hatch from eggs that the adult moths lay on the leaves of young plants. They eat their way through the leaves, leaving a messy, greenish brown excrement behind. Be sure to arrange the row cover to allow plenty of room for the crop to grow, but seal the lower edges with soil or stones to keep the pests out. Metal 'staples' can also be purchased to secure the row covers.

THE SMALL, JUICY HEADS *of early summer cabbage can be cut when they feel firm and hearty. After harvesting, cut a ½in. cross in the top of the stump and it should resprout in about five weeks.*

Broccoli

Harvest heads and shoots

Continue harvesting broccoli as heads and sideshoots form. Cut the main head about 6in. below the top, while the buds are tight, before yellow flowers open. Depending on your region, sideshoots will continue to develop for a few more weeks. By cutting the shoots frequently you will encourage more to develop.

Cabbage

Water in dry spells

As long as cabbage is watered thoroughly immediately after transplanting, little additional water is needed. In prolonged dry spells, however, provide a thorough soak every ten days. And when hearts begin to form, generous watering will greatly improve head size, but as heads mature avoid excessive watering after a dry spell, which can cause heads to split.

Harvest spring and summer cabbage

In mild-winter and mid-temperate regions, spring and early summer cabbage can be harvested now. Round-headed varieties such as 'Gonzales' and 'Super Red' should be cut when the heads are full and firm. Pointed varieties such as 'Caraflex' can be cut as greens before they have hearted up, but by this time they should be producing tight, firm heads.

Cauliflower

Blanch heads

Cauliflower thrives in cool temperatures and should still be growing well in cold-winter regions. Some varieties are 'self blanching'—that is, their leaves tend to curl around the heads as it forms. Other varieties, however, need some encouragement to keep the head covered and prevent it from turning green. Once heads reach about 2in. in diameter, tie leaves loosely around it using soft string or rubber bands. Check the heads every 2–3 days and loosen the string or rubber bands as necessary to allow the head to expand.

Harvest heads

Cut the cauliflower heads once they reach the appropriate size for the variety, but while the curds are still firm and white.

Kale

Sow kale for salads

Mature kale is well known as a winter vegetable, but it can also be grown as a baby leaf for salads. One of the best varieties for this use is 'Toscana', an Italian variety with very dark green, strap-shaped leaves with a deeply puckered surface. It adds an interesting color and texture to summer salads and has a spicy, peppery flavor. Sow thinly in short rows at intervals between now and mid summer, either in the vegetable garden or in a container. Leaves are ready for picking within about 30 days, and they should be cut when they are young and tender.

LEGUMES

Fava beans

Harvest young pods

Harvest beans when they are small, before the flesh becomes starchy and the skin bitter. Take pods from the base of the plant first and work your way up. It is best to use scissors or hand pruners to remove the pods; sometimes they hang on tightly to the stem and you can uproot the plant while trying to tug them off.

HARVEST GARDEN PEAS *carefully, to avoid uprooting the vine; the pods should be bright green and plump with developing seeds. Until the weather gets hot, regular picking will encourage further production.*

INOCULATING BEANS AND PEAS

Beans and peas have the capacity to convert nitrogen from the soil atmosphere into a usable form for the plants with the help of beneficial bacteria that grow on their roots. Although they occur naturally in the soil, it is helpful to inoculate beans and peas with the bacteria to encourage nitrogen fixation, which will increase crop production. Bean and pea inoculants are readily available from seed companies and garden centers.

Lima beans

Sow outdoors

In mild-winter and mid-temperate regions, continue to sow lima bean seeds outdoors. Sow varieties 1in. deep and 3in. apart in rows 2–3ft. apart. Thin bush varieties to 6in. apart. Pole varieties should be thinned 6–10in. apart and provided with a sturdy support for the bean vines to grow on. They can also be grown on poles spaced to form a tee-pee; sow several seeds at the base of each pole, thinning to 3–4 plants per pole.

Peas

Water growing plants

Once flowering has begun, plants must have enough water for the pods to swell properly. During dry spells, check the soil moisture (dig under the surface near the plants to see if the soil is damp at root level) and if necessary give the crops a good soaking once or twice a week. Apply a 2in. layer of organic mulch over the root area, to lock in the moisture. Harvest mature pods promptly, to encourage more production. As daytime temperatures begin to rise, flowering and pod formation drop off significantly.

Harvest as ready

Harvest peas as they mature. Pick pods of snow peas when they get 3–5in. long, but before seeds fill out. Harvest garden peas and snap peas when the seeds have developed but before the pods become dry or yellow. Take care pulling pods from the vine to avoid damaging plants; using scissors or hand pruners may be helpful.

Remove finished vines

In mild-winter regions where the weather has turned warm by now, most pea vines have finished their productive life and should be removed to make room for late crops.

After the harvest, cut off the stems at ground level; do not pull up the spent crops. This is because the clusters of small, white nodules found on the roots are full of nitrogen-fixing bacteria. If left in the ground, these nodules will gradually break down, releasing the nitrogen they have taken from the air back into the soil for the next crop to use.

Snap beans

Sow outdoors

Sow bush varieties 1in. deep and 2in. apart in rows 2–3ft. apart. After they germinate, thin seedlings to 4–6in. apart. Continue to sow seeds every couple of weeks from now until mid summer for a succession of beans. Sow pole varieties about 3in. apart along their supports, thinning so that they are 6–10in. apart. Pole bean varieties tend to produce a crop over a longer season than bush types.

Support climbing varieties

Bush varieties of snap beans are the most commonly grown, but there are climbing varieties available, too. The simplest, most traditional support structure is a tee-pee (made of bamboo or wooden poles) or a double row of poles, at least 6ft. tall, spaced 8in. apart. Grow one plant per pole to avoid congestion.

Climbing beans can also be trained up a trellis, over arches, or along fences to show off their beautiful, white or lilac flowers and interesting pods. Whichever way you choose, they will usually need some initial encouragement to get them growing on the support. Tie in young shoots because they can unwind from poles in windy weather.

Protect newly germinated seedlings

If unexpectedly cold weather is forecast after sowing your beans, cover the plants with a floating row cover or even newspaper until it is warmer. Windy weather is another problem, since it can desiccate leaves and damage any climbing stems that weren't tied to their support. Plant early sowings in an area protected from winds, if possible.

GETTING POLE BEANS TO CLIMB

The young stems of pole beans sometimes have trouble getting an initial hold on their supports, particularly where smooth bamboo poles are used. Winding a little rough textured twine around the base of each pole gives stems something to cling on to.

Wind fast-growing shoots carefully around the poles and tie them in loosely where necessary, as they usually need a little help to get climbing. It is important to twine the shoots in the right direction, otherwise they will simply unwind themselves again. Looking at it from the beans' point of view (that is, looking up from below), the stems twine in a clockwise direction; if you are looking down on the top of the stems they twine counter-clockwise.

POLE BEAN SUPPORTS *can make an attractive garden feature. This slender obelisk frame made of thin, galvanized metal is strong enough to take the weight of heavy climbers.*

ROOT AND STEM CROPS

Beet

Harvest roots when young

For the best flavor and texture, pull roots when they reach tennis-ball size; any larger and they develop an unpleasant, woody texture. Harvest succulent and tender baby beets as soon as they are large enough to eat, usually around golf-ball size.

Before lifting, use a garden fork to loosen the soil beneath, but take care not to damage the roots, particularly if they are intended for storage.

Carrot

Lift baby roots

Carrots are ready for harvesting 12–16 weeks after sowing, although the timing depends on whether you prefer tender baby carrots or larger roots. In light soils or in raised beds, young carrots can be pulled up carefully by hand, but in heavy clay or when roots are larger, they are best lifted by gently easing them up with a fork to avoid damaging or breaking the roots. Bruising the roots will encourage the development of soft rot during storage. Carrots are often easier to harvest if you first soak the soil with water before you lift them.

Fennel

Weed and water bulbs

Keep fennel well watered during dry spells. Weed the crop regularly, hoeing between the rows and hand weeding close to the plants, to avoid damaging the shallow roots. As the bulbs start to swell, use a hoe or trowel to mound the soil up around the roots to make them sweeter.

Potato

Finish mounding soil

Cover spring-planted potato tubers with more loose soil, mounding it over the row for the last time in the next few weeks, leaving them in a rounded ridge about 12in. high. Mulching the row with well-rotted garden compost or clean straw will further protect tubers from turning green and will help retain soil moisture.

A CROP OF YOUNG BEETS *should be harvested by easing a fork or trowel under the soil, enabling you to lift the swollen roots gently out of the ground.*

Check early varieties

In cooler regions, early-planted potatoes may be producing tubers of a usable size already. Once the plants have started flowering, scrape some of the soil away or burrow your fingers into the soil and check to see how big the tubers are; usually at this time you are looking for potatoes the size of an egg. With care, you can take enough tubers for an early meal without disturbing the plants. Lift just a few tubers from each plant and return the soil so the rest of the crop can continue to grow. The first meal of homegrown new potatoes is always an eagerly anticipated treat. No need to peel the potatoes, just rinse them and the skins should slip right off.

In warmer regions, potatoes may be ready to harvest. Dig potatoes when at least two thirds of the topgrowth has died back. Use a fork and gently lift the soil. Once the potatoes are gathered, brush off excess soil and sort them carefully; those that were injured during digging should be used promptly. Allow others to dry and then store them in a cool, dry, dark place. If the soil isn't too wet, you can leave the potatoes in the ground to harvest as they are needed.

Rutabaga

Sow direct outside

Rutabaga requires a long season to produce a crop and is best planted from early to mid summer for a fall or early winter harvest. It grows best in full sun and well-drained, moisture-retentive soil, with plenty of organic matter, such as compost or well-rotted manure, added. Since rutabaga is a member of the cabbage family and prone to clubroot if grown on acid soil, check the soil's pH before sowing and add a dressing of lime, if necessary, to increase the alkalinity. A moderate dose of a balanced fertilizer prior to sowing is a good idea.

Sow seed thinly where the crop is to grow in well-prepared soil about ½in. deep in rows 18–24in. apart. After germination, thin seedlings to 4–6in. apart. Water deeply each week if the weather is dry; rutabaga needs about 1in. of water per week. Good varieties for the kitchen garden include 'Laurentian' and 'American Purple Top'.

Sweet potato

Plant slips

In warm regions, finish planting rooted cuttings (slips) of sweet potatoes. Sweet potatoes do not perform well in areas with cool summers. Use certified, diseasefree slips to avoid diseases.

Turnip

Encourage steady growth

Water the developing plants every 5–10 days during dry spells to avoid irregular growth, which can lead to splitting roots. Hoe or hand weed around the plants frequently to prevent competition for nutrients and water.

LEAFY GREENS

General

Continue to harvest cool-season greens such as arugula, lettuce, and spinach until they begin to bolt (develop seed stalks). Once this happens, the leaves turn bitter. Remove the plants to make room for summer crops such as chard, which tolerates warm weather better than most greens.

Chard

Sow seed outdoors

In mid-temperate and cold-winter regions, sow chard (also called Swiss chard) seed where the crop will grow. It grows best in full sun and well-drained soil, but will tolerate some shade. Because chard plants, particularly those with colorful stems, are so attractive, they make useful additions to flowerbeds and mixed containers.

In the garden, sow seed 2–3in. apart and ½in. deep, in rows 18–24in. apart. Thin seedlings to a final spacing of 12in. apart; the thinnings can be used in salads.

Harvest leaves from earlier sowings

In mild-winter regions, harvest outer leaves from earlier sowings once they are about 6in. long. Continue to harvest frequently to encourage the production of new leaves from the center of the plant. Chard is more tolerant of heat than most other leafy greens and, except in the warmest regions, can usually be harvested throughout the summer.

Lettuce

Cut as leaves and heads mature

Harvest lettuce by cutting rather than pulling—the stems will often sprout fresh leaves if cut off close to ground level, provided conditions are not too hot and dry. Loose-leaf types are particularly good at this. If just a few leaves are needed, cut the outer leaves, leaving the inner leaves

'LOLLO' LETTUCE AND CURLY ENDIVE *make a striking pattern, grown in interweaving bands. Cut off lettuce close to ground level and it may sprout fresh leaves if conditions are right.*

to continue to grow. In hot weather, harvest in the morning, putting leaves straight into a bucket of clean water to prevent wilting.

Many varieties will store well in the fridge for at least a couple of days in a plastic bag, if rinsed first, but wash the leaves again before use.

Spinach

Keep the soil moist

In cooler regions where spinach has yet to bolt, keep it well watered at all times, as hot, dry conditions lead to the plants going to seed at the expense of growing leaves. Once a plant has bolted, there isn't much you can do except pull it up.

Spinach is probably the most versatile of the leaf crops, producing delicately flavored, soft-textured leaves that are particularly good in salads. They are also delicious when lightly sautéed, added to an omelet, or baked in a quiche. Whatever size of leaves you harvest, rinse and place them in a plastic bag to keep them fresh. Store spinach in the fridge until you need it.

Protect spinach from insect pests

Use a floating row cover to protect plants from infestation by leaf miners and flea beetles. Both pests feed on leaves: Leaf miners eat the inner leaf tissues, creating irregular tan lines, and flea beetles' feeding causes numerous small holes.

CUCURBITS

Cucumber

Sow seed or transplant seedlings outdoors

The two main types of cucumbers are slicers—those with smooth, thin skins that are best eaten fresh; and picklers, which are usually harvested when small to be used for making pickles and relishes. Picklers can also be eaten fresh, so if you have room for only one type, a pickling variety may be the best option.

In cold-winter regions, it is finally time to transplant seedlings from indoors to the garden after proper hardening off. In all regions, cucumber seed can be sown directly in the garden as soon as the soil has warmed to

about 70°F. Sow seed of vining types 1in. deep and 2in. apart, in rows 3–5ft. apart. Thin seedlings to 8–12in. apart when they are large enough to handle. Bush varieties can be planted closer together or in containers.

Melons

Plant outdoors

In cold-temperature regions, plant fully hardened-off melon plants in their final positions, setting each one so the top of its rootball is just below soil level—do not plant too deeply as this encourages rotting. Space plants 18in. apart, in rows 4ft. apart. Choose a warm, sunny spot in humus-rich, light, well-drained soil. On heavier soil, use raised beds filled with free-draining soil that will warm up more quickly. For best results, warm up the site by covering with black plastic a week or two before planting. Rather than removing it, you can cut holes and plant the melons through the plastic; it serves as a mulch to discourage weeds and retains soil moisture.

Summer squash

Train trailing plants

Check the spread of trailing types by training them over a support such as a fence or trellis, tying plants in regularly as they grow. This is important where space is limited, as they can quickly cover a huge area of ground and smother other crops if left alone.

Hand pollinate flowers

Sometimes the earliest flowers do not set fruit well, but this can be avoided by hand pollinating. Female flowers have a round swelling at the base, while the male ones have a straight stem. Pick off a male flower and carefully remove or fold back the petals, then push it gently into the female flower so that the pollen is transferred.

Feed and water as fruits develop

As fruit starts to form, give plants a liquid fertilizer every week or two, or sprinkle a balanced fertilizer near the base and water in. Watering is most important as the fruit is developing; the more the plants get at this time, the better quality the fruit will be. Water generously every ten days in dry spells, soaking the soil deeply. Keeping the roots moist also helps to prevent powdery mildew.

Winter squash and pumpkin

Feed plants regularly

Apply liquid fertilizer every couple of weeks, or scatter a balanced fertilizer around the plant shortly after planting. Water every ten days during hot, dry spells.

Aim for large fruits

If you are growing a large cultivar, remove the growing tip of the main stem once three fruits have set, since limiting the number of fruits gives them a better chance of reaching a large size. If your main aim is to grow the largest possible pumpkin or squash, leave one fruit on each plant and give it extra water and fertilizer. As the fruit swells, place it on pieces of wood or brick to keep it off the wet soil to avoid rotting or being attacked by pests such as slugs.

FRUITING CROPS AND CORN

Corn

Sow seed outdoors

In cold-winter regions, sow corn outdoors. In warmer regions, continue to sow blocks of corn at two-week

BIOLOGICAL CONTROL

Biological controls—the use of one organism to control or reduce the population of another—is effective for many vegetable pests. Natural predators, such as lacewings, predatory mites, or *Trichogramma* wasps feed upon or parasitize other insects or mites that can cause significant injury to crops. Beneficial microbes, such as the many varieties of *Bacillus thuringiensis* (Bt), control specific pests by producing toxins that poison the pest, but do not harm other organisms.

Many biological controls can be purchased and released or spread in the garden when pest populations rise. It is critical to identify the pest correctly so that the appropriate biological control for that pest can be obtained. Purchase biological controls when the pests are seen to be building up and introduce them to your plants according to the manufacturers' instructions. Watch your plants for symptoms of infestation to determine if pest populations are rising. If predators or parasites are introduced before there is a sufficient population of the pest, they may leave your garden to seek their prey elsewhere. Biological controls are a natural way of keeping pest numbers down and limiting the amount of damage that they do.

SUMMER SQUASH ARE FORMIDABLE GUZZLERS *in hot weather and should never be allowed to dry out in summer when new fruit is developing. Regular watering is essential for quality fruit.*

FEED CUCURBITS WITH A LIQUID FERTILIZER *every couple of weeks as fruit starts to form. Given the right care, this new bud and growth (above) will grow into an impressive pumpkin.*

TO GROW LARGE PUMPKINS *or squash, leave one fruit on each plant and give it extra water and fertilizer. They are by far the most impressive vegetables you'll ever grow.*

intervals for an extended harvest season. Choose a sheltered, sunny site for planting. Corn is not fussy about soil and will grow well, provided the soil is well drained and has good fertility. Prepare the soil by adding well-rotted manure. Sidedress newly planted rows with a balanced fertilizer.

Appropriate plant spacing is crucial to achieve good pollination; only pollinated kernels will swell to fill the cobs. They are most successful when grown in blocks because the pollen is less likely to be blown away from its target. Plant at least four rows at the same time, or make blocks at least four rows deep and wide, with each plant 15–18in. apart. Water deeply once a week, especially when kernels are developing.

Eggplant

Plant out young plants

In all regions, now that all danger of frost has passed and the weather has settled, eggplants can be transplanted to the garden. If you have not raised your own plants from seed, young plants are usually available from garden centers. Set plants 12–18in. apart. To accelerate growth, spread a black plastic mulch over the soil to absorb heat, or cover plants with a floating row cover.

Eggplants make attractive and productive container plants. A 12in. pot filled with well-drained growing mix is

sufficient for one eggplant. Be sure to keep it watered and fertilize it every two weeks with a balanced liquid fertilizer.

Okra

Plant out young plants or sow seed

Young okra plants that were sown indoors can now be planted in the garden. Space seedlings 12in. apart, taking care not to disturb the roots. Okra needs a warm soil for healthy growth. In cold-winter regions, spread sheets of black plastic over the planting area two weeks before transplanting to warm the soil and plant through slits.

Alternatively, sow okra seed ½in. deep and 2in. apart, thinning to 6in. apart when large enough to handle.

CORN POLLINATION

Corn is unusual among vegetables because it is pollinated by wind rather than by insects. The male flowers are called tassels and appear in a tuft at the top of the stem. The female flowers are held in rows in the developing cob, and each has a slender strand called a silk that emerges out of the end of the cob. The pollen from the tassels is shed in the wind and drifts down to land on the silks of the female flowers. Growing the plants in a block ensures that the pollen is more likely to come into contact with the female flowers than if they were growing in individual rows, where it could be blown away. You can help the pollination process along by giving the stems a gentle shake on a still day to help release the pollen.

YOUNG OKRA PLANTS *can reach quite a size, about 4ft. high, and need plenty of space, so don't crowd them. Position them carefully when growing your own.*

Support plants with bamboo canes if necessary. Keep well watered and fed with a tomato fertilizer.

Peppers

Plant out young plants

Finish hardening off and transplanting peppers to the garden where they will grow. Space plants 12–18in. apart. Like eggplants, peppers make attractive container specimens. Many varieties of pepper, especially those with small, colorful fruit, add interest to beds of flowering annuals and herbs.

Peppers require well-drained, moisture-retentive soil, so dig in plenty of well-rotted organic matter before planting. Like tomatoes, both sweet and hot peppers need sunshine and warm temperatures to produce a good crop. In cooler regions, choose a warm site such as a sheltered raised bed or plant against a sunny wall that will radiate the sun's heat back onto the ripening fruit.

Tomato

Finish transplanting outdoors

In all regions, tomatoes can still be planted for a late crop. If possible, schedule your transplanting for a mild, overcast day to minimize transplant shock.

Feed and water regularly

Tomatoes are thirsty and hungry plants, and the soil should be kept evenly moist. Avoid fluctuations between wet and dry conditions, which can result in the fruit splitting. Allowing the soil to dry out can cause blossom end rot (pictured on page 30). Feed tomatoes regularly using a tomato fertilizer that contains high levels of potassium to encourage good fruiting. Always use according to the manufacturer's instructions.

Bush and trailing tomatoes need little attention, but vine types are better grown in cages or on stakes. Snap or cut off sideshoots, as this concentrates each plant's energy on the fruits that grow from the main stem. Remove any yellowing, lower leaves as they appear.

Avoid blossom end rot

Never allowing plants to go short of water is the key to avoiding this damaging disorder. If plants are allowed to wilt while they are flowering, it is almost inevitable that the fruits that were forming at this time will be affected. The actual cause of the rot is a lack of calcium in the fruit, triggered when insufficient water is available to transport it through the plant.

Blossom end rot causes the base of the tomato opposite the stalk to become sunken and shriveled, with a dry, black or very dark brown discoloration. The top part of the fruit may still be edible, but the rot usually extends into the center of the tomato.

Blossom end rot typically subsides or disappears once plants are supplied with water on a regular basis. Mulching helps to minimize soil water fluctuations.

PERENNIAL VEGETABLES

Asparagus

Stop cutting spears

It is time to stop cutting established asparagus 6–8 weeks after the start of the harvest. This gives the plants time to build themselves up for next year's crop. Give beds a dressing of balanced fertilizer once cutting has finished.

Look for asparagus beetle

Asparagus beetles are small, black beetles with yellow spots, and they can do a great deal of damage to asparagus plants. You can often find rows of their small, black eggs laid up the stems of spears as you cut them.

Rub off any eggs you find and destroy any beetles or their grayish larvae as soon as you see them.

Globe artichoke

Harvest main heads

In warmer climates, where artichoke is grown as a perennial, heads can be harvested as they become ready. Large terminal heads are produced first, followed by smaller secondary heads. Harvest plump heads with hand pruners before the scales start to open or they will become tough. If you don't intend to eat the head immediately, leave a length of stalk attached and stand it in a glass of water in the fridge, where it will keep fresh for several days.

Rhubarb

Pull young stems

Harvest rhubarb from established plantings as soon as the leaves open fully, until the stems become tough, stringy, and green. Remove no more than half the stalks

at one time. Trim and discard the leaves—they are poisonous. Leave the remaining stems to allow the plant to produce sufficient foliage to build up food reserves for a good crop next year.

To remove a stem, hold it at the base, pull down, and twist. Do not harvest from new plantings.

TO PULL RHUBARB (top), grab the stem at its base, close to the crown of the plant, and pull it down with a slight twist. Stems come away easily. Remove no more than half the stems at one time.

GROW RHUBARB (above) in a sunny position and in well-drained, moisture-retentive, fertile soil that has been prepared with lots of organic matter. Harvest as soon as the leaves open fully.

EATING ARTICHOKES

Many gardeners are not sure how to prepare artichokes for eating, but they are well worth the trouble! Cut the stem off with a sharp knife, just below the lower scales. Remove any brown or damaged scales at the base. Using a pair of scissors, cut off the tips of each scale—they carry a thorny point, which can be very sharp. Wash under running water, opening the scales out slightly to allow the water into the center. Boil the entire head in a large saucepan of water until a scale near the base of the stem comes away easily when pulled—this usually takes 30–40 minutes depending on size. Remove from the pan and turn upside down to drain for a few minutes.

Eat the artichoke by pulling away scales, starting from the outside; dip the base of each scale in butter and scrape off the fleshy portion with your teeth. Continue until you reach the papery inner leaves and remove these to expose the 'choke'—the fuzzy, hairy center of the flower. Remove and discard these silky fibers, carefully using a teaspoon to scrape them off the base and reveal the flat green 'heart', which is the tastiest part.

| Grow your own tasty tomatoes

A summer salad is somehow incomplete without the splash of color and the intense, sweet–tart flavor and aroma of ripe tomatoes—preferably picked sun-warmed and taken straight from the plant to the plate.

The multitude of tomato varieties available in seed catalogs is almost overwhelming. There are tomatoes of all shapes and sizes, from tiny, grape-sized ones to huge beefsteaks; from round or pear shaped to those whose shape more closely resembles a banana. Even their color provides you with a choice: In addition to fire-engine red, there are yellow, orange, pink, mahogany, and even striped varieties to choose from.

While all the major seed companies offer an extensive range of different tomato varieties, even wider choices, including long-established heirloom varieties and some extraordinary shapes and colors, are available from specialist suppliers. Varieties may be determinate or indeterminate in their growth habit. Determinate types grow to a certain size and produce the bulk of their fruit over a short period. Indeterminate varieties continue to grow until frost kills the vine, producing smaller quantities of fruit over a longer period.

Make sure you pick the right variety of tomato for your conditions. If you are really short of space, look for tomatoes that have been specially bred for growing in pots, window boxes, and even hanging baskets. You should be able to find something suitable and enjoy growing and eating your own tomatoes no matter how big or small your garden is.

CHERRY TOMATOES (above) bear small, round fruit, which make a tasty addition to summer salads and pasta dishes.

Recommended varieties

'Sungold'
A golden-orange cherry tomato that bears ½–1in. diameter fruit with exceptional sweet–tart flavor. Plants are indeterminate.

'Gold Nugget'
A very tasty cherry tomato with a bushy, determinate habit that produces an early crop with good yields. The crack resistant, 1in. diameter fruit is golden-yellow.

'Cherokee Purple'
This indeterminate heirloom has relatively short vines and bears full-flavored, medium to large fruit with a slightly flattened shape. It is deep red to purple with darker shoulders.

'Celebrity'
This widely adapted, disease-resistant selection has medium to large, bright red, globe-shaped fruit with a firm texture. It ripens in mid season and is determinate.

'Roma'
This popular paste tomato produces heavy crops of 3in. long, pear-shaped fruit that has a very meaty texture and few seeds. The vines of this determinate variety are compact.

'Gardener's Delight'
An indeterminate cherry tomato with exceptionally sweet flavor. The plants bear long trusses of 6–12 bright red, ¾–1½in. diameter fruit that is resistant to cracking.

'Olivade' (F1 hybrid)
These large, dark red plum tomatoes are very early to mature and are borne in profusion on the indeterminate plants. The 3–3½oz. fruits are juicy, with good flavor.

'Rutgers'
Developed in the 1920s, this heirloom is very productive, has excellent flavor, and is resistant to numerous diseases. Bears medium-sized, bright red fruits on determinate vines.

'Marmande'
A popular French heirloom variety with large, ribbed, sweetly flavored fruit, which are great sliced on a sandwich or for cooking. Plants are indeterminate.

fruit | GENERAL ADVICE

Remove tent caterpillars | Prune out and destroy tent caterpillar nests found in fruit trees before they defoliate the tree or spread to others.

Continue training fans | Continue tying in suitably placed shoots on fan-trained trees.

Continue trapping codling moth | Monitor codling moth traps and replace them if necessary. If there are a lot of moths on the wing, the sticky surface of the trap sometimes becomes covered with insects and reduces its effectiveness.

Continue spray program for pests and diseases | Consult with your local extension service for an appropriate spray schedule and continue to apply preventive controls as advised.

Water fruit where necessary | Make sure fruits aren't drought-stressed at this time of year, especially those that are newly planted or growing in pots or against a wall.

Keep weeding | Continue to weed regularly around all tree and soft fruit to prevent competition for water and nutrients. Where trees or bushes are growing in a lawn, maintain a circle of bare (or mulched) soil extending at least 12in. from the main stem to prevent competition from the grass.

FIGS AND OTHER FRUIT TREES *will benefit from regular weeding at this time of year. Give figs plenty of water throughout summer.*

fruit | WHAT TO DO NOW

TREE FRUIT

Apples and pears

Train fan-trained trees

If you are training a fan from a feathered maiden (a branched, one-year old tree), the branches that were selected in winter (see page 53) should now have developed sideshoots of their own. Select two or three of these sideshoots and spread them equally on the wire system and tie them with string—ideally two above the branch and one to train downwards. On more established fans, remove any sideshoots that are making vigorous upright growth from the first tier of branches. Encourage weaker stems as these will be more fruitful.

Thin fruits

At the beginning of early summer there will be a natural shedding of fruitlets known as the 'June drop.' This is the tree's way of making sure it doesn't carry more fruit than it can manage to ripen satisfactorily. However, to obtain large fruit, you may need to thin them out some more, leaving well-placed fruit that can develop fully. Wait until the June drop has taken place before doing so.

Prop up branches

To prevent branches from breaking under the weight of a heavy crop, prop branches up with sturdy supports.

Apricots

Thin crowded fruits

If there is a heavy crop, thin the fruit to about 3½in. apart when they are the size of hazelnuts.

Water trees where necessary

Water newly planted trees frequently as their root system becomes settled. More established trees need watering only during dry spells.

JUST BEFORE CHERRIES START TO RIPEN (top), *erect some netting over the fruits to protect against birds. A framed net is best because the netting can be kept taut, which helps prevent birds from getting caught up in it.*

TREE FRUITLETS (above), *such as these young apricots, are vulnerable to late frost in cooler regions, but by early summer should be safe. Wait to thin until after the June drop has occurred.*

Cherries

Net against birds

Erect netting to deter birds before fruits start to show some color—trees may be stripped if left unprotected.

Check early varieties

Cherries are a very nutritious fruit, with high levels of the antioxidant vitamins A, C, and E. They are also an excellent source of several minerals including calcium, phosphorus, potassium, and iron.

Harvest early cherries as soon as they start to ripen. The earliest varieties in sheltered areas will start cropping soon. Pick during dry weather, by the stalks rather than the body of the fruit, which bruises easily.

Although sweet cherries are best enjoyed fresh, both sweet and sour cherries can be preserved by canning, freezing, drying, or making into jams.

Prune fan-trained trees

Shorten all new growth to 3in. long, to encourage sunlight to ripen the developing fruit. Also remove shoots growing directly into or away from the wall or fence, and prune out a proportion of old or unproductive twiggy growth, tying in well-placed replacement shoots.

Prune freestanding sweet cherries

Examine established trees for any diseased or damaged wood and remove it with clean cuts. No further pruning is usually necessary.

Prune sour cherries

Because of their different cropping habit, sour cherries need heavier pruning than sweet cherries to keep them productive. Prune out a proportion of the older stems of both fans and freestanding trees, training new replacement growth, while allowing sunlight to penetrate the canopy.

Figs

Water frequently and start feeding

Give figs plenty of water. If you are growing the fig in a container, watering will probably be necessary each day during summer. Apply a high-potassium fertilizer (such as tomato fertilizer) every two weeks until the figs start to ripen. One of the advantages of figs is that you don't

IT'S TIME TO START CHECKING *early varieties of cherries—if they are not ready to harvest, they will be soon. Pick fruit by the stalks, to avoid bruising the tender flesh.*

have to worry about pollination; the fruit develop without the need for fertilization.

Pinch back new shoots

Shorten new growth to five or six leaves, to stimulate the production of embryonic figs in the tips of the shoots. These will develop into fruit that will ripen next year.

Harvest early crop

Figs grown in mild-winter climates often produce an early summer crop on the previous year's wood, which may begin ripening at this time; a second crop on new growth will be produced in late summer. Allow fruit to ripen completely on the tree for best quality.

PINCH BACK THE TIPS OF FIG BRANCHES *in early summer to produce compact growth and encourage a good crop next year.*

Peaches and nectarines

Thin fruit

When they are hazelnut size, thin the fruitlets out to 4in. apart and then, when walnut size, to 8in. This allows them to mature to their full size and obtain maximum sugar levels. Aim to have the fruits spaced equally over the plant, removing ones that will become trapped and bruised against a branch or wall when ripe.

Train fans

On young trees, tie in the shoots that are growing at the tip of each rib to extend their length. Select three or four new shoots that have branched out along the ribs and cut the others back to one bud or leaf. One shoot can be tied downwards and a couple upwards.

On established fans, tie in the new shoots as they grow. Pinch back all secondary shoots to one leaf, and to about six leaves on shoots that were left in early spring.

Pick up fallen leaves

Gather up and destroy leaves that have been affected by peach leaf curl and have fallen from the trees. This helps to prevent the spores remaining near the tree to infect the following year's growth.

Plums

Train fans

Remove the central leader from a tree to be fan trained in its first summer; tie canes to the horizontal wire supports and the remaining sideshoots to the canes. Tie in new shoots that develop from these stems to fill any gaps.

Look out for the first signs of 'shothole'

Shothole fungus can affect all stone fruits. Small, circular patches on the leaves start to develop now, and by the end of the season the patches will have turned brown and fallen out, leaving the foliage peppered with tiny holes. This disease is most severe when mild wet winters are followed by long wet springs. Remove and destroy infected leaves and twigs as soon as symptoms appear.

Thin plums

Thin out plum fruitlets where necessary to obtain a satisfactory crop (see apples and pears, page 125).

Quinces

Water in dry spells

Water in periods of drought, even when well established. Quince is relatively low-maintenance but requires moist soils, and supplementary watering is often necessary.

FRUIT SUCH AS NECTARINES (above) and peaches should be thinned. If this proves difficult without damaging neighboring fruit, slice the unwanted one in half; it will soon wither.

PEACH LEAF CURL is caused by a fungus that attacks peach and nectarines as buds open in spring. Remove and destroy infected leaves as they fall. Spores overwinter in crevices in the tree's bark.

Blackberries

Water in dry spells

Water young plants during dry spells. While mature plants shouldn't need extra irrigation, their fruit size will benefit from watering if the weather is particularly dry.

Tie in new canes

Secure newly produced canes to their supports to prevent them from being damaged by wind.

Black currants

Water in dry spells

Throughout the growing season, water black currants during dry periods.

Blueberries, cranberries, and lingonberries

Water during dry periods

Using rainwater where possible, water plants during dry spells, especially in hard-water areas.

Gooseberries

Remove suckers and prune established plants

Remove suckers around the base of the plant as they appear throughout summer. Cut shoots back to five leaves when the plant has produced 8–10 leaves. Like red and white currants, gooseberries fruit on old wood.

Water in dry spells

Container-grown gooseberries in particular frequently struggle in dry conditions, so monitor their watering requirements carefully.

Pick fruit for cooking

Harvest gooseberries in two main pickings. A few weeks before the gooseberries are fully ripe, pick every other fruit and use to make pies, tarts, and sauces. The gooseberries that are left to ripen and develop their full sweetness can be enjoyed raw.

TIE NEW BLACKBERRY CANES (top) *carefully into position along the wires, spreading them out as much as possible. Use a figure-eight knot and don't tie them too tightly.*

FROM A HEALTHY MATURE BUSH *you can expect 8lb. of gooseberries (above) each season; from a cordon about 2lb. Pick the fruit with its stalk to prevent the skin from tearing.*

Raspberries

Remove suckers

Cut out suckers between the rows of summer raspberries. This makes weeding easier, maintains good circulation of air, and helps keep the space between rows clear, for easier harvest.

Pick early varieties

The first summer raspberries should be ready to pick (see left); do it on a dry day as they deteriorate when wet. Varieties of red raspberries that produce early crops include 'Killarney', 'Prelude', 'Comet', and 'Reveille'.

Red and white currants

Support cropping plants

Tie the plants to canes using twine to stop the branches from flopping onto the ground from the weight of the fruit.

Water when necessary

Red and white currants will benefit from extra watering during the growing season if it is particularly dry.

Prune established bushes

Shorten new growth back to five leaves. Red and white currants fruit on old wood, so this summer pruning encourages small fruiting spurs to develop on the branches of the currant bushes for next year's fruit.

Harvest when ripe

When the fruit first turns red it is not yet fully ripe, so pick it only once it has sweetened, which may be 2–3 weeks after it turns red (or white). Cut the strigs (bunches of fruit) using scissors, being careful not to damage the spur. Fruit can be stored in a refrigerator for a week or two after picking.

PRUNE RED AND WHITE CURRANTS' NEW GROWTH *to five leaves in summer, to encourage the formation of small fruiting spurs on the main branches for the next year's crop.*

Strawberries

Mulch plants with straw

If you have not already done so, place straw around strawberry plants to keep the fruits clear of the soil. Spreading sheets of newspaper beneath the straw helps to prevent weeds from emerging.

Harvest fruits

Pick strawberries when they are bright red all over, ideally during the warmest part of the day—this is when they are at their tastiest.

Plants have a short but heavy cropping period over 2–3 weeks; there are early, mid, and late-fruiting varieties. Everbearing strawberry varieties produce small flushes of fruit from now to early fall and are useful for a prolonged season of picking. The crops aren't as heavy as the summer-fruiting varieties; the fruit is smaller; and the plants are less likely to produce runners.

Remove moldy fruit

Any strawberries affected by botrytis (gray mold) should be removed promptly to prevent it from spreading. Also strip off affected blossoms and leaves. Botrytis is common in wet or humid weather.

De-blossom everbearing varieties for a late crop

To extend the season and concentrate strawberry production in late summer and early fall, remove the early summer flowers from perpetual varieties.

DIFFERENT TYPES OF CURRANTS

Currants are members of the genus *Ribes*. Black currants include *R. nigrum*, which is native to Europe, as well as *R. odoratum*, native to North America. Both thrive in colder regions and produce flavorful black fruit on large, 5–6ft. tall deciduous shrubs that benefit from annual pruning. Fruit of the European species is borne on one-year-old wood, while on the American species it is produced on spurs on two-year-old wood. The fruit ripens in mid to late summer.

Red and white currants, whose only significant difference is fruit color, include cultivars derived from several species native to Europe and Asia, such as *R. petaeaum*, *R. rubrum*, and *R. sativum*. These are attractive shrubs that grow best where winters are cold and summers mild.

Fruit color ranges from dark to light red or pink, and pale yellow to white. The fruit forms on drooping stalks called strigs; harvesting is done by cutting the entire strig. To maximize fruit production, maintain a good supply of spurs on two- and three-year-old wood.

ROOTING STRAWBERRY RUNNERS

GROW NEW STRAWBERRY PLANTS *from the old ones by potting up healthy runners, which usually arise in prolific numbers from the main plant.*

PEG DOWN A YOUNG PLANTLET *into a small container of fresh potting mix. Use a wire hoop as a peg to keep the runner in direct contact with the soil.*

CUT THE RUNNER *from the main plant after a few weeks, when the plantlet has taken root. Continue growing the plantlet on its own making sure to water it regularly.*

Start picking alpine varieties

Alpine strawberries produce tiny fruits from now until late fall. They are usually red but some varieties are white or yellow. They are very sweet, aromatic, and have superb flavor, but are not as juicy as the everbearing and summer-fruiting varieties.

Remove runners

Unless they are wanted for propagation, remove strawberry runners with hand pruners. Runners—long stems with baby plants attached to them—compete for water and nutrients and crowd out the main plant. They also make it difficult to keep the strawberry bed tidy and weed free as they grow in the pathways. If you need to increase your plants, some of the runners can be retained and rooted (see above). Alternatively, allow some runners to develop into new plants within each row and eliminate those that form outside the row. Spacing between rows should be about 4ft., to provide easy access for harvest. This is called a matted row system, and is a productive cropping method for June-bearing varieties.

VINE FRUIT

Grapes

Remove lower buds and stems

Prune out buds or stems that appear low down on the trunk of grape vines trained on supports. This process is called 'bud rubbing' and is important as these water shoots will deprive the plant of necessary nutrients and water. Between now and mid summer, pinch out the growing tips (or on long rows use a hedge trimmer) on the tops of the vines to prevent them getting too high and shading neighboring rows.

Train cordon vines

Tie in the leading shoot to its vertical cane with soft twine in a figure eight and shorten the other main shoots to five or six leaves. Prune back any sideshoots on these main shoots to one leaf.

Care for young plants

In their first year after planting, water grape vines during dry periods. Once fully established, those in cooler

EARLY SUMMER *is the season every strawberry grower longs for— when they finally get to sample their delicious fruit. Strawberries are at their best when eaten immediately after picking.*

regions shouldn't need watering as their deep-rooting system makes them tolerant of drought, and mulching will reduce loss of soil moisture through evaporation. Remove all flowers for the first couple of years after planting to prevent overcropping on young vines.

Mulch to retain moisture

Suppress weeds and retain moisture by mulching around the base of the plants. White gravel is a useful mulching material because it reflects sunlight back into the canopy of the grape vine, while black gravel is also suitable as it absorbs the heat from sunlight, helping to warm the soil. Avoid mulching around the vines with manure because this encourages surface rooting and contributes to luxuriant vegetative growth.

Foliar feed where necessary

Grape vines can be prone to magnesium deficiency, which can be treated with a foliar feed of Epsom salts or a fertilizer containing trace elements. An application of dolomitic limestone may also be helpful. Symptoms of magnesium deficiency are yellowing between the leaf veins (interveinal chlorosis) while the margin of the leaf remains green. Later in the season, the edges of the leaves turn brown or rust colored.

Thin dessert fruits

Remove individual dessert grapes to allow the berries to ripen fully and to improve air circulation. Use scissors with long, thin blades to snip off berries when they are small, removing about one in three per bunch.

TUCK OR TIE IN ALL NEW GROWTH *on a grape vine (top) to the parallel fixed wires. Remove any buds or shoots that develop low down on the trunk.*

REMOVE ALL NEW GROWTH *on a grape vine (above) that appears above the top wire. Shorten any sideshoots that grow from the new branches to one leaf.*

NUTRIENT DEFICIENCIES

Plants usually get all the nutrients they need from the soil, but in some cases they are not able to do this. This is often because the soil pH is either too high or too low and nutrients become chemically bound or 'locked up' so that even though they are present in the soil, they become unavailable to plants. Most plants prefer a pH that is close to neutral, because the essential nutrients are all relatively available in this range. Maintaining the correct pH is one of the best ways to guard against nutrient deficiencies.

The main nutrients needed by plants are nitrogen, phosphorus, and potassium, but there is a whole range of other elements required in only tiny amounts. These include iron, magnesium, manganese, boron, and copper, among others. These are known as trace elements and their shortage often shows as yellowing or browning of leaf edges, or between the leaf veins. Different nutrient deficiencies produce characteristic symptoms. Iron deficiency, for example, shows up as yellowing between the veins on young leaves, while a general yellowing of older leaves may indicate a nitrogen deficiency. Other deficiencies, such as copper and manganese, cause stunting.

One way to remedy trace element deficiencies is to apply them as a foliar feed, as leaves will absorb them even when the roots are unable to do so. Look for a trace element fertilizer that has been specially formulated for foliar application, otherwise it could scorch the leaves.

Kiwi

Water young plants

During their first two growing seasons, young plants need regular watering. More established plants require less, but yields will be significantly increased if plants are watered thoroughly during dry spells.

Train plants to their supports

When the central shoot of a young plant reaches the top of its support, train it along the horizontal wire, removing the tip when it reaches the end. If the main stem of the plant lacks vigor its first season, cut it back by about half during the dormant season and begin training the following year. To train, allow the central shoot to develop sideshoots along the horizontal wires, thinning these to 20in. apart. Train the sideshoots to the outer wires, then remove their tips. These sideshoots will form permanent fruiting arms. Pinch back any shoots that arise from them to four or five leaves. These will flower and fruit in subsequent years.

Prune established vines

Although established kiwi should be pruned during the dormant season (usually late winter) to shorten and thin lateral branches, summer pruning is required to keep vigorous growth in check and increase light penetration.

Shorten shoots with fruits developing at their bases to five or six leaves past the last fruit. This will divert energy into the developing fruits. Cut out any shoots growing from the base of the vine. Once harvested, cut fruited shoots back to 2–3in., to develop a spur system.

PRUNING KIWI VINES *is done both in the dormant season and in summer, when you should cut back the fruiting shoots to five or six leaves to divert energy into fruit production and allow in sunlight.*

KIWI FRUITS *develop only on female plants; however, a male plant is needed by most varieties for pollination and fruit production. Be sure the male plant is growing within 35ft. of the female.*

| Grow your own herbs

No garden is complete without herbs. They add flavor to so many dishes, and their wonderful fragrances can be appreciated when you brush past their foliage or squeeze their leaves between your fingers in passing. Most herbs are very easy to grow and are undemanding—in fact, many herbs have better flavors and more powerful aromas when they are growing in poor soil conditions. Moist, fertile soils promote lots of lush, leafy growth, but this has lower concentrations of the oils that give herbs their flavor than growth produced in leaner conditions.

The majority of culinary herbs come from Mediterranean regions, and they like a warm, open, free-draining position in full sun.

MANY HERBS (above) are not only a source of nourishment but also provide decorative interest in the garden for much of the year.

HERB POTS (right) can be stuffed full of your favorite herbs and then positioned in a handy spot for quick and convenient harvesting.

Recommended herbs

Basil
Sow seed indoors in mid spring and set plants outside only after all risk of frost is over, or sow directly in the garden in a sunny site in early summer. Grown as an annual.

Marjoram
Pot marjoram (or oregano) is a perennial, while the closely related sweet marjoram is grown as an annual. Both like an open, sunny site. Sow sweet marjoram indoors and plant out in late spring.

Sage
Sage has a characteristic strong aroma, and its spikes of blue flowers are popular with bees. Grow in an open position in free-draining soil and replace plants when they become leggy. Perennial.

Chives
These have a mild onion flavor and attractive flowerheads of papery purple blooms, which are also edible. Sow seed in mid spring, or divide clumps in early fall. Perennial.

Parsley
Sow the slow-germinating seed indoors in early spring and plant out in mid to late spring. Plants left to overwinter will quickly bolt in their second year. Biennial.

Thyme
Creeping or low-growing bushy perennial with flowers that are alive with bees in summer. Thyme likes well-drained soil and a sunny spot; propagate by cuttings or division.

Fennel
The seeds can be used as well as the leaves. Fennel prefers moist, fertile soil. Sow seeds in situ. Perennial.

Rosemary
This evergreen shrub likes a warm, sheltered site. Is usually propagated by cuttings; can be raised from seed.

Cilantro/Coriander
An annual with pungent leaves and seeds. Sow seeds in situ and keep plants moist. Tolerates light shade.

mid summer

This season you can start to really enjoy the fruits of your labors. Raspberries, blackberries, plums, cherries, snap beans, new potatoes, cucumbers, summer squash, peppers, and tomatoes are ready or nearly ready to be picked, and if you've timed your sowings right, there are plenty more crops to come.

Weed growth may slow down a little after the frantic pace of early summer, but you still need to keep weeding constantly and to watch out for pests and diseases, too. Take action at the first sign of trouble and you may prevent big problems from developing. Plenty of watering will likely be needed in all areas of the garden; if you added lots of organic matter to the soil earlier in the season you will now see the benefit, as it helps retain soil moisture instead of letting it drain away.

It may be high summer, but it is also time to start thinking ahead and start crops for the fall garden, such as broccoli, cabbage, cauliflower, and Brussels sprouts.

vegetables | GENERAL ADVICE

Feed hungry crops | Fast-growing vegetables will benefit from sidedressings of a balanced fertilizer. Container-grown vegetables also need regular liquid feeds.

Look out for pests and diseases | Many crops are targeted by pests at this time of year. Insect pests, including flea beetles, caterpillars, squash bugs, and leaf-mining insects, are beginning to cause serious damage. To avoid significant damage, use preventive measures and act promptly if pests appear. During summer, blight on potatoes and tomatoes may necessitate fungicide sprays. In dry seasons, powdery mildew on squash, cucumbers, and pumpkins can be a problem. Careful watering to keep the soil moist can limit damage.

Arrange for absences | Make arrangements with a neighbor to water and harvest your vegetables if you go on vacation for more than a few days.

Continue sowing | Continue making successional sowings of turnips, radish, snap beans, beets, carrots, kohlrabi, and bunching onions (scallions).

Sow seeds for fall crops | Start plants of cabbage-family crops in prepared seedbeds outdoors for transplanting into the fall garden.

POLE VARIETIES OF SNAP BEANS *will continue producing for several weeks as long as they are harvested regularly. If you go away on vacation, invite a neighbor to harvest and enjoy the beans.*

vegetables | WHAT TO DO NOW

ONION FAMILY

Leek

Keep crops moist and weed free
Weed leeks regularly, preferably using a hoe. During long, dry spells, water thoroughly but not frequently—a good soaking every ten days will do.

Continue to blanch stems
Continue drawing soil up around the stems of leeks to increase the length of the blanched portion. This is not essential, and deep-planted leeks will have a good length of white stem anyway.

Onion and shallot

Begin harvesting
Both onions and shallots are ready to harvest when the leaves turn yellow; the exact time will depend on the sowing or planting time. You can take one or two shallot bulbs out while they are in growth to use fresh, without disturbing the rest. For the general harvest, use a fork

HOE YOUR LEEK BED *regularly to keep weeds at bay, being careful not to damage the plants, and water them thoroughly every ten days during long spells of dry weather.*

to loosen the bulbs from the soil, then spread them out in the sun to dry, ideally on wire mesh above the ground so the air can circulate around them. Separate shallots into individual bulbs first.

Once the bulbs are thoroughly dry, gently knock off any loose soil, then store them in a net bag and keep in a cool, dry shed or garage. The skins should be brown and papery, and the remnants of stems and leaves make a convenient tool for bunching or braiding them together and hanging them so they are ready for use.

HARVESTING ONIONS AND SHALLOTS

ONIONS AND SHALLOTS *can be lifted as soon as you need them, although they store better if allowed to die back first.*

PUSH A GARDEN FORK *under the plants and lever the soil up as you pull the bulb out of the ground by its neck.*

BULBS CAN EITHER BE LEFT *to dry out in the sun or taken directly to the kitchen for immediate use.*

CABBAGE FAMILY

General

In mild-winter and mid-temperate regions, sow seeds of broccoli, Brussels sprouts, cabbage, and cauliflower in a well-prepared seedbed outdoors, or indoors under lights, for transplanting into the garden in late summer.

In cold-winter regions, move young plants of these crops into the garden, following the same spacing used in spring. Cabbage-family vegetables frequently perform best in the fall garden, maturing as temperatures begin to drop, when many insect pests are less prevalent.

Broccoli

Harvest sideshoots
In cold-winter regions where summers are mild, continue harvesting sideshoots of broccoli after the main head has been cut.

Cabbage

Feed cabbage
Apply a sidedressing of high-nitrogen fertilizer to cabbage planted out over the last few weeks, to boost growth. Cultivate between rows with a hoe and remove weeds from within the row by hand.

KEEP BRASSICAS FREE OF COMPETING WEEDS *by regular hoeing and hand weeding. Remove any collars that have been put in place and take care not to damage the vulnerable stems.*

Cauliflower

Transplant seedlings
In cold-winter regions where summer temperatures are mild, transplant seedbed-raised seedlings as soon as they are large enough to handle, ideally at around six weeks old. Space plants 24in. apart within the row, with 30in. between rows. Water them before and after you transplant to reduce shock. Ensure that the soil is kept moist at all times during the growing season.

Kale

Sow directly in the garden
Thoroughly prepare the soil before sowing by raking the surface to a fine, crumbly texture. Use a length of string as a guide and make a ½in. furrow to sow the crop. Spot sow the seed, placing three seeds 8in. apart in each row, with 18–24in. between rows. The seedlings should appear within 7–10 days. Thin to one plant per spot. Alternatively, thinly sow seed in a 4–6in. wide row. When seedlings are large enough to handle, gradually thin them, using thinnings in salads. Eventually thin to 8in. apart.

Kale has many advantages over other brassicas. It tolerates a little shade, is completely frost hardy, and is not so vulnerable to the pests and diseases that afflict the others. It can also be grown in virtually any soil, including wet and poor ones. However, adding well-rotted organic matter, such as manure or garden compost, or hoeing a granular fertilizer such as pelleted chicken manure into the surface, will improve the crop.

WORK A GENEROUS AMOUNT *of well-rotted farmyard manure or garden compost into the soil before planting brassica crops, to provide a steady supply of nutrients for these heavy feeders.*

Kohlrabi

Sow seeds now

Kohlrabi is a quick-growing brassica with a swollen stem that has a very pleasant flavor if it is harvested while still young. Sow in rows 12–18in. apart and thin seedlings to 4–6in. apart. Keep the soil moist.

Begin pulling the stems for eating when they reach the size of golf balls; do not let them grow much above tennis-ball size or they may be woody and fibrous. They reach a usable size in about seven weeks from sowing.

LEGUMES

Lima beans

Start picking

In warmer regions, lima beans will begin to mature and can be harvested. Wait until the pods have fattened up and the seeds have filled out inside the pod. Harvest while the pod is still fresh green. Hold the vine firmly with one hand as you remove the pod with the other, to avoid damaging the vine.

Keep weeding and watering

Continue to hoe weeds around plants regularly and water thoroughly in dry weather, to encourage further seed formation and development.

Snap beans

Start picking

Harvest pods as soon as they are large enough. Pods that snap crisply in half are at their peak; flabby pods that don't break cleanly or are stringy are past their prime. Harvest beans regularly, to prolong cropping. Colored varieties of beans such as 'Royal Burgundy' or yellow 'Rocdor' have pods that are easy to spot among the green foliage, making picking easier.

Continue sowing seeds of bush varieties

Make successive sowings of fast-maturing bush varieties to ensure a continuous harvest into fall.

Water plants for good flower setting

Weed around the plants regularly and water thoroughly in dry weather, particularly once the flowers begin to form. Sufficient water around the roots is essential to get the flowers to set a good crop of pods; dryness at flowering time is the prime cause of poor yields. A thick mulch around the base of each plant is a good way to help prevent loss of soil moisture and restrict the growth of weeds.

Remove growing tips of pole varieties

Once the beans reach the top of their supports, pinch out the growing tips. This encourages sideshoots to develop, and it prevents them from becoming top-heavy.

FRESHLY HARVESTED LIMA BEANS *with their butter texture and mild flavor are a delicacy. They are also an excellent source of dietary fiber and several mineral nutrients.*

PICK SNAP BEANS *once the plants start cropping in summer. The young pods will be sweetest, and regular picking will stimulate the growth of more beans.*

ROOT AND STEM CROPS

Beet

Sow now for overwintering
In mild areas, you can try your luck by sowing an overwintering crop from now to late summer, to mature the following spring. Soak seed overnight to hasten germination. The foliage of some beet varieties becomes a beautiful dark red in cold weather.

Carrot

Mound soil over carrot shoulders
Using a hoe, draw soil up around the tops of carrots to prevent their shoulders from turning green.

Sow seeds for a late crop
Make a final planting of carrots for a fall harvest. To speed germination when conditions are warm and dry, moisten the planting furrows well prior to sowing the seed and cover the seed with premoistened potting mix.

Celeriac

Water in dry spells
Water plants every 5–10 days if no rain falls. Remove the lower leaves to expose more of the crown; also pull off and destroy any blistered leaves, which may be a sign of attack by the celery leaf miner larvae.

Potato

Continue harvesting early potatoes
Carefully harvest tubers as you need them, by pulling back the surface soil without disturbing the entire plant. Remove only one or two tubers per plant at a time and allow the rest to continue to develop.

Rutabaga

Weed and water plants
Keep the crop well weeded, to avoid competition for water and nutrients. Take precautions against pests such as cabbage worms and flea beetles by covering the crop with a floating row cover.

WHEN SOWING BEET SEED, *the best way to encourage it to germinate quickly is to soak it overnight. Sow short rows every 14 days through late summer, to provide a continuous crop.*

SWEET POTATO TUBERS *form just beneath the crown of the vine and benefit from an inch of rain or irrigation water each week. Avoid damaging the vine or tubers when weeding.*

An irregular water supply can lead to poor growth and to root splitting, so water the developing plants every 5–10 days in dry spells. This also helps to prevent powdery mildew from forming on the leaves.

Sweet potato

Keep plants weeded and watered
Continue to weed sweet potato plantings by hoeing around plants to prevent competition for water and

nutrients. Soon the vines should cover the ground and the need for weeding will be minimal. Provide plants with about 1in. of water per week. Mulching around the plants helps retain soil moisture and reduce weed growth.

Turnip

Continue sowing seeds

Plant turnip seeds for a fall crop from now through late summer. Turnips produce a crop in 4–8 weeks, depending on the variety, and can withstand some frost, but they should be harvested before the ground freezes. Their flavor is improved by cool temperatures.

WHEN HARVESTING CHARD, *use sharp hand pruners to snip away the leaves, being careful not to cut too close to the plant. When harvesting the whole plant, make the cut 2in. up the stem.*

LEAFY GREENS

Chard

Weed and water

Weed and keep the soil moist during dry weather for the best leaves, but established plants will withstand some drought. Chard is very easy to grow; even neglected, it still looks good and produces leaves. Some varieties, such as 'Bright Lights', have colorful stems.

Keep harvesting leaves

Gather large leaves for cooking as you need them, but do not cut too close to the plant. You can cut the whole plant for cooking but make the cut 2in. up the stem so the stump can resprout.

Cut back bolted plants

Plants may bolt in hot weather or if they are not regularly cut, but they are so vigorous they can be chopped back and will soon start producing good, tasty leaves again.

Chicory

Water and feed plants

Water plants during dry weather and apply a nitrogen-rich fertilizer if growth begins to flag.

Blanch leafy varieties

The bitter taste of chicory is sometimes welcome in salads, but it can be reduced by blanching, where light is excluded from parts of the plant. To blanch the whole plant, cover it with a bucket, which will exclude all light completely and turn the entire plant white in color.

Red radicchio and sugar loaf varieties of chicory both usually form hearts of leaves, although a proportion of any crop will always fail to do so. Because of this heart-forming habit, these chicory varieties tend to be naturally self-blanching; to enhance this, tie the leaves together. Blanch only as many plants as you are likely to need, as they will deteriorate if left covered or tied for too long. It should take about ten days for blanching to take place.

CUCURBITS

Cucumber

Protect plants from cucumber beetles

Use floating row covers to protect plants from striped cucumber beetles, which spread a serious disease called bacterial wilt. Unless you are growing a parthenocarpic variety (one that produces fruit without pollination), remove the covers when flowering begins, to allow for pollination. If plants develop wilt symptoms—wilting and rapid dieback of leaves—remove and destroy them immediately, to reduce further spread.

Water and harvest plants regularly

Water cucumbers regularly once the crop starts to swell, a mulch will help prevent water evaporation from the soil. Check plants every day and harvest them as they mature, to encourage further production; cucumbers become overripe rapidly in warm weather.

Melons

Feed and water crops

Keep the soil moist around the roots at all times. A regular water supply is very important for successful crops, but don't allow the soil to become waterlogged. Apply a high-potassium liquid feed every 10–14 days.

Thin fruits

Melon plants will not be able to ripen a large number of fruit. Once they reach golf-ball size, thin the fruit to leave three or four well-placed melons per plant.

Look out for mildew

Powdery mildew forms a white coating over leaves, especially at the shoot tips. Remove any affected leaves promptly and destroy them.

Summer squash

Harvest regularly

Always use a sharp knife to cut summer squash cleanly from the plant. If you are tempted to try to twist or pull the fruit off, you will invariably damage the plant itself or else the fruit.

Cut squash when they are young and tender; they quickly grow large, and seeds and skins may become tough. Try to cut the fruit before the flower has fallen off. It is important to pick squash frequently, to encourage more fruit to form. If a squash escapes your notice and becomes large before you pick it, it can still be used; try stuffing it with a mixture of vegetables and bake it topped with breadcrumbs or cheese, or grate it for making a delicious bread. Many squash plants have very prickly stems, so it is a good idea to wear long sleeves when picking the crop, to avoid skin irritation.

Keep plants well watered

Summer squash need watering frequently in dry spells, to keep the plants growing and cropping well. Mulching around plants helps reduce moisture competition from weeds and prevents moisture loss through evaporation.

Winter squash and pumpkin

Support developing fruit

As the fruits swell, place a piece of wood or tile beneath them to keep them off the wet soil and away from slugs. Alternatively, mulch plants with clean straw. Give regular liquid feeds if your aim is to grow giant fruit.

MELON FLOWERS *ideally need to be pollinated all at the same time. Open up greenhouses to allow pollinating insects in, or lend a hand by picking a male flower and pushing it into the center of a female one.*

THE TASTIEST SQUASH *are picked when young and small. Slice them off using a sharp kitchen knife. Never try the twist-and-pull approach as it is likely to damage the plant.*

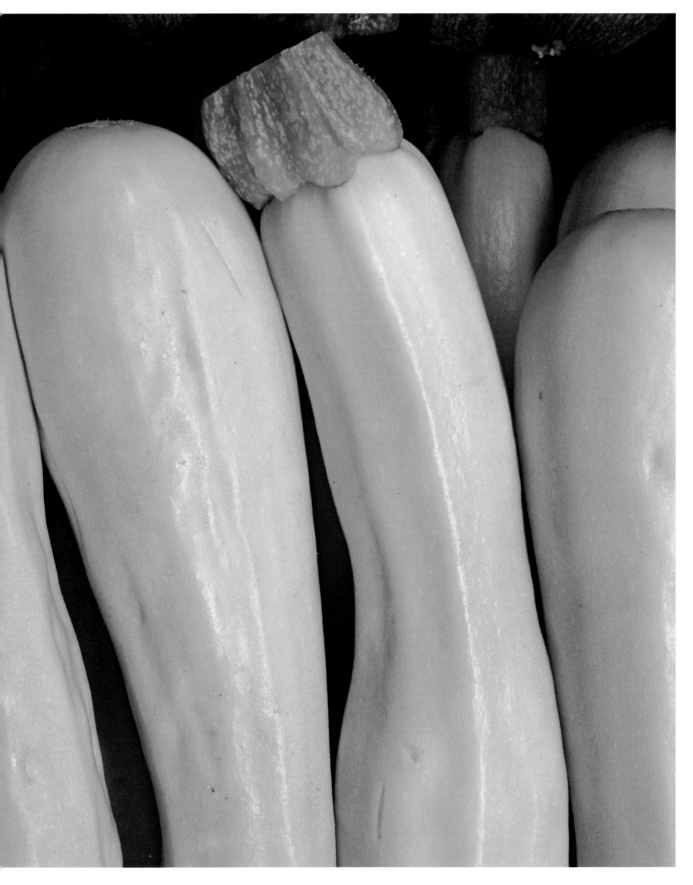

FRUITING CROPS AND CORN

Corn

Provide support
On windy sites, corn may start to rock, which loosens the roots and hinders growth. Mound soil over the bases, to foster the growth of stabilizing adventitious roots.

Keep the soil moist
Water corn plants during dry spells, especially while they are flowering.

Eggplant

Weed and water
Keep eggplants well weeded. Water plants thoroughly every 7–10 days during dry spells, and mulch to discourage weeds and reduce surface evaporation.

Protect plants from insect attack
Use floating row covers to protect plants from damage by flea beetles and Colorado potato beetles.

Okra

Harvest pods regularly
Cut okra pods when bright green, firm, and 2–3in. long. They can become stringy quickly so eat when young.

Peppers

Train plants and feed regularly
Peppers usually form compact plants but some may need supports—if necessary, use cages or stakes, similar to those for tomato plants (see page 72). Feed peppers with tomato fertilizer, and water regularly while flowering and fruiting.

Tomato

Continue training plants
Continue to remove sideshoots from staked plants and to tie the main stems to their supports. If you are growing tomatoes in cages, guide any stems that start to grow out of the cage back inside.

PREPARING OKRA FOR COOKING

Okra is a popular and traditional vegetable in the South. This tender perennial, which is grown as an annual in the vegetable garden, bears large, attractive flowers that resemble hibiscus. The pods have a glutinous texture used to thicken soups and casseroles and are a vital ingredient in gumbo. The pods are usually covered with fine hairs, but 'Clemson's Spineless' has smooth skin. Inside, there are creamy white, edible seeds.

The pods should be washed only if necessary and dried before cooking. They can be used whole or sliced and added to soups and stews, stir-fried with other vegetables, or tossed in seasoned flour and fried. To minimize the slimy texture, use very young pods and stir-fry them whole.

Watch out for blight
Blight is a fungus disease that attacks potatoes and tomatoes in warm, wet conditions. Brown spots appear on the leaves, which quickly yellow and wilt, and brown, rotten patches spread rapidly to the fruit. Remove and destroy affected plants as soon as symptoms are seen.

Pick fruit as they ripen
Harvest tomatoes when fully ripe and evenly colored, but don't leave mature fruit on the plant for long or it will soften and split. If any of your tomatoes display symptoms of blossom end rot (see page 30), pick the fruit and use it immediately, simply cutting out the damaged area. This disorder is usually caused by an irregular water supply; mulching your plants and regular irrigation should remedy the problem.

PERENNIAL VEGETABLES

Asparagus

Keep weeding beds

Remove weeds from the beds and give a topdressing of balanced fertilizer if you have not already done so.

ALLOW ASPARAGUS SPEARS *(top) to develop their fernlike foliage, which serves to build up the roots for next year's crop. Keep the bed weeded, but do not harvest any more spears this year.*

CONTINUE TO MONITOR PLANTS *for asparagus beetle (above) and, if they appear, remove them by hand.*

Support stems on windy sites

The fernlike stems and leaves of asparagus should be allowed to develop fully to build up the plants' resources for future crops. In windy positions in the garden, stake stems with twigs or bamboo canes as they are brittle and can be easily snapped off at the base.

Continue to remove asparagus beetle

Keep picking off and destroying any adult asparagus beetles and their larvae found near the crop.

Globe artichoke

Water young plants

Weed and water well plants in their first year. Although mature plants are drought tolerant, better yields can be obtained if they are watered during dry spells, especially during the period when flower buds are forming.

Harvest small heads

On established plants in warmer regions, small secondary heads develop in the sideshoots of the main stem, below the main head. These will not be as large as the main head, but they make a useful second crop and can be picked as soon as they are big enough, before the sepals start to open.

GLOBE ARTICHOKE *is a regal-looking plant and makes an attractive addition to any ornamental vegetable garden. If one large head is required, remove the sideshoots on each flower stem.*

| Plant a pesto garden

by Kris Wetherbee

A classic culinary pleasure from the summer garden is pesto, an uncooked fresh herb paste with origins based in basil. And while Genoa, Italy claims credit for its basil beginnings, its true origins begin in the kitchen garden.

Pesto has five basic ingredients: fresh herbs, nuts, garlic, cheese, and oil. Basil is the classic herb of choice, but there are many variations that can be made with aromatic herbs such as parsley, chervil, chives, cilantro, marjoram, oregano, rosemary, summer savory, and mint. Pesto can also be pumped up with other ingredients. For example, give pesto a twist with tomatoes or arugula, mix in roasted sweet peppers, or add heat with chili peppers.

Most pesto herbs grow best in full sun to partial shade and well-drained soil. Pesto herbs that originate from the Mediterranean, such as basil and rosemary, grow best in full sun. For herbs such as chervil that shun direct sun in warmer climates, provide afternoon shade or seek out patches of filtered shade under the canopy of taller, sun-loving herbs such as fennel or rosemary.

Annual herbs such as cilantro and dill can be directly sown from seed. In fact, some annual herbs are more susceptible to premature bolting when grown from transplants. Perennials are best grown from purchased plants, especially if you're eager for any kind of harvest the first year.

Pesto herbs that thrive during the cooler seasons of spring and fall include chervil, chives, cilantro, and

ALTHOUGH BASIL *is the classic pesto herb, many other herbs such as parsley, cilantro, rosemary, and summer savory can be used singly or in combination to make delicious pestos.*

PARSLEY IS A BIENNIAL HERB *that thrives in cooler weather, as does the spicy flavored arugula. Try combining their flavors in a spring pesto that is sure to please.*

BY USING VARIOUS COMBINATIONS *of freshly harvested herbs with the other essential pesto ingredients—garlic, nuts, and oil—you can develop your own pesto recipes. A food processor makes it easy.*

parsley. For summer-loving basil, it's best to transplant or direct-seed after the soil has warmed above 55°F and the danger of frost has passed.

A yearly application of compost or organic fertilizer will supply most herbs with the nutrients they need. Basil and other annual herbs need a slightly richer soil for continual harvests; sidedress annual herbs with additional well-rotted manure or a complete organic fertilizer when seedlings are about 6in. tall.

You can begin to harvest a few leaves from most pesto herbs when they are 6–8in. tall. In fact, the more often you harvest, the busier and more productive your plants will become. Pinching top and side stems will encourage the development of more stems and leaves. Frequent harvests also help delay flowering and prolong leaf production. Herbs such as basil, marjoram, and oregano can be cut back by two thirds when the plant reaches 12–18in. tall. The remaining plant will regrow and be ready to harvest in another two to four weeks, allowing you to harvest continually throughout the summer.

Traditional pesto was made with a mortar and pestle. Now the food processor has turned pesto production into effortless fun. Start with clean, dry leaves and, with a pulsing action, coarsely chop herbs, whole garlic, grated cheese, and nuts, scraping down the sides as needed. Slowly add olive oil while the machine is running and process into a paste or the consistency you prefer.

Single-herb pestos are great, and no herb dominates this category better than basil. But you can also create an entirely new taste sensation by mixing herbs in a pesto. Enticing combinations include arugula with parsley; cilantro, chives, and parsley; rosemary, oregano, and basil; or lemon basil, chives, and mint. Keep in mind that as herbs are the main ingredient of pesto, the combination of herbs will influence its overall character and flavor.

PESTO—A FRESH HERB PASTE—ADDS *garden-fresh flavor to a wide range of dishes, from chicken or fish to vegetables and pizza. Using different herbs, singly or in combination, provides endless variety.*

fruit | GENERAL ADVICE

Feed trees in pots | Liquid feed fruit trees in containers with a high-potassium fertilizer such as a tomato one.

Check tree ties | As tree trunk girth increases, tree ties may start to restrict growth so adjust where necessary.

Control weeds | All fruit trees grow better if they are kept free from competing weeds around the base. Hand weeding and hoeing are the most effective, non-chemical methods of controlling weeds, along with mulching. Avoid using string trimmers near the base of trees because it can rip the bark and in extreme cases kill the tree.

Water trees thoroughly | In dry weather, don't let fruit trees suffer from lack of water. It is particularly important to water newly planted trees throughout their first growing season as their roots establish; they need 1–1½in. of water every 7–10 days. The canopy of a tree in full leaf can prevent light rains from reaching the roots. Give fruit trees a thorough soaking so the water penetrates deeply into the root zone. Light watering does more harm than good by encouraging roots to grow in the upper layer of soil, which is most prone to drying out.

Check for pests | A variety of fruit tree pests, including peach tree borers, San Jose scale, spider mites, pear slug, and various plant bugs, may infest your garden at this time of year. Be on the lookout for them and, if necessary, consult your local extension office for effective and safe pesticide recommendations.

CHERRIES are one of the earliest tree fruits to ripen and their flavor is delicious. Keep an eye out for pests feeding on the leaves.

fruit | WHAT TO DO NOW

TREE FRUIT

Apples and pears

Thin fruits

In a good year, apples and pears can set a lot of fruit. Unless the crop is already very small, which can be due to late frosts or poor pollination as a result of bad weather during flowering, the fruit on apple and pear trees will need thinning if it is going to ripen fully and if biennial cropping and broken branches from heavy yields are to be avoided. Thinning fruit on these trees should therefore be carried out now.

When thinning apple trees, remove the king fruit, which is the apple at the center of the cluster of fruit and is generally misshapen. Thin dessert apples to leave one or two fruit every 4–5in., and cooking apples to leave one fruit every 6–8in. On freestanding pear trees, thin the fruit out to two every 4–5in., and on restricted forms such as cordons and espaliers to one fruit every 4–5in.

THIN APPLES *in mid summer so fruit will ripen fully. Thinning also prevents biennial cropping and broken branches from heavy yields.*

MAYPOLING

Trees heavily laden with fruit may require support as the fruit swells and develops. Maypoling is one method that can be used for trees with a sturdy central leader. Strings are looped around the center of the lateral branches and tied upwards to the tree's central leader. Alternatively, stake individual branches if they look as though they may break.

Water in dry weather

Water apples and pears during dry spells and from the time the fruit starts to swell, particularly if they are on restricted rootstocks. The most effective method of doing this for rows of fruit trees is to place a drip irrigation line or soaker hose under the trees. Large established trees will be more resistant to periods of drought than newly planted trees and require less watering.

Control bitter pit on apples

If bitter pit has been a problem in past years, spray apple trees with calcium, to help prevent the issue from recurring. The disorder shows later in the summer as sunken brown pits on the surface of the apples, which extend into the flesh. It is a similar problem to blossom end rot on tomatoes (see page 30), being caused by a shortage of calcium. It is usually due to a lack of water interfering with the distribution of calcium within the plant, so maintaining a regular water supply to your apple trees is of key importance.

Apricots

Start picking fruit

Apricot trees should begin to bear fruit 3–4 years after planting. Like peaches, apricots are likely to be ready for picking between now and late summer. The fruit is ready when it feels soft and parts easily from the tree. Apricots can be stored fresh for only a few days, so they are best consumed right away. Alternatively, they can be dried or made into preserves.

Cherries

Harvest fruit

Cherries are an excellent source of vitamin C, fiber, antioxidants, and many other important nutrients. The majority of sweet cherry varieties are ripening now and sour cherries are soon to follow. Sweet cherries typically grow to 25ft. tall, sour cherries are somewhat shorter, so unless you are growing your cherries on dwarf rootstocks you are likely to need a ladder to reach the fruit.

To harvest, twist the fruit stalk, handling the ripe fruit carefully by its stalk, as cherries are easily bruised, and bruised fruit deteriorates quickly.

Sweet cherries are best eaten shortly after picking, but can be kept in the refrigerator for a couple days. They can also be frozen or made into preserves. Sour cherries are harvested the same way as sweet cherries, but they remain tart when they are ripe. They are great for baking into pies and other desserts and for making jams and preserves. Sour cherries can also be dried or canned. A cherry pitter is a useful tool if you plan to preserve your cherries or use them for baking.

Figs

Protect fruit from birds

Cover figs with a net as harvest time approaches or the birds will harvest the crop before you have a chance to.

RIPENING FIGS *will attract birds, which enjoy the succulent fruit. Be sure to protect your crop with a bird net as the fruit begins to color so that some fruit will be left for you.*

SWEET CHERRIES *are ripe and ready for harvesting by mid summer. Pick them by their stalks, to avoid bruising the fruit, and eat them soon after picking to enjoy them at their best.*

Feed and water container-grown trees

Give figs in pots a balanced liquid fertilizer every ten days or so during the summer. Water plants regularly.

Peaches and nectarines

Harvest ripe fruits

Most peaches and nectarines will be ready now or in late summer, though the exact harvest time is dependent on individual varieties and weather conditions. The fruit is suitable for picking when it has fully colored and the flesh near the stalk feels soft. To pick the fruit, cup it in the palm of your hand and gently lift—it should come away easily from the tree. The tree will require regular visits for picking as the fruit will not ripen all at once.

Peaches and nectarines are best eaten directly after being plucked from the tree. Alternatively, they can be stored in a cool place for a few days after picking. Fruit harvested just before ripening will last longer and can be left to mature in the fruit bowl or be placed in a single layer in a shallow box, but they are unlikely to achieve their full potential in terms of juiciness and flavor. Monitor harvested peaches and nectarines carefully; brown rot—a fungal disease—can spread rapidly through a box or bowl of fruit, causing it to turn soft, brown, and inedible (see box, page 153).

Expect 20–27lb. of fruit from a mature, healthy, fan-trained tree that hasn't been damaged by frosts or peach leaf curl. A freestanding peach will produce as much as 44lb. of fruit.

WHEN PEACHES ARE RIPE *and ready to harvest, they should come away easily from the tree by simply cupping the fruit in your hand and gently lifting.*

PLUM VARIETIES *that crop heavily benefit from having their fruit thinned out in mid summer. This will boost fruit size, reduce biennial bearing, and avoid branches snapping under the weight.*

Trap wasps

Wasps are strongly attracted to ripening peaches and nectarines, so hanging wasp traps around the branches may help to keep down the damage. Remove any damaged fruit promptly as it will attract even more wasps to the tree and more fruit will be ruined.

Feed wall-trained fruit

Peach and nectarine trees trained against a wall will usually benefit from an application of high-potassium liquid fertilizer every ten days or so during the time that the fruits are forming and ripening.

Plums

Thin fruits and support branches

Fruits may require thinning to ease congestion and weight in the canopy, as well as to boost fruit size. It is often essential to prop up branches with sturdy supports in mid to late summer, as the weight of fruit can otherwise snap them.

Water trees

If the weather is dry, water trees from now right through until the fruit is harvested. Keeping the soil evenly moist will allow the fruits to reach a good size and help to prevent them from splitting.

Pick plums as they ripen

Early plum varieties such as 'Early Laxton' should be ripening now. If they are to be eaten raw, pick the fruit when they are fully ripe for the sweetest flavor. You do not need to be quite so fussy about the ripeness of plums that will be used for cooking.

BROWN ROT OF STONE FRUIT

Plums, peaches, nectarines, and cherries are all susceptible to a fungal disease known as brown rot. The fungus can attack blossoms and fruiting spurs early in the season, but it often goes unnoticed until summer, when it spreads to the ripening fruit. Green fruit may display small, circular, light brown spots. As the fruit matures, these spots turn brown and are covered with spores that appear as feltlike masses. When conditions are right, the entire crop of fruit on affected trees can be destroyed in a couple of days.

To avoid brown rot, remove any affected fruit as soon as it is noticed. Damaged fruit may dry up into 'mummies' which, if not removed, will allow spores to overwinter in the tree to reinfect it the following spring. The regular application of a fungicide beginning in early spring as soon as blossoms begin to color is often necessary to control brown rot. Consult your local extension agent for appropriate spray recommendations.

Blackberries

Pick ripe berries

Harvest blackberries and related berries such as tayberry and loganberry as they ripen. Blackberries are best picked when the fruit is fully ripe and separates easily from the stem. They do not hold up well after harvesting, so enjoy them while they are fresh or use them to make jam.

Black currants

Harvest fruits as they ripen

In some varieties, the fruit matures uniformly and should be gathered by cutting the strigs (bunches of fruit) as they turn black. Other varieties ripen at different times, with the currants at the top of the strig ripening first. The fruit should therefore be painstakingly picked individually. Protect fruit from birds.

Blueberries

Protect plants from birds

Cover fruiting blueberry bushes with nets, to keep birds at bay. Otherwise, birds will pick the fruit off well before it is ripe, leaving you with nothing to harvest.

Pick ripe fruits

Harvest blueberries a day or two after the color changes from green to dusky blue. Pick over the plant several times as not all the fruit ripens at once. The berries can be eaten fresh or they can be dried, frozen, made into preserves, or used in cooking. They are rich in antioxidants and vitamins and very low in calories, so have many health benefits.

Cranberries and lingonberries

Keep the soil moist

To keep the roots damp at all times, regularly water these plants, preferably with rainwater to maintain the acid conditions they need. A layer of mulch will help prevent moisture loss through evaporation as well as inhibit weed growth. The fruits will not be ripe until early to mid fall, but the bushes can be netted against birds now.

HARVEST BLACK CURRANTS *from mid summer onwards, but remember to net the crop if you don't want to share a good proportion of it with the birds in your garden.*

Raspberries

Gather fruits and cut out weak canes

Continue to harvest raspberries as they ripen. Select the best of the new season's canes and tie them onto the supports; cut off at ground level those canes that are coming up in the pathways or are weak and spindly.

Red and white currants

Pick fruit by the strig

Harvest the fruit by cutting the whole strig (bunch) as soon as most of the currants on it are ripe. It is difficult to pick currants individually because they are more delicate than black currants and easily squashed.

Strawberries

Renovate established June-bearing strawberries

Once all the fruit of June-bearing varieties has been picked, and provided none of the plants are being used

for propagation, the strawberry bed should be renovated. Remove straw used around the plants and mow down or cut off the leaves, taking care not to damage the crowns, which will soon produce new growth. Rake up and remove all the old straw and foliage.

Having selected the most vigorous young plants to keep, discard excess plants that have become matted or grown out into the spaces between rows.

Propagate plants from runners

If more strawberry plants are required, they are easy to propagate from the runners that are freely produced by the plants (see page 131).

Choose runners from healthy, vigorous plants, selecting a maximum of three or four from each. Pinch off the tip of the runner just beyond the first plantlet—the one nearest the parent plant. Peg the plantlet down either directly into the soil, or preferably into a small pot filled with soil or potting mix, which has been plunged into the soil almost up to its rim.

Keep the pot watered throughout the remainder of the summer so the plantlet can form a good root system.

Allow newly planted everbearing strawberries to develop

Stop removing blooms from newly planted everbearing varieties and allow the fruit to develop for a fall crop.

PINCH OUT THE GROWING TIPS *on grapes before the rows get too high, and let more sunlight into the canopy by shortening the sideshoots back to one leaf.*

ON CORDON VINES, *allow just one bunch of grapes to develop on each lateral branch. Remove all the others using hand pruners so that the vine concentrates its energy into those remaining.*

VINE FRUIT

Grapes

Prune sideshoots

Using your fingers or hand pruners, pinch out the growing tips of vines back to a leaf or bud, when they reach the top wire, to prevent the rows from becoming too high and shading others. Shorten sideshoots (produced in the leaf axils of the fruiting arms) back to one leaf, to get more sunlight into the canopy and to improve air circulation.

Remove grapes that will not ripen

If the vine is carrying immature bunches of grapes that clearly will not have time to develop and ripen for harvest, remove these to allow the plant to put its energy into the fruit that will be able to ripen.

Kiwi

Continue summer pruning

If not already done, shorten fruiting shoots to five leaves past the last fruit, to divert energy into the developing ones. After harvesting in fall, this fruited shoot will be cut back to 2–3in. to develop a spur system. Continue to train main shoots along the horizontal wire supports.

| Grow your own blueberries

by Lee Reich

Plant a blueberry bush and you get delectable and very healthful berries as well as a beautiful landscape plant. In spring, clusters of small, white or pinkish blossoms dangle from the stems like upended urns. Blueberry leaves retain a healthy, fresh appearance all summer and then turn fiery crimson in fall. After leaves fall, cold temperatures bring a reddish cast to the bare stems.

Three species of blueberries are generally grown for fruit production. The fresh blueberry of markets is mostly highbush blueberry (*Vaccinium corymbosum*, USDA Hardiness Zones 4–7), a shrub growing 5–7ft. tall, bearing relatively large, tasty berries. Rabbiteye blueberries (*V. ashei*, Zones 7–10) are adapted to warmer climates and drier conditions. They grow as tall as 15ft., with the best varieties bearing flavorful fruits that maintain quality

BLUEBERRIES (*top*) *are among the most nutritious crops you can grow, and they are ornamental as well. Following their spring flowers, clusters of fruit develop, gradually ripening over several weeks in summer.*

THE FRUIT (*above*) *of lowbush blueberries, left, are small compared to those of highbush blueberries, right. The plants differ in size as well; lowbush plants are 18in. tall, while highbush species may grow 7ft. tall.*

ALTHOUGH CONSIDERED PARTIALLY SELF FERTILE, *blueberries will produce more abundant crops and larger berries if two or more cultivars are planted.*

BLUEBERRIES ARE ACID-LOVERS. *For healthy growth, the soil should have a pH of 4–5, otherwise plants tend to suffer from iron deficiency. The soil should also be moisture retentive but well drained.*

in hot weather. The third species, lowbush blueberry (*V. angustifolium*, Zones 3–7), spreads by undergound runners and reaches only about 18in. high so it makes a tasty and attractive ground cover. So-called half-high blueberries are hybrids of lowbush and highbush species that combine some of the best qualities—flavor, stature, cold hardiness—of the parents.

Blueberries are partially self fertile, so you will harvest more and larger berries if you plant two or more cultivars. For supreme flavor, allow berries to remain hanging on the plant for a few days after they turn blue.

Blueberries are low maintenance as long as they have full sun and soil to their liking. The soil must hold moisture and be well drained, high in humus (but not in fertility), and very acidic. Digging a generous bucketful of peat moss into each planting hole is a start in creating these soil conditions. Unless soil already is at the needed pH of 4–5, spread pelletized sulfur over the area of the planting and dig it into the planting hole. After planting and thereafter, maintain a mulch, 2–3in. deep, of some organic material, such as wood shavings or chips, pine needles, or leaves. The organic mulch will suppress weeds, maintain soil moisture, and, as it decomposes, replenish humus. Watering plants as necessary during the first couple of years helps them establish quickly.

Blueberry plants are beset by few insect or disease problems, but their ripening fruits are relished by birds. You could take your chances that birds will share the bounty with you, or else you can hang various bird deterrents, such as flash tape or other shiny objects or fake predators or scare-eye balloons, near the plants. The surest way to keep birds at bay is with a net. Birds can usually find their way inside of a net merely draped over the plants. Most effective is a walk-in cage whose top and sides are covered with 1in. or less mesh netting while the berries are ripening.

Prune annually after bushes are a few years old. Remove some of the oldest stems, in order to make way for new ones, and thin out excess new stems as well as those that are crowded, damaged, or drooping too much. Spread sulfur, as needed, to maintain acidity and fertilize annually with soybean meal at 2lb. per 100 sq. ft. (or equivalent nitrogen fertilizer).

late summer

The harvest continues, sometimes threatening to swamp the kitchen with its overflowing bounty. Later-maturing crops such as corn and the first winter squash join the rest of the summer crops; cucumbers, tomatoes, peppers, and eggplants add to the haul. You may be tiring of endless snap beans and summer squash now, but they will be welcome through the winter months so fill your freezer with the surplus produce.

As the earlier crops finish, their remains must quickly be cleared to make way for the next plantings and sowings. Fall crops need nurturing to bring them to maturity; thin, water, and feed them where necessary.

Soft fruits are still going strong, with late-fruiting raspberry and strawberry varieties extending the season; there are luscious plums and peaches to pick, and both sour and sweet cherries. Apples and pears will start ripening now, too, and the early varieties may be ready to pick and enjoy straight off the tree.

vegetables | GENERAL ADVICE

Tidy after harvest | Clear spent crops promptly to eliminate pests and diseases and expose weeds.

Sow a cover crop | If you have spare time and space and the soil is sufficiently moist, sow a cover crop (green manure) to improve soil fertility and workability. Crimson clover and mustard are good for sowing now.

Keep harvesting | The more you pick fruiting crops such as summer squash, beans, and tomatoes, the more will be produced. Allowing crops such as beans to develop a few mature pods provides a signal to the plant that its job, which is to produce seeds for next year, is achieved and it will cease production. Even if you have a surplus of produce at present, keep picking to ensure a supply later, when it will be more welcome. Share your surplus with neighbors or a nearby soup kitchen.

Sow extra crops | As space becomes available, sow quick-growing crops of beet, kohlrabi, radishes, fall lettuce, and turnips.

Look out for slugs and snails | When plant growth is lush and there are plenty of hiding places during the day, slugs and snails continue to be a nuisance at this time of year. Keep weed growth down and remove spent crops and debris promptly, to help keep them at bay.

Water when necessary | There can be heavy downpours in late summer, but long, hot, dry spells are not uncommon. Keep vegetables growing strongly and crops tender by watering when necessary. A soaker hose is often the most economical way to water; it applies moisture near each plant's roots and little water is wasted by evaporation.

Remove diseased leaves | Clear away leaves affected by fungal diseases such as blight and mildew promptly. It is better not to compost diseased material; if the

IMPROVE SOIL WITH GREEN MANURES

Cover crops (also called green manures) are fast-growing crops that are sown specifically to improve the soil. The plants are cut down and incorporated back into the soil where they break down and release their nutrients. Scatter the seed of a cover crop over a piece of spare ground. In late fall, before plants flower and stems get woody, cut them down to ground level using shears or a string trimmer. Allow them to wilt for a few days, then turn them into the soil with a spade or rototiller. Alternatively, some cover crops can be sown in late summer or fall and left in the ground over winter before being cut and incorporated into the soil in spring. These help to prevent nutrients from being washed away by winter rains.

Suitable plants to grow as cover crops include several clovers, rape, oilseed radish, mustard, vetch, and cowpeas.

compost pile reaches high enough temperatures the spores will be killed, but not all parts of the pile will heat up sufficiently to ensure this.

Pot up herbs for winter | Although herbs dry successfully, fresh ones have a much better flavor. If you want to be able to pick a few sprigs through the winter months, this is a good time to pot up some herb plants. In early to mid fall, they can be moved into a bright spot in the house and can be picked sparingly through winter. Rosemary, parsley, thyme, marjoram, mint, and summer savory are among those that can be potted up now.

YOU CAN ENSURE *the greatest productivity from snap or string bean plants by harvesting the beans regularly. Pick the beans when they are still small and tender, before the seeds inside the pods get large enough to be noticeable.*

vegetables | WHAT TO DO NOW

ONION FAMILY

Garlic

Harvest as soon as crops are ready

These crops are ready to harvest once the leaves have turned yellow and toppled. While some varieties are ready earlier, many are maturing now.

Choose a spell when the weather looks settled and dry for a few days. Loosen the bulbs by inserting a fork under the roots and lifting slightly; after a day or two, lift the bulbs completely and spread them out to dry. Ideally raise them off the ground on wire mesh, for air to circulate freely. Bulbs that are not properly dried will rot in storage.

Once the bulbs are thoroughly dry, gently rub off any loose soil and leaves and inspect them for damage. Any that are damaged or those with soft necks should be put to one side for immediate use. Store firm, sound bulbs in net bags in a cool, dry shed or garage, preferably hanging up for good air circulation. They can also be braided together in ropes; although these look attractive enough to hang in the kitchen, this is not a good place to store them as it's too warm and humid.

MAKE A GARLIC ROPE

Choose firm, dry bulbs with a good length of stem. They can be braided together, but it's easier to use a piece of strong twine, about 4ft. long, and doubled into a loop. Twist the end of the loop around the neck of a large bulb and feed the rest of it through to form a secure noose; this will make the base of the rope. Hang the twine up and twist the neck of the next bulb around several times so it lays close against the twine and the rest of the neck lies along it. Continue adding bulbs to make an evenly filled rope.

LIFT GARLIC BULBS *when it is likely to be dry for a few days, then leave them to dry out thoroughly. Cut off the stems of the bulbs, unless you plan to braid them together.*

ONCE THE GARLIC BULBS HAVE DRIED OUT, *you can gently split some of the individual cloves apart for planting your next crop. Keep these in a cool shed or garage for planting in the fall.*

Leek

Harvest baby leeks

Young leeks are particularly sweet and tender, and baby leeks can be pulled for use as soon as they are large enough. However, let most leeks continue to grow, to ensure a harvest of good-sized plants from late summer right through fall (through winter in mild regions).

Onion and shallot

Sow bunching onions

Sow seeds of bunching onions (scallions) for a crop that matures in fall or very early spring. Bunching onions do not form large bulbs, but are very hardy and produce edible stems and leaves over a long season.

Sow overwintering varieties

In mild-winter regions, sow a suitable variety (such as 'Walla Walla') for overwintering in rows 12in. apart. Overwintered onions are worth growing in mild areas and some losses can be expected, but they will give a very early crop next year where they are successful.

CABBAGE FAMILY

Broccoli

Plant fall varieties

Good broccoli varieties for fall production include 'Gypsy', 'Premium Crop', 'Marathon', and 'Arcadia'. Follow the same spacing as for spring. Broccoli is ready to harvest 40–80 days from transplanting, depending on the variety.

BROCCOLI *should be transplanted to the garden now for a late crop. As the florets mature, cooler fall temperatures sweeten their flavor. After cutting the main head, continue to harvest sideshoots.*

Cabbage

Plant out fall varieties

Set out young cabbage plants for fall and winter cropping into prepared, firmed soil. Space the rows 18–24in. apart, with plants 18in. apart within the row.

Harvest firm heads

In cold-winter regions, cut summer cabbage as they become large enough to use.

Cauliflower

Sow or transplant fall varieties

In mid-temperate regions, transplant cauliflower seedlings to the garden for a fall harvest. In mild-winter regions, sow seed directly in the garden.

Kohlrabi

Sow for a continuous supply of bulbous stems

Continue to sow short rows of kohlrabi directly in the garden. Thin seedlings to 4–6in. apart.

| Grow your own brassicas

The brassica family includes many crops that form the mainstay of the vegetable garden. Although it is often referred to as the cabbage family, it includes kale, broccoli, Brussels sprouts, and cauliflower as well as cabbage. In addition to these leafy and flowering crops, the root crops rutabaga, radish, and turnip are brassicas, too. This makes the brassica family a very large and diverse group.

However, all brassicas do share a number of cultivation requirements. They like similar soil conditions and are prone to the same pests and diseases, so it is convenient to group brassicas together in the crop rotation scheme. Whatever brassicas you are growing, the following tips will help to ensure you get good results from this diverse, delicious, but occasionally difficult family.

BRASSICAS (above) are among the most useful of all vegetable crops, providing a fresh, nutritious harvest year-round.

CABBAGE (right) can be grown in both spring and fall, and it is among the most versatile of crops in the kitchen.

Success with brassicas

Nutrients

Brassicas are hungry crops and require large amounts of nitrogen. They thrive on soils that have been improved with generous quantities of organic matter such as well-rotted garden compost or manure. They also like an open, sunny position.

Avoiding clubroot

One of the most important factors in growing good brassicas is avoiding the disease clubroot. This is a soil-borne fungus that affects only plants of the cabbage family, and it can do serious damage. It thrives in acid soil, which is why brassicas should be grown in neutral or alkaline soils. In many gardens, this means applying garden lime to the area in which brassicas are to be grown, in order to bring the soil pH up to the correct level of 6.5–7.5. Also, to deter clubroot, follow a crop rotation plan (see page 25) to ensure that brassicas are not grown on the same piece of ground in successive years.

Clubroot is often brought in on the roots of plants that have been raised elsewhere, on infected ground. For this reason, you should either raise your own plants from seed or buy them from a reputable source, making sure they have been raised in sterile potting soil. Accepting kindly meant gifts of brassica plants from friends or neighbors is one of the most common ways for clubroot disease to be introduced.

KEEP CABBAGE SEEDLINGS *(top right) free of competing weeds by regular hand weeding or hoeing. Take care not to damage the stems.*

WHEN HARVESTING CAULIFLOWER *(right), retain some of the leaves around the head to protect it during handling and storage.*

Plant firmly

When planting any brassica, make sure that the ground is gently firmed around each plant. Although walking on the soil destroys its structure, brassicas need firm planting, so don't be afraid to use your feet when planting to settle soil around the base of the stems.

If brassicas such as cauliflower, Brussels sprouts, and broccoli work themselves loose, they will develop poor root systems and leaf structure so that they flower prematurely and produce small, poor-quality heads. After planting, tug gently at a leaf—the leaf should tear rather than the plant move in the soil.

Brassicas need good amounts of space between plants to allow air to circulate around them and to help prevent diseases from taking hold. For the same reason, it is also important to remove weeds and any old, withered leaves as they appear.

Protect against pests

The best defense against several serious brassica pests, including cabbage loopers, imported cabbage worms, and flea beetles, is covering the plants with floating row covers. Biological controls such as Bt and Trichogramma wasps are also effective against cabbage worms

To avoid damage by aphids, use a strong water spray to dislodge them; insecticidal soaps are another effective control for this pest.

DRYING BEANS FOR WINTER USE

There are many types of beans that can be grown in the kitchen garden. Snap beans (and similar types such as filet beans, yard long beans, and wax beans) are grown for their young pods that are eaten before the seeds develop fully. Shelled beans, such as fava beans and lima beans, are grown for their edible seeds, which mature in the pod then are shelled (removed from the pod) for fresh eating. Some beans are grown primarily for their dried seed—their mature seeds are dried in the pod, shelled, and stored for winter use. Lima beans and fava beans can be used either as fresh shelled or dried beans.

Drying is an easy, low-tech way to put up beans for winter use. Once the bean seeds mature, allow pods to remain on the vines to dry until the pods turn brown and brittle—but before they open up and release the seeds. To harvest, either pick the pods and spread them out on a screen to dry for a couple of days, or cut the plant at ground level and hang plants upside down to complete their drying for 2–3 days.

Shell the beans when they are completely dry—test one by biting it, if you can barely dent it with your teeth, it should be sufficiently dry. If beans are not dry, they will mold in storage. If you are concerned about the beans' dryness, you may want to dry them further in a food dehydrator. Sort beans as you shell them, saving only unblemished seeds for storage. Pasteurizing beans will kill any insects or their eggs that may remain on the harvested seeds. This can be done by spreading the beans in a single layer in a shallow pan and placing them in an oven, preheated to 160°F for 30 minutes. Store beans in clean, airtight containers, in a dry, cool place out of direct light.

The following are among the most popular beans for drying:
Cannellini (white kidney bean): Italian heirloom, can also be eaten fresh shelled
Cranberry: sweet-flavored heirloom
Great Northern: mild-flavored, white beans for soups or stews
Navy: small, white beans for baked beans, soups, or chili
Pinto: medium–large bean, tan with darker streaks, used for chili and refried beans
Red kidney: large, red beans used for chili, soups, refried beans, and salads
Soy: nutritious and versatile, used in soups and salads, also tofu, soy milk, cheese, etc.

LEGUMES

Lima beans

Harvest pods

Lima beans should be producing well at this time. Harvest when the seeds fill out and the pods expand but are still bright green. If left too long on the vine, lima beans get tough and mealy.

Shell lima beans prior to eating. To remove the beans from the pod, press on the seam of the pod with your thumb; it often opens with this pressure and seeds will pop out. Alternatively, use a paring knife to cut off the end of the shell and open it from that point. Lima beans are best eaten fresh, soon after they are harvested, but can be frozen for winter use.

Peas

Direct sow for fall harvest

Growing peas in the fall garden can be a bit tricky because they must produce a crop that is harvested before a hard frost.

About two months before your first expected frost, sow peas directly in the garden. For more precise timing, use the days to maturity listed on the seed package and count backwards from the first expected frost adding 10–14 days for your harvest. Even if your harvest is cut short by frost, you can enjoy some late-season peas.

Select varieties of pea such as 'Super Sugar Snap', 'Sugar Bon', or 'Oregon Sugar Pod II' that are resistant to powdery mildew, which may be present at this time of year. Use the same spacing as for spring-sown peas (see pages 41–42).

Thin and support young plants

Thin peas to 2–3in. apart when seedlings are large enough to handle. Provide support for vining varieties and keep the plants well watered in dry spells.

Snap beans

Keep harvesting

Continue to pick beans as soon as they are ready, before they become stringy. If you don't want to do this with a knife, use two hands to pick the beans, holding the stem with one hand while you pull the bean with the other. If you tug at a bean with only one hand, you can easily uproot the plant.

ROOT AND STEM CROPS

Fennel

Harvest bulbs when large enough

Dig up plants from now to mid fall, as soon as the bulbs are sufficiently large, using a fork to loosen the roots carefully before lifting. Alternatively, when harvesting, cut the bulb off just above ground level and leave the stump in the ground. Young feathery shoots will soon appear and these can also be used in the kitchen.

Potato

Start lifting tubers

Potatoes can be harvested after their tops die back. The harvest can be delayed as long as the soil is well drained, and insects or slugs are not a problem. You may prefer to dig some for use now and leave the rest until fall. They should all be harvested before the first frost.

To dig potatoes, carefully insert a garden fork into the ground next to the plant, taking care not to spear the tubers. Any mildly damaged potatoes should be eaten promptly. Throw out any that have gone green through exposure to light because these are potentially poisonous.

Deal with scab

Potatoes affected by common scab—a fungal disease— have corky, raised, brown patches on the skins. This is not a serious problem and the affected potatoes can still be eaten—they just need to be peeled more deeply than usual to remove the scabs. If the whole crop is affected, however, you may want to select a resistant variety to grow next year.

Dry and store harvested potatoes

Leave dug potatoes outdoors to dry for several hours then knock off loose soil and place them in a dark room at 65–70°F to cure for a week. Store cured potatoes in a bucket or bin in a dark, cool room, ideally around 40°F, with high humidity. Check them frequently.

FLATTISH FENNEL BULBS *(top) are nearly as rewarding as rounded ones and can be harvested for the table as soon as they are ready. The foliage can be used as an herb dressing.*

LIFT POTATOES *(above) as soon as they are ready if your garden suffers badly from slugs. Soil-dwelling slugs are a nuisance as they eat and burrow into the tubers.*

Radish

Sow for succession

Continue sowing short rows every 14 days for a nonstop harvest through fall. Keep the seedlings well watered, to avoid them becoming woody or bolting due to dry conditions.

Sow winter radish

Winter radishes are hardier than the summer varieties

and are generally larger with thicker skins. Sowings are best made now, as plants sown earlier than this are more likely to bolt. When grown in well-drained soil in a reasonably sheltered site, winter radishes can be left in the ground through the winter in mild regions and be pulled as required. Sow in rows 10in. apart and thin to 4in. apart in the row.

There are several varieties of winter radish available: 'Round Black Spanish' forms a large, round, black-skinned root and has peppery, white flesh; long-rooted 'China Rose' has rose-pink skin and white flesh; 'Chinese White' produces 8in. long, white roots with a blunt tip; and 'Tama White' is a diakon-type radish that can grow to 18in. long and 3in. in diameter.

THE GLOSSY TEXTURE OF SWISS CHARD (above) is enhanced by the glowing color of the leaves and stems, giving them ornamental appeal in the vegetable garden. They remain productive for many weeks.

LEAFY GREENS

Chard

Make another sowing
Although earlier sowings will often produce well into winter, a further sowing of Swiss chard made now, particularly in mild-winter regions, will produce a good crop for fall, winter, and even early spring. Continue to harvest leaves of established plantings.

Clear bolted crops
Plants that have been productive through the summer will often bolt over the next few weeks. It is best to pull these plants up and compost them now, and let new sowings take over.

Chicory

Harvest blanched plants
Cut blanched plants immediately once the cover is removed, as they will soon start to revert to their dark green coloring and bitter taste. Stored in a cool place, the cut leaves have better keeping properties than lettuce.

Lettuce

Sow outside for fall crops
Sow varieties that are suitable for cropping in fall. To prolong the harvest, they can be protected with floating row covers as the weather cools later in the season. Lettuce can also be sown in a cold-frame for harvesting in winter. 'Igloo', 'Buttercrunch', 'Winter Density', 'Black Seeded Simpson', and 'Little Gem' are all suitable for sowing now. Water the furrow before sowing to cool the soil because lettuce seed becomes dormant if temperatures are too high.

Sow mixed leaves
Continue sowing seed mixtures for baby salad leaves. Make your own mix from several varieties of lettuce, spinach, mustard, oriental greens, and herbs, or use one of the commercial packets that are already mixed for you.

Spinach

Sow seed and keep plants watered
In mild-winter regions, make another sowing of spinach for a late fall or early winter harvest. Water spinach regularly in dry spells to ensure that fresh, young leaves continue to develop.

Control downy mildew
Yellow patches on leaves, which may be slightly furry underneath, are a sign of downy mildew. This is common on spinach, especially late in the season. Remove the affected leaves immediately and thin out plants if necessary, to provide better air circulation.

General

Continue to keep beds weeded and well watered as fruit forms. Maintain a mulch to inhibit surface evaporation. Monitor cucumbers, melons, squash, and pumpkins for cucumber beetles, which spread bacterial wilt. Late in the day—when bees are not active—apply rotenone, to help prevent beetle infestations; do this at weekly intervals. If plants display symptoms of bacterial wilt—wilting and dieback—remove and destroy them immediately, to prevent further disease spread.

Cucumber

Pick early in the day

Once the cucumbers are sufficiently large, cut them off using a sharp knife and pick before the strongest heat of the day, for maximum crispness. Harvest regularly, because leaving mature cucumbers on the plant will stop the development of new ones.

Melons

Thin fruit

Reduce the crop to four fruits per plant. Allowing too many fruit to remain will reduce their size and quality.

LATER VARIETIES OF MELON (above) will be ripening now—they emit a strong scent, and may start to crack and soften around the stalk when ready for harvesting.

HARVEST CUCUMBERS when the fruit tips are rounded and no longer pointed. Cut them off using a sharp knife or hand pruners and do so before the strongest heat of the day, to pick them at their crispiest.

Support ripening fruit

Place fruit on blocks of wood to lift them off the soil, to prevent rotting.

Check fruit for ripeness

It is sometimes difficult to tell when a melon is ready for harvest. Many varieties start to crack and soften around the stalk when they are ripe, but the best test is usually smell. A ripe melon emits a strong, aromatic scent. Watermelons often turn white or yellow on their underside and the tendril closest to the fruit shrivels as it becomes ripe. Other indications of ripeness for watermelon include the rind losing its shininess and developing a dull appearance, and when thumped soundly with a finger the melon emits a dull thud.

Remove mildewed leaves

Pick off leaves affected with powdery mildew as soon as they are noticed. Keep the plants moist at the roots, but avoid watering over the foliage.

Summer squash

Continue harvesting

Keep cutting summer squash frequently, so that the plants continue to produce more; cut as soon as they reach a usable size. They are usually more tender and tastier to eat if they aren't allowed to grow too large—the flesh of very large squash can become fibrous and stringy.

HARVEST A FEW BUTTERNUT SQUASH *or other winter squash to eat now, once they reach full size. Leave others on the vine to continue to ripen and develop a tough skin for storage.*

If you miss harvesting a zucchini, and it does become large, you needn't toss it in the compost pile. Instead, consider using it to make zucchini bread. Or hollow it out and stuff it with a mixture of seasoned vegetables or vegetables and meat, top it with cheese or breadcrumbs and bake.

Winter squash and pumpkin

Prepare for stored fruits

Cut off winter squash and pumpkins for eating fresh as required, but to store well over winter they must be fully ripened and cured. Leave fruits that are to be stored on the plant for as long as possible so that they can ripen fully and develop a tough skin.

FRUITING CROPS AND CORN

Corn

Test cobs for ripeness

Once the tassels on the ends of the cobs turn brown, you can start testing for maturity. Peel back the husk to check the corn; the kernels should be plump. Prick a kernel with your thumbnail; a milky liquid should ooze out if it is ready. If the liquid is thin and watery it is too early, and if it is thick and pasty the cob is past its best. It is vital to harvest corn at just the right stage for maximum sweetness and flavor. As soon as the cob

is picked, the sugar in the kernels starts to change to starch, so for the very best flavor you should cook and eat—or freeze—the sweet corn within minutes of picking. If not eaten right away, standard varieties of corn will remain fresh for a few days if kept refrigerated. Super-sweet and sugar-enhanced hybrid varieties maintain their sweetness for up to two weeks.

Eggplant

Harvest ripe fruit

Pick eggplants as soon as they are full size for the variety and have developed their full color; for most varieties, the skin is glossy purple-black, but there are also red, white, and striped ones. Don't allow the fruit to dull on the plant; this is a sign of overmaturity, and it will be leathery and dry.

Control red spider mite

Biological controls can be used to keep red spider mite under control. Increase the humidity by misting plants regularly, as red spider mite dislikes humid conditions.

Okra

Continue picking pods

Okra pods can quickly become stringy and tough, so pick frequently. They take 3–5 days to develop after flowering and grow 3–4in. long. Harvest with a sharp knife when pods are bright green, firm, and dry, and handle carefully because they bruise easily, which reduces their shelf life. Dull and yellowing fruit are past their best but must be picked to encourage continued cropping.

HARVEST CORN *in late summer, testing the cobs for maturity once the tassels turn brown. Pick only what you want to eat that day, preferably as close to cooking time as possible.*

HOW TO GROW BABY CORN

Baby corn is a relatively new concept; it is simply corn cobs that are picked at a very early stage, before the kernels are mature. Grow the plants as you would for normal corn, but harvest the cobs within one or two days of the silks emerging from the end of the cob. At this stage the whole cob is sweet and crunchy. Remove the green sheaf and cook the cob, either whole or sliced according to size, by quickly stir-frying, or serve it raw in salads. Since fresh-picked baby cobs are much sweeter and tastier than the canned varieties, they are well worth growing.

Peppers

Pick sweet peppers as required

Peppers can be picked while still green and immature or be left to change color on the plant. Some varieties develop their ripened color more quickly than others.

Harvest hot peppers

Like sweet peppers, hot peppers can be harvested green or can be left to ripen, which enhances not only their flavor but also their heat. Handle hot varieties with care as the juice can burn your skin. If you are harvesting or processing a lot of hot peppers, consider wearing plastic gloves. Discard the seeds for a milder flavor.

Tomato

Watch for blight

Blight becomes more of a possibility as the summer progresses; it is at its worst in wet seasons. Keep an eye on tomatoes and remove affected plants promptly, spraying the remaining plants with an appropriate fungicide as a preventive. Check with your extension service for their recommendations and always follow the label instructions.

Keep harvesting fruits

Pick tomatoes as soon as they are fully ripe. Try to break the fruit off complete with the green calyx attached, as they keep better like this. Water the plants regularly; sudden watering after a dry spell can result in the fruit splitting. Cut down on the watering slightly while the fruit is ripening, as this produces a sweeter flavor.

EGGPLANTS *(top) make a lively, surprising addition to the container garden, and they are not all black or purple. There are also white, red, or striped ones. Use at least a 12in. pot for a single eggplant.*

PICK OKRA PODS *(above) often to avoid them becoming tough and stringy. Ideally, okra should be eaten as soon as it is harvested because it doesn't store particularly well. Very young pods can be eaten raw.*

PERENNIAL VEGETABLES

Asparagus

Keep weeding

Keep asparagus beds free of weeds. It is important that weeds are kept under control because they can be very difficult to eradicate in perennial beds.

| Grow your own edible flowers

It may be a surprise to discover that many flowers can be used in the kitchen. Some petals have a strong peppery or fruity taste while others impart more subtle aromas and flavors. Flowers wilt quickly, especially in hot weather, so pick in the morning if possible and move to a cool place indoors for preparing. Spread them on a piece of paper towel so any small insects can be removed. In most species, the flowers are too tough to eat whole, so place the removed petals in a small plastic bag and seal with a little air so they don't get squashed. The petals should keep like this in the fridge for several hours. Avoid washing flowers, to avoid damage, but if they're wilting place in a bowl of water to revive them.

BORAGE AND CALENDULA *(above) grace the garden in summer, but their petals can also be picked for the plate.*

EDIBLE FLOWERS AND LEAVES *(right) give a salad an extra peppery, fruity, nutty taste—and look beautiful, too.*

Recommended edible flowers

Calendula (*Calendula officinalis*)

A hardy annual with double and single varieties in shades of orange and yellow. Deadhead to prolong flowering or use successional sowings. Petals add color to salads.

Bush marigolds (*Tagetes tenuifolia*)

Bush marigolds (such as varieties 'Lemon Gem' and 'Tangerine Gem') are very easy to raise from seed, and young plants are readily available from garden centers. The petals have a distinctive, zesty flavor and add a splash of sunshine-yellow to salads.

Clary sage (*Salvia sclarea*)

Strictly speaking it is not the flowers that are of interest here but the purple and pink bracts. Select the younger ones as these are brighter and will not yet have become papery. Their flavor is negligible but they make a decorative garnish.

Nasturtium (*Tropaeolum majus*)

A wonderful flower for use in the kitchen as both the leaves and petals of nasturtium have a strong, peppery taste, which takes a few seconds to develop on the tongue. The flower color can vary from deep red to butter-yellow. The seedheads can also be collected and pickled to use as a substitute for capers—pick while green and fresh.

Heartsease (*Viola tricolor*)

This delicate wildflower is small enough to use whole. Just snip as much of the calyx off as is possible without causing it to fall apart. It is pretty frozen in ice cubes and used in summer drinks. Cultivated violas and pansies can also be used but are best bought as bedding plants. Winter-flowering pansies will offer a supply of petals when little else is available.

BORAGE

Borage (*Borago officinalis*) is an annual that produces star-shaped flowers that are usually blue, but may be white or pink. Traditionally, the cucumber-flavored leaves have been an ingredient in interesting mixed salads, and the dainty flowers have been candied for decorating pastries or used fresh for garnishing salads and drinks. However, recent findings suggest that both the flowers and leaves contain trace amounts of a number of pyrrolizidine alkaloids. These compounds, which are similar to those found in comfrey and coltsfoot, are known to cause liver damage, particularly if consumed over an extended period. Thus ingestion of borage flowers or leaves is not recommended.

fruit | GENERAL ADVICE

Feed trees in pots | Continue giving a high-potassium fertilizer to fruit trees growing in pots.

Deal with wasps | Hang wasp traps on the branches of trees bearing ripening fruit. Wasps will damage ripe fruit and make it inedible, and there is also the risk of being stung if you unsuspectingly pick fruit with wasps inside. Remove any damaged and overripe fruit promptly, as these help to attract wasps.

MAKE A WASP TRAP

Take an empty, plastic, 2-liter soda bottle and cut the top off at the shoulder, discarding the cap. Put the top to one side. Place something sweet to attract the wasps in the base of the bottle; sugary fruit juice works well. Position the top of the bottle back on the base, but turning it upside down to form a funnel.

If you want to hang the trap in a tree, make three holes in the sides of the bottle, below the level of the funnel, and thread string through to form a hanging loop. Seal the edges of the top and base with tape if necessary, and place the trap where wasps are a problem. They will have no trouble entering the bottle through the funnel, but it will be almost impossible for them to find their way back out again.

Deal with brown rot | Fruits affected by brown rot turn soft, brown, and wrinkled, forming a feltlike mass of fungal spores on the fruit surface. If left unpicked, the fruit dries into 'mummies' which often remain on the tree through winter. Remove any fruit affected by brown rot, including those that have fallen, and destroy them to reduce reinfection next spring.

RIPENING APPLES *and other fruit will be attractive to wasps and birds, so take the necessary action to avoid damaged crops.*

fruit | WHAT TO DO NOW

TREE FRUIT

Apples and pears

Summer prune restricted forms

Cordons, fans, and espaliers are usually pruned in late summer as their growth slows down for dormancy during winter. Pruning at this time of year allows sunlight to get into what would otherwise be a crowded and congested canopy. This helps the wood to ripen and to initiate the development of fruit buds for next year.

Cordons: A cordon has a trunk that is straight or, if it is an oblique cordon, one that is angled at 30–45 degrees. It is trained against horizontal supporting wires and the leader should be tied to a cane fixed to these. If the leader has reached the required height, prune it back now. Prune sideshoots back to one or two buds past the basal cluster (the group of leaves at the base of the stem).

On an established cordon, prune most of the new growth back to one or two buds past the basal cluster, using a pair of sharp hand pruners. Ensure that the wood has ripened and is no longer green. If growth is less than 8in. long, leave it to develop further, then prune it in late fall or winter. Shorten any shoot that has developed directly from the main stem, cutting it back to three or four buds above the basal cluster, to encourage a system of fruiting spurs to develop. Prune any weak or wispy growth to just one leaf past the basal cluster.

Espaliers: Trees being trained as espaliers should have two shoots being trained against canes at a 45-degree angle; these canes can now be lowered to horizontal. Prune the tip only if the shoot has reached the end of

RESTRICTED FORMS *like a cordon apple tree benefit from summer pruning. Vigorous trees put on less growth when pruned at this time of year and it helps prevent biennial fruiting.*

PRUNE THE SIDESHOOTS *back to one or two buds past the basal cluster using sharp hand pruners. Ensure that the wood has ripened and is no longer green.*

PRUNING IN SUMMER *allows sunlight to get into an otherwise congested canopy, which helps the ripening of the wood and development of fruit buds on restricted forms.*

the wire. On an established espalier, prune sideshoots of more than 10in., which have formed from existing spurs back to one bud past the basal cluster. Shorten new growth directly from the horizontal-branch tiers to three or four buds above the basal cluster. Remove spurs or shoots on the central trunk.

Fans: Prune new growth back to a couple of buds above the basal cluster. Remove any dominant shoots that are attempting to take over as the central leader. If the tree is predominantly a spur bearer, shorten some sideshoots to one or two buds past the basal cluster. Fill empty spaces by tying in other sideshoots and pruning back the tips.

Pyramid: A feathered maiden (a young, branched tree) being trained as a pyramid should have the leader and lateral branches shortened by two thirds to downward-facing buds. On established trees, maintain the shape by removing vertical growth and keeping growth at the apex short. On lateral branches, cut back new growth to 8in. to a downward-facing bud.

Pick apples as they are ready

To pick an apple, cup it lightly in your hand, lift gently, and give it a slight twist. The fruit should come away in your hand with the stalk intact. If it doesn't, then it isn't ready for picking. Never pull at the fruit because this can break the fruiting spurs. Place the apples gently into a box or basket, being careful not to drop or bruise them.

Specially designed bags or baskets that hang from the shoulders are useful if lots of apples are to be harvested.

Harvest pears

Pick pears just before they are fully ripened. They should be firm and swollen, with a subtle color change to their skin. Test early varieties by tasting one of the fruit for sweetness, yet firmness. Later varieties should part easily from the tree when lifted and gently twisted. Pears will continue to ripen and become sweeter after they are picked. Check picked pears daily to see if they are ready for eating; they can quickly become overripe.

WHEN IS AN APPLE READY FOR PICKING?

With most fruit, the obvious method of testing whether it's ready for picking is to taste it. This is certainly possible with some of the early apples such as 'Ginger Gold' and 'Lodi', which can be eaten fresh off the tree. However, some later-maturing apples require a period of storage before being at their best for eating—a bit like a fine wine—and so other methods of identifying their maturity for harvesting are required. The telltale sign of an apple being ready is a few windfalls lying beneath the tree. The fruit should have swelled to a good size and started to color up. Cut the apple in half and look at the pips (seeds); if they have changed from white to brown then the apple is close to harvest time.

HOW TO STORE APPLES FOR A LATER DATE

A LINED FRUIT BUCKET *is the ideal tool for collecting an apple and pear harvest. Discard rotting and damaged fruit as you go along, to make sure you collect only the best fruit.*

WRAP APPLES *in paper or perforated freezer bags, or lie each of the fruit unwrapped on a tray away from the others. Make sure you keep all the stalks intact.*

PLACE THE WRAPPED APPLES *and pears in a crate or pallet and store them in a cool, dark place. Inspect the fruit regularly and remove any rotting fruit immediately.*

Apricots

Keep picking fruit

Although the main harvest season for apricots has passed, continue harvesting late varieties of apricots as they ripen, when they will feel soft and part easily from the tree with a gentle lift betweeen the fingers.

Apricots are best eaten fresh from the tree, but they can be stored in the refrigerator for about two weeks. You could also can, freeze, or dry some of your harvest.

Cherries

Continue harvesting

Harvest both sweet and sour cherries as they ripen. Sort the fruit and discard any that show evidence of brown rot. This disease will spread rapidly through a basket of ripe cherries.

Remove diseased branches and unwanted shoots

Prune out branches and stems of cherries displaying evidence of bacterial canker. Disinfect pruners between cuts. On fan-trained trees, remove unwanted shoots and tie in others to maintain desired shape.

Figs

Harvest ripe fruit

Figs are ready for harvesting when the skin is soft, sometimes split, and hanging limply from the branch. Occasionally a sugary liquid is secreted from the eye of the fig. In this condition, pick and eat raw right away.

Select next year's fruit

It is important to understand how a fig tree produces fruit, as this affects how it is pruned. Figs grown in cool-temperate climates are usually borne in the tips of wood produced the previous season. Embryonic figs—about pea size—appear at this time of year in the growing tips of shoots. They should overwinter on the tree (although they may be damaged by harsh frosts and cold winters) and ripen into figs ready for harvesting this time next year.

The tree will also be carrying larger, unripened figs that formed in spring. In most regions, these won't ripen before the onset of winter and also won't overwinter successfully as they are too prone to cold damage, so remove them now.

CHERRIES ARE VULNERABLE *to bacterial canker infections; to check its spread, prune out diseased branches after harvest (top) when the weather is dry.*

PINCH OUT WAYWARD GROWTH *regularly on cherry trees trained as fans (above) and tie in well-placed shoots, to keep the restricted shape of the fan in control.*

Peaches and nectarines

Prune fan-trained trees

Because peaches and nectarines bear most of their fruit on year-old wood, you will need to 'reinvent' the fan form each year. To avoid stimulating excessive vegetative growth, prune during the growing season. After harvesting, cut out some of the older wood and shoots that fruited last year. Tie in some new growth from the current year as replacements, as these will be the branches that produce next year's crop. Remove shoots that are overcrowding the fan or detracting from the form, and cut out any diseased wood.

Plums

Harvest fruits when ripe

Pick the fruit carefully so as not to bruise them, then eat fresh, freeze them, or make into preserves.

Quinces

Leave fruit to ripen

Quinces need a long, hot summer to ripen well. They should not be harvested yet but left on the tree as long as possible, picking them just before the first frosts.

SOFT FRUIT

General

Continue to pick fruit of black currants, red and white currants, and gooseberries as it ripens. Blackberries and late raspberries are best eaten fresh shortly after picking, although they also make good preserves. Blackberries and raspberries are great for cooking, traditionally teamed with apples for desserts.

Blueberries

Protect fruit and pick it as it ripens

Cover the bushes by draping netting over the plants, to protect the berries against birds, or there will be no crop left for you to pick.

Harvest blueberries now, handling them gently so as not to spoil the grayish 'bloom' on the fruits' surface.

Store fresh blueberries in the refrigerator for up to a week. To freeze, spread washed fruit in a single layer on a cookie sheet; once frozen, store in freezer bags.

Water plants

Continue to water blueberry plants, preferably with rainwater. Keep the soil moist at all times.

Cranberries and lingonberries

Keep soil moist

Continue to keep the soil damp at all times around cranberries and lingonberries, using rainwater. The fruit will normally start ripening shortly.

Raspberries

Remove fruited canes

Cut out fruited summer canes once they have finished cropping and tie in new canes to the supporting wires, leaving three to four young canes per 1ft. of row.

Pick fall-fruiting varieties

Harvest fruit as it ripens. Do not allow overripe fruit to remain on the plants because it may attract insects. Fall-fruiting raspberries carry their fruit on the current season's canes, instead of last year's growth (like summer-fruiting types). Good varieties include 'Heritage', 'Fall Bliss', 'Caroline', and 'Fall Gold'.

Strawberries

Clean up beds and fertilize

If you have not already done so, clear away straw and old foliage from fruited strawberry beds. Apply a sidedressing of a balanced fertilizer.

Order new plants

Strawberries can be planted in the fall as well as spring, provided they are heavily mulched over winter. Order strawberry plants from specialist suppliers so they can be planted in the next few weeks. Strawberry plants deteriorate markedly after a few years. Aim to replace one third of your strawberry bed each year—that way you will always have a crop and your plants will be replaced before they become worn out.

BLUEBERRIES *(above) are just bursting with goodness. It's so simple for gardeners to grow them at home and pick them fresh off the bush as they ripen. Do so with care to avoid spoiling their grayish bloom.*

Prepare beds for planting

Dig over the planting site, adding well-rotted organic matter, removing weeds, and breaking the soil down to a reasonably fine tilth. If you haven't tested the soil lately, now is a good time to do it; you will have plenty of time to work in the soil amendments before planting in early spring. If you have already tested it and adjusted its pH as necessary, simply rake in a dressing of balanced fertilizer and smooth the soil surface.

Plant rooted runners

If you have rooted strawberry runners, these can now be lifted and planted in their permanent positions. Runners that were pegged down into pots sunk into the soil will transplant more readily than those lifted from the open ground, as they suffer much less root disturbance. Be sure to water newly planted runners well.

Pick everbearing strawberries

Continue to pick fruits of everbearing varieties as they ripen and remove damaged or moldy fruit promptly. Everbearing strawberries can continue cropping until mid or late fall if conditions are right; cover the plants with floating row covers as the weather deteriorates. Good varieties include 'Tribute', 'Tristar', and 'Quinault'.

Grapes

Harvest fruit as it ripens

Grapes are ready for picking when they feel soft to the touch and taste sugary. The skins on white grapes often change from deep green to a translucent yellow and they become much thinner. The best way for an amateur to tell when wine grapes are ripe is by tasting them—only when they are at their sweetest, containing maximum sugar, are they ready.

Another guide to determine when to harvest your grapes—at least for varieties that produce seeds—is seed color. As grapes mature, their seeds change from green to brown. Cut open a few grapes to determine when this occurs. Cut them in bunches with each stalk attached.

Protect fruit from wasps

Ripe grapes are very attractive to wasps, which are drawn to the high sugar content of the fruit; hundreds of wasps can infest a planting, creating a serious nuisance. Use wasp traps (see page 176) or cover the vine with a fine netting, to keep them at bay. Netting also helps to stop birds from getting to the fruit.

CUT OUT ALL ONE-YEAR-OLD RASPBERRY CANES *using sharp hand pruners after they have fruited. They are easy to recognize as they are brown at the base—the current year's canes are green.*

TIE IN THE NEW CANES OF SUMMER-FRUITING RASPBERRIES *to the sturdy wire supports as soon as the fruited canes have been pruned out, spacing them evenly or wrapping into bundles.*

| Encouraging natural pest control

Ask any group of gardeners to list the benefits of eating homegrown food, and you can bet that somewhere near the top of most people's lists would be the fact that it has been grown naturally and has not been sprayed with a battery of unknown chemical compounds. While garden chemicals available today have undergone rigorous testing to ensure they are safe when used as directed, most gardeners would still prefer to eat untreated produce, especially if feeding children.

If you are to win the battle against garden pests without resorting to the sprayer at frequent intervals, you need to enlist all the help you can. Fortunately, there are many naturally occurring allies that you can encourage

A POND (above) *provides a habitat in which toads, frogs, and newts can breed and is also a water supply for insects, birds, and other animals.*

SNAILS AND SLUGS DAMAGE *most plants (right), so at dusk pick them off by hand, with the help of a flashlight, and destroy them.*

CLOSED BIRD HOUSES (above) with one small entrance hole of no more than 1¼in. across attract bluebirds and other birds.

FROGS (left) reside in warm yet damp, shady places often a considerable distance from ponds, except when breeding in water.

into the garden. These are unlikely to eliminate your problems entirely, but they will keep pest numbers down.

Natural predators

The majority of garden pests are insects. A wide range of natural predators will eat caterpillars and adult insects—birds such as robins, chickadees, and nuthatches; wasps; hoverflies; lacewings; ladybeetles (ladybugs); and centipedes. Frogs and toads enjoy feasting on slugs and snails as well as insects.

You can attract natural pest controllers into your garden by providing them with an appropriate habitat, and a food supply. A garden pond is perhaps a useful feature, as this provides a home for frogs and toads, and a drinking water supply for many other creatures. (Ensure that at least one side of a pond has a shallow 'beach' area for land animals to escape if they fall in.)

Turn a small corner of the garden into a wild area, with piles of stones, logs, and leaves, wild flowers and ground-cover plants. Garden centers and specialist, mail-order suppliers provide wildlife homes such as frog and toad houses, nest boxes for birds, bats, and beneficial insects, and many wildlife organizations offer plans for building your own.

Attracting predators

Grow nectar- or pollen-rich flowers that will attract beneficial insects, such as beebalm (*Monarda didyma*), Joe Pye weed (*Eupatorium fistulosum*), wild columbine (*Aquilegia canadensis*), and fennel (*Foeniculum vulgare*).

Putting out food for garden birds year-round will ensure they visit your garden regularly. Peanuts are a useful high-energy food, but supply them only in special feeders, as young birds, particularly, can choke on loose nuts, and squirrels are very adept at

grabbing large quantities of them. Other suitable foods for birds include mealworms, dried fruit, cheese, stale bread, cracked corn, and seeds such as sunflower, thistle, and millet. Suet—animal fat—is another easily digestible food for birds that is particularly valuable for helping them survive winter, when little food is available in the garden.

Landscape plants that produce seeds and berries that mature at different times during the year will help sustain a population of birds. Do not remove seedheads of annual and perennial flowers prematurely. For example, allow the spent blooms of black-eyed Susans (*Rudbeckia* spp.) and purple coneflowers (*Echinacea* spp.) to remain in fall, so birds can feed on them into winter.

Remember to be extra careful about using garden chemicals—some could be harmful to the creatures you are trying to encourage.

early fall

Though the days may still be hot, they are getting noticeably shorter, and soon there will be that first, faint, unmistakable fall chill in the air. It's time to gather in the harvest in earnest, particularly in colder regions. Fungal diseases can spread quickly in the moist air, so dying leaves and rotting fruits should be disposed of promptly, before they spread infection to the rest of the crop or are left to infect next year's garden. Late-ripening fruit will be a magnet for wasps, so take extra care when picking. Store crops carefully for fall and winter use, selecting only undamaged specimens. As each crop is gathered, clear away the remains to the compost pile, uproot weeds, and begin soil preparation for next year.

This year's sowing season is not quite over yet: In most regions, winter radish, lettuce, and other leafy greens can be sown for some welcome late-fall and early-winter salads. In mild-winter regions, there are many other crops that can yet be planted.

vegetables | WHAT TO DO NOW

Garlic

Plant cloves

Because warmth is needed to ripen the bulbs, garlic must be grown in a sunny site, in rich soil that is moisture retentive but with good drainage. Avoid planting on freshly manured ground, which could cause rotting.

Just before planting, thoroughly rake the top 1–2in. of soil and incorporate a balanced fertilizer. Split garlic bulbs into individual cloves and plant each one with the pointed end up, spacing them 4in. apart with 9–12in. between the rows. The tips of the cloves should be hidden just below the surface.

Leek

Harvest leeks as required

Continue to lift leeks as required, as soon as they are large enough. Since these are hardy vegetables that can be harvested throughout winter, gardeners can leave most of their leeks to be enjoyed during the winter months rather than eating them all now, when there are still plenty of alternative crops available.

Onion and shallot

Plant onion and shallot sets or seeds

In mild-winter and mid-temperate regions, fall-planted onion sets will give an early crop next year, but they are not appropriate for soils that are prone to waterlogging during winter.

Prepare the soil thoroughly and rake in a dressing of a balanced fertilizer. Plant in rows 12in. apart, spacing the sets 2–3in. apart in the row. Make a shallow furrow, deep enough for the tips of the sets to show just above the soil, and push the sets lightly into the base of the furrow before drawing the soil back around them with a trowel

and firming them in. If the weather is very dry, water the sets after planting.

Onion seed can also be planted now. Sow seeds thinly in rows 12in. apart and cover them with ¼in. of soil. They should germinate in a week or two. As the young onions

BIRD PROBLEMS

Blackbirds as well as other garden birds can sometimes pull newly planted onion and shallot sets out of the soil. Taking off the loose, papery skin at the top of the set can help to prevent this, as the birds grab hold of this skin to tug at the bulbs. Check the beds shortly after planting and replant and refirm any sets that have been pulled up. If the problem persists, cover the newly planted bed with row covers or netting while the roots get established.

LEEKS ARE SIMPLE TO HARVEST: *Using a garden fork, just lift leeks as required when the stems are sufficiently thick. Then rub off the excess soil and trim the leaves and roots.*

grow, thin them to a final spacing of 2–3in. apart; you can use the thinnings as green onions.

Plant shallots in the same way as onions, but spacing the sets 4–6in. apart in the row. 'French Red' and 'Dutch Yellow' are good varieties for fall planting.

CABBAGE FAMILY

Broccoli

Harvest regularly
All types of broccoli should be picked when the flower buds are well developed, but before the flowers actually open. If possible, cut broccoli in the morning before the heat of the day sets in; if this is not possible, submerge the spears in cold water, to remove the field heat. Cut the florets from the plant using a sharp knife, harvesting central spears first.

Harvesting the main head will encourage sideshoot formation for further harvests. As the weather cools florets remain in good shape on the plant for a longer time, so harvest just what you need at one time, but harvest frequently.

Cabbage

Transplant cabbage
In mild-winter regions, continue to transplant cabbage to their final positions. Firm the young plants in well, especially when grown on light soils, pressing the soil around the plant stem.

Harvest fall cabbage
Cut fall cabbage as the heads expand and become firm.

Prepare for colder weather
Some varieties of cabbage are prone to cold-weather damage. These should be harvested and stored before the first frosts. Varieties that are well suited to fall gardens because they will tolerate frost include 'Danish Ballhead', 'January King', and 'Ruby Ball'.

To provide additional protection from wind and frost for the cabbage left in the ground, draw soil up around the base of each plant before the first heavy frosts. Such 'earthing up' protects the plant stem.

BROCCOLI HEADS *(top) are ready to cut when the buds are well developed but before the flowers actually open. Regular picking of florets encourages more cropping.*

HARVEST CAULIFLOWER *(above) while the heads are still firm and tight, and before the curds have started to separate, to ensure best quality. Size of the head will depend on the variety.*

Cauliflower

Harvest as required
The fall varieties that were sown in summer are ready to harvest between now and late fall. They range from large-headed varieties such as 'Giant of Naples' that may be 12in. in diameter to more compact types such as 'Fremont' and 'Amazing' that produce heads that are 6–7in. in diameter.

Kale

Plant seed
In mild-winter regions, there is still time to sow a late planting of kale for harvesting in early winter. Sow seed thinly in rows spaced 18–24in. apart. When they are big enough to handle, thin seedlings to 8–12in. apart.

LEGUMES

Lima beans

Continue to harvest

In warmer regions, continue harvesting lima beans for fresh use. Pick the pods when the seeds cause them to bulge, but they are still bright green.

If you want dried beans for winter soups, allow some of the pods to remain on the vines to dry. Harvest these when the pods turn light brown and brittle, but before they open and release their seeds.

Peas

Weed and support new crop

Continue to weed peas sown for a fall crop and provide a trellis or other support for taller, climbing types.

Snap beans

Continue picking

Most snap beans will still be producing a crop, although production will be slowing in cooler regions. If a late sowing of beans was made in mid summer, these will provide a welcome picking of fresh, young, tender beans in fall, often until the arrival of the first frosts.

Clear spent crops

Once the snap bean crop is finished, clear away the plants and remove the above-ground growth to the compost pile. If pole varieties were grown, remove, clean, and store the supports.

ROOT AND STEM CROPS

Beet

Lift roots for storing

Where winters are relatively mild and soils are light and free draining, beets can be left in the ground over winter, but many gardeners, particularly those who live in colder regions, find it more convenient to lift the roots over the next few weeks and store them. When harvesting the beets, coax the roots up carefully with a fork and gently

SAVE YOUR OWN BEAN SEED

At the end of the season, allow some pods to remain on the plants to ripen their seeds. Leave the pods on the plants for as long as possible, until they become dry and crisp. The seeds can then be shelled out; reject any damaged, very small, or nontypical seed and store the rest in a cool, dry place for sowing next spring. You can store them in a paper bag or in a lidded jar with a silica sachet, to absorb any moisture. If your bean variety was an F1 hybrid, the beans grown from the seed will not be true to type; open-pollinated varieties may also have cross-pollinated with nearby varieties to produce variations.

knock off excess soil. Inspect the roots for damage and select only sound ones for storage. Twist or cut off the leaves 1–2in. from the top of the root, wearing rubber gloves to avoid staining your hands. Then carefully place the roots, not touching each other, in boxes of sand or peat moss. Store in a cool shed or garage. Any damaged roots should be used right away.

Carrot

Harvest as needed

Dig summer-sown carrots as needed. Roots may be left in the ground for later use; they are not injured by frost. In mild-winter regions, they can be left in the ground for harvesting throughout winter, but in cooler regions it is better to dig the carrots before the ground freezes.

HARVEST BEETS *when the roots reach tennis-ball size for the best flavor. If they are allowed to grow any larger, they may develop an unpleasant, woody texture.*

Celeriac

Mound soil around plants

Draw soil around the swollen stem-bases of celeriac, to keep the flesh white.

Potato

Continue harvesting

Carefully dig up potatoes for storage. It is best to do this when the soil is relatively dry. The tubers may continue to increase in size as long as the weather is good, so you will get a heavier crop by leaving them in the ground as long as possible. However, the longer they stay in the soil, the more liable they are to become diseased or damaged.

Radish

Continue sowing

Although it is early fall you can continue to sow summer radishes, which are quick to mature. Also make a sowing of a winter radish variety for use in late fall and winter.

LIFT POTATOES (top) *as soon as they are ready if your garden suffers badly from slugs. Store only undamaged potatoes with loose soil removed, and check them regularly for signs of rot.*

TURNIPS CAN BE STORED (above) *in a cool, frost-free basement or garage. They will last longer in storage if they are placed in a shallow box and covered with moist peat or sand.*

Rutabaga

Harvest roots

Rutabaga roots can be harvested as soon as they are large enough to use. This may be as early as late summer, but since the plants take quite a long season to mature—up to seven or eight months—the majority of roots are ready for use only over the fall and winter months. Much depends on growing conditions, the variety grown, and the time of sowing. The roots become noticeably sweeter after exposure to a few frosts.

Harvest the roots as required, carefully pulling or lifting them from the soil. Unless you have very light soil, a fork will probably be necessary.

Rutabaga can be left in the ground for pulling as they are needed throughout the winter, but if you lift a few roots and store them in wooden boxes of moist peat or sand you will have some available for use when the ground is frozen solid and cannot be dug.

Sweet potato

Harvest roots

Dig sweet potato roots before frost. Although a light frost shouldn't damage the roots, it will kill the vine. If this happens, harvest at once. A hard frost will damage roots.

Lift the roots by inserting a fork into the soil near the base of each vine. Because they are easily bruised, take care in handling them. Brush off excess soil and separate damaged roots, which should be used right away.

Cure roots for storage

Place undamaged roots in a temperature of 80–90°F for about ten days. On top of a refrigerator can be a convenient, warm location. The curing process helps convert the starches in the root to sugars, which improves flavor. To store your crop, place the cured roots in a cool, dark room, ideally where temperatures are 50–60°F.

Turnip

Store lifted roots

Turnips can be lifted throughout fall for immediate use or storage. Brush away wet soil; place the roots in a shallow wooden box and cover with moist peat or sand, like rutabaga. Store in a cool, frost-free place. Use damaged roots right away, as they will not store well.

LEAFY GREENS

General

In mild-winter and mid-temperate regions, sow greens for late fall and winter harvest as room becomes available in the garden. Fast-maturing varieties of lettuce and other greens such as arugula, corn salad (mâche), and buckler-leaf (French) sorrel provide abundant variety for fresh salads. To extend the season in mid-temperate regions, use floating row covers to protect plants from early frosts.

Chicory

Harvest plants

Chicory and endive are ready for cutting now. Continue to blanch plants to remove excessive bitterness. When forced, the deep roots of witloof chicory produce chicons. To force plants outdoors without having to dig up the roots, cut off the leafy head to leave a 2in. stub. Use a hoe to draw soil over these stubs, and within a few weeks chicons will form under the soil, particularly if a hot cap or cloche is used to provide extra warmth.

Better results are often achieved by forcing indoors, where plants are lifted and planted in a box of moist peat or sand, with the leaves trimmed to ½in. from the roots. Cover the roots with 9in. of peat and put the box in a warm, dark place. Blanched chicons will be ready for cutting in about four weeks.

SPICY GREENS *(top) have an especially fine flavor when you grow them yourself and they are eaten within hours of harvesting. They are available in a range of colors, leaf types, and flavors.*

CUT-AND-COME-AGAIN LETTUCE *(above) offers delicious leaves over a period of several weeks and constantly picking leaves, rather than lifting the whole plant, keeps them immature and tender.*

Lettuce

Harvest heads as soon as they are ready

Continue cutting lettuce and picking leaves from cut-and-come-again crops. Remove damaged or dying outside leaves from plants as soon as they are seen, in order to prevent the rest of the plant from succumbing to fungal diseases. Remove and compost plants that bolt, or start to go to seed. The leaves become very bitter once flowering has initiated.

Sow varieties for overwintering

In mild regions, hardy varieties of lettuce are worth growing outside in a sheltered spot. Suitable varieties for overwintering include 'Winter Density', 'Arctic King', 'Rouge d'Hiver', and 'Brun d'Hiver'.

Prepare the soil thoroughly and rake it to a fine consistency before sowing. Sow in furrows spaced 12in. apart. Thin the seedlings in stages to leave them 6–8in. apart. Row covers will help the plants survive the winter temperatures and will give an even earlier spring crop. Depending on conditions, lettuce should be ready for cutting from early spring onwards.

Sow seed in cold-frames

In many colder regions, an unheated greenhouse or cold-frame provides a suitable environment for growing overwintering varieties of lettuce. These can be sown now for harvesting throughout most of the winter and will provide an early harvest in spring, even without the assistance of artificial heat.

Spinach

Sow winter varieties

In mild-winter and mid-temperate regions, sow spinach in drills 12in. apart and gradually thin the seedlings to 9in. apart in the row. Fall-sown spinach will provide an early spring crop.

CUCURBITS

Cucumber

Continue picking

As in summer, harvest cucumbers as they are ready.

Melons

Protect plants from cold weather

Late varieties of melon may need protecting with floating row covers during the first cool nights of fall, while they finish ripening during the warmer daytime.

Summer squash

Continue picking crops

Keep picking until either the plants are exhausted and cease to produce fruit, or the first frosts kill them off. Flowers can also be harvested to be stuffed or fried. Mildew is common late in the season; badly mildewed plants are not worth saving and should be discarded.

Winter squash and pumpkin

Start harvesting

Fruit for immediate use in the kitchen can be cut off the plant as required. If winter squash and pumpkin are to store well over winter, they must be fully ripened and cured. To do this, allow the fruit to remain on the vine until frost threatens. A light frost will not usually damage fruit, but harvest before a heavy frost, leaving about 1in. of stem. Keep fruit in a warm, sunny place for a week or two, to cure; a greenhouse or sunroom is ideal.

After curing, store them in a cool, dry, frost-free place such as an unheated basement or garage. Depending on the variety, fruit that has been fully cured should last for up to six months.

SQUASH FLOWERS (top) are quite delicious and need to be picked just as they are starting to open. Take them straight to the kitchen. They can be stuffed and fried in batter.

ALLOW PUMPKINS (above) to remain on the vine to develop and mature until frost threatens. Harvest them leaving 1in. of stem attached and cure the pumpkins in a sunny, warm room.

ALTHOUGH MOST PEPPERS *can be enjoyed green, many varieties change color and develop fuller flavor as the fruit matures. Colors range from green, yellow, and orange to bright red and deep purple.*

FRUITING CROPS AND CORN

Eggplant

Encourage fruit ripening

In cooler regions, remove any fruit that forms after late summer, because it's unlikely to mature. This will channel the plant's energy into ripening the larger fruit. Cover plants with a floating row cover on cool, fall nights. Harvest the fruit as soon as it reaches full size and develops its appropriate mature skin color.

Okra

Continue harvesting

Continue to pick okra pods as soon as they reach a suitable size, before they become stringy. Once the plants have finished cropping, pull them up and add them to the compost pile.

Peppers

Ripen and harvest fruit

If frost threatens, cover outdoor plants with row covers to protect them and help ripen their remaining fruit at the end of the season. Hot pepper plants can also be uprooted and hung upside down in a dry shed.

TOMATOES, ESPECIALLY SMALLER-FRUITED VARIETIES, *add color to beds of annual flowers such as marigolds (above), zinnias, and calendula. They can also be paired with flowers in a container.*

Tomato

Pick remaining fruit

Before the first frost, green fruit should be picked and ripened indoors. To ripen a few tomatoes at a time, place them in a drawer along with a couple of ripe apples or bananas. These give off the gas ethylene, which is responsible for initiating the ripening process.

PERENNIAL VEGETABLES

Asparagus

Cut back yellowed ferns

When the foliage of asparagus turns yellow, cut it back to ground level. Depending on the weather and your region, the foliage may still be green, in which case leave it a bit longer while it builds up the plants for next year.

Globe artichoke

Cut down stems

Once the foliage of globe artichoke has turned yellow, cut the stems down to ground level. In mild regions, where globe artichoke is grown as a perennial, cover the crowns with mulch before the first frost.

| Preserving the herbal bounty

by Kris Wetherbee

No gardener should have to resort to store-bought herbs, especially when you can capture the flavor of fresh herbs year-round by drying your own. Dried herbs are among the handiest staple ingredients found in kitchens today. They pack loads of flavor and can be used in a pinch to enliven any dish.

Preserve an herb's flavor by harvesting it in the early morning, preferably after the dew has dried but before the heat sets in. Overcast days are ideal. Harvest only clean, pesticide-free herbs for culinary use. If herbs are splotched with mud or dirty, then rinse them with a hose several days before harvesting so they can dry off before you bring them into the kitchen.

Use scissors or hand pruners to cut the stems and handle herbs as little as possible, being careful not to

TO PRESERVE HERBS *for winter use (top), harvest them at their peak, cutting them early in the day for maximum flavor. Handle them as little as possible, to avoid bruising the leaves.*

FOR HERBS WITH LARGE LEAVES, *such as bay (above), remove the leaves from the stem before placing them in a food dehydrator.*

bruise the leaves. Remove any dead or wilted leaves that may be mixed in with your harvest. Gently shake the stems to remove debris but don't wash the leaves. Adding moisture at this point will lengthen the drying process and possibly encourage mold.

The easiest way to preserve fresh herbs is to hang them in bundles until dried in a dark, warm, dry location with good air circulation. Keep bundles no thicker than 1in. in diameter and secure them by tying with string, twist ties, or rubber bands. This method works best for rosemary, sage, oregano, and other herbs with long stems. Herbs will dry in several days to two weeks, depending on the type of herb and the temperature and humidity of the location in which they are kept.

A food dehydrator is easy and super efficient, drying just about any herb in 30 hours or less. Most herbs dry in less than eight hours in a dehydrator equipped with a fan. Leaves can be left on the stem when drying small-leaf herbs such as thyme, oregano, and basil. Place only the leaves on the drying trays for bay, sage, and other large-leaf herbs.

Another way to preserve fresh herbs is by 'freeze drying' them in the refrigerator. This method works well for herbs that tend to lose their true essence when dried, such as chives, tarragon, dill, chervil, and cilantro. Even the flavor of rosemary is enhanced when dried this way. Place whole or chopped herbs in a small paper bag or lunch sack and refrigerate. Herbs will dry in 2–4 weeks, yet retain their bright color and flavor.

Always completely dry herbs before storing. You can tell an herb is sufficiently dried when a leaf easily crumbles when crushed between your thumb and finger. Avoid overdrying your herbs—they shouldn't turn to dust when they are crushed.

The best containers for storing dried herbs are made from glass or ceramic and come with airtight lids. (Plastic is air-permeable and not a good choice.) Store dried herbs in a cool, dark, dry area such as a cupboard or drawer. Keep herbs away from heat or humidity sources such as a stove, microwave, sink, or dishwasher, and avoid exposing dried herbs to direct sunlight.

In general, most dried herbs will retain their flavor for up to one year or more when stored in proper conditions. An herb's potency is best judged by its aroma. Crush the dried herb in your fingers. If its aromatic appeal is weak or nonexistent, it's time to recycle it in the compost pile.

MANY HERBS, *including rosemary, basil, parsley, oregano, and thyme (all shown here), are easily preserved by drying in an oven or food dehydrator. Store dried herbs in airtight glass or ceramic containers.*

fruit | GENERAL ADVICE

Continue the fall harvest | Apples and pears are abundant now and lingonberries and cranberries should be beginning to ripen.

Deal with wasps | Hang wasp traps around trees with ripening fruit. Wasps tend to become more of a nuisance as the season progresses, until the first frosts.

Control diseases | Remove rotting and damaged fruits promptly to prevent the spread of diseases. Also remove damaged or diseased twigs and branches.

Prepare for fruit storage | Plan to store, freeze, dry, or make preserves with some of the bountiful harvest of fall fruit for enjoyment through the winter months.

IT'S HARD TO BEAT THE FLAVOR *and crispness of a freshly picked apple. For eating fresh, harvest the fruit when it is fully ripe; but for storing, harvest slightly earlier.*

fruit | WHAT TO DO NOW

TREE FRUIT

Apples and pears

Harvest fruit

Pick apples and pears as they ripen, and before fall storms bring them down as windfalls. Handle the fruit carefully, cupping it in your palm rather than grasping it, and lift it off the tree with the stalk intact. If the stalk remains on the tree, the fruit isn't ready for picking. Never pull at the fruit, because this can break the fruiting spurs. Some varieties need eating within one or two days of picking, while some of the later fruits can last for months and so are suitable for long-term storage.

APPLES ARE READY FOR PICKING *when there are a few windfalls lying beneath the tree. The fruit should have swelled to a good size and have started to color up. The pips (seeds) should be brown.*

STORING FRUIT

Fruit such as apples, pears, and quinces store best in a well-ventilated, airy place that has an even temperature, preferably 37–45°F, but certainly frost free. A shed or garage is often ideal. Only store perfectly sound fruit.

There are two main methods of storage. The traditional one is to wrap individual fruits in tissue paper, newspaper, or waxed paper, and place them in a single layer in a shallow tray. Trays can be stacked on top of one another if there is a gap between them, to allow air to circulate.

A more modern method is to place around half-a-dozen apples in a plastic bag, seal the end with a twist-tie, and make several holes in the bag with the tip of a ballpoint pen, allowing one hole for approximately every 1lb. of fruit. Although this method prevents the fruit from shriveling, the fruit may rot more easily. All stored fruit needs to be checked regularly and any showing signs of rot must be removed immediately.

Pears are often stored unwrapped because they need to be carefully examined frequently, to ensure they are eaten as soon as they are perfectly ripe; they quickly go past their optimum condition.

Peaches and nectarines

Harvest late fruit

Pick late varieties of peaches and nectarines as the fruit ripens. For best quality, allow the fruit to ripen fully on the tree. Unlike apples and pears, which increase in sugar content after harvest, peach and nectarines do not improve once picked.

The fruit is suitable for harvesting when it has fully colored and the flesh near the stalk feels soft. Handle the fruit very carefully when picking, to avoid bruising. Cup it in the palm of your hand and lift it to see whether it separates easily from the tree. The tree will require regular visits for picking over a period of several days as the fruit will not ripen all at once.

Plums

Harvest fruit

Continue to pick plums as they ripen. Some varieties of plum ripen much earlier, in summer, but there are others that are not ready until early fall. 'Fall Rosa', 'Golden Nectar', 'Empress', and 'Damson' are all late varieties that extend the season after the early plums are finished.

Quinces

Harvest fruits before the frost

Although quinces ripen well in hot, sunny summers, they are very unlikely to produce fruits that are edible straight off the tree. Leave the fruits to hang on the tree as long as possible, but harvest them before the first frosts. Quinces are very astringent and are best consumed after cooking.

One of the quince's assets is that the fruit can be stored until mid or late winter before it will spoil, so the season of use is much extended. Arrange the fruit on slatted trays or in cardboard boxes in a cool, dark but frost-free location.

Quinces are strongly aromatic and if stored near other produce their aroma may taint it. To avoid this, store them in a separate place.

APPLE VARIETIES

There are hundreds of varieties of apples; selecting the best for your garden depends on several factors including: size of tree, fruit quality, harvest season, disease and pest resistance, and pollination requirements.

- The size of the tree is largely a function of rootstock and pruning technique. While dwarf trees are great for small-scale landscapes and for easy harvesting, standard trees can add significant beauty to the landscape.
- The flavor among varieties of homegrown apples ranges from tart to very sweet, and it is a matter of personal taste which you grow. Most varieties are delicious for eating fresh, and many are also recommended for baking, drying, storing, or making sauce.
- Harvest season begins in mid or late summer with early varieties such as 'Lodi' and 'Yellow Transparent' and extends through mid fall with late varieties such as 'Pink Lady', 'Winter Banana', and 'Granny Smith'. By selecting early-, mid-, and late-season varieties, your garden can produce fresh apples over several months.
- Apples require cross-pollination—the presence of a second apple variety that flowers at the same time—in order to

AN ASSORTMENT OF APPLE VARIETIES *demonstrates a wide range of fruit size and color. Varieties also differ in flavor, texture, harvest season, and suggested uses.*

produce a good crop. Consult your extension service or reliable fruit tree nursery for suggestions of compatible varieties for pollination that are suited to your location.
- Varieties that have been bred to resist diseases and pests are less likely to need spraying. 'Freedom', 'Liberty', and 'Jonafree' are good varieties that bear resistance to several important diseases including apple scab, cedar-apple rust, fireblight, and powdery mildew.

QUINCES *are a delicious and useful fruit. Their aromatic flavor is excellent when cooked with apples, and their high levels of pectin make them indispensable for the setting of jams and fruit jellies.*

HARVESTING LATE-SEASON BLACKBERRIES *is one of the pleasures of early fall. It is a wonderful activity that shouldn't be rushed, especially as you will want to sample the produce fresh off the canes.*

SOFT FRUIT

Blackberries

Continue harvesting fruit

Although production will be slowing and is over for some varieties, continue picking fruit of late-maturing varieties as it ripens. Some varieties of blackberries can be picked until the first frosts. The fruit is more prone to developing molds in damp, cool weather, so remove diseased fruit as soon as it is noticed.

Blackberries are extremely nutritious; they are very high in fiber, low in fat, and are an excellent source of vitamins A and C and other antioxidant compounds. For the greatest nutritional benefits, eat blackberries raw; they add a burst of flavor to a bowl of ice cream or cereal. Alternatively bake them into pies or cobblers, or freeze them or make jams or jellies to enjoy later.

Prune after harvest

Once all the fruit has been picked, remove the one-year-old canes of blackberries. It may be easier to cut fruited canes in sections so as not to damage the new growth. Tie in the new canes, or bundle them together, to prevent them from being whipped by winds over winter.

Black, red, and white currants

Prepare for planting

Prepare the site now so it is ready for planting new bushes in late fall or early spring. Work the soil thoroughly, adding plenty of well-rotted organic matter.

Prune black currants

Cut out about one third of the older stems, removing them right down to ground level. Also cut out any weak, damaged, or diseased shoots. The aim is to encourage strong new growth that will bear fruit in future years. Pruning can be carried out from now until late winter.

Blueberries

Continue harvesting

Late blueberries may still be producing ripe fruits, provided they are protected from birds. Harvested berries can be stored in the refrigerator for up to a week. Keep the plants well watered, using rainwater whenever possible, and when the soil is thoroughly moist apply a mulch over the roots. Chipped bark, pine needles, or leafmold are suitable mulches for these acid-loving plants; do not use mushroom compost as it contains lime.

Cranberries and lingonberries

Harvest fruits

Cranberries and lingonberries take longer to mature than blueberries. Their first fruits should be ripening now, and you can continue picking until mid fall. Harvest cranberries and lingonberries when their fruit is light red to dark red; green fruit is unripe and has a bitter flavor. Light red lingonberries will continue to develop color in storage. The fruit stores well in a plastic bag in the refrigerator, but make sure the fruit is dry and that all damaged fruit is removed.

Raspberries

Pick fall-fruiting varieties

Harvest fall raspberries from now until the first frosts. In colder areas, it is worth covering the plants with row covers or high tunnels, to extend the cropping season.

Strawberries

Continue to harvest everbearing and alpine varieties
Both everbearing and alpine strawberries will continue to produce flowers and bear fruit until frost; check them regularly for ripening fruit. Even though it is not produced in large quantities at one time, these delicate fruit add much flavor to fall desserts. The berries become more prone to rotting as the season progresses, so pick the beds over frequently and remove all damaged or rotting fruits.

Plant new outdoor beds

Although strawberries are usually planted in early spring, they also can be planted now in beds prepared in summer, following the same directions for planting strawberries in early spring (see page 58). Be sure to allow sufficient time for the roots to become established so that alternate freezing and thawing of the soil will not cause plants to heave.

Thin and fertilize established beds

Remove extra plants that have developed in established beds; allowing plants to grow too closely together will reduce the quality and size of next year's crop. If growing multiple rows, maintain at least 18in. of open space between rows. Sidedress rows with a balanced fertilizer.

CRANBERRIES *make good subjects for containers where garden soil doesn't have a sufficiently low pH or where it is not wet enough to satisfy their cultivation needs.*

LINGONBERRIES *bear clusters of spherical, red berries. They naturally occur in moist, acidic sites but, with care, the gardener can replicate such an environment at home.*

HARVEST KIWI *before the fruit softens; its seeds will have turned black-brown. 'Passion Poppers' (top) is a hardy kiwi developed by Kiwi Korners of Pennsylvania. Unlike fuzzy kiwi, hardy kiwi has smooth skin.*

HARVEST GRAPES *(above) by cutting entire bunches from the vine; most fruit in a bunch ripens simultaneously.*

Grapes

Protect fruit from wasps
Continue to protect the ripening fruit from wasps by using wasp traps or by covering the vines.

Harvest bunches when ripe
Pick bunches of grapes only when they are fully ripe, so that they achieve maximum sweetness.

Kiwi

Harvest fruits
Pick kiwi just as they start to soften. Hard fruits can be allowed to ripen indoors; storing them with ripe fruit like apples and bananas will encourage ripening.

| Grow your own native fruits

by Lee Reich

Native fruits offer more than just delectable and interesting flavors. These plants are more locally adapted and less susceptible to pest problems than many non-natives. Many native fruits also sport growth habits, leaf colors, and/or shows of flowers that make them ornamental plants in their own right. Except for blueberry, native fruits are mostly overlooked in American markets and gardens.

The cultivation of blueberries is covered in detail under its own heading throughout this book, while the following are some other, perhaps less appreciated, natives bearing good fruit.

THE BLUE-BLACK FRUIT *of the American elderberry (top) has a sweet, mild flavor that is valued for making pies and preserves. Harvest the berries by combing through the clusters with a dinner fork.*

THE FLAVOR OF JUNEBERRIES *(also called serviceberries) is sweet with a hint of almond. Birds enjoy the fruit too, so cover plants with a net if you expect a harvest of any size.*

Beach plum
(*Prunus maritima*, Zones 3–6)
Native to the Atlantic Coast, beach plum is drenched in fleecy, white blossoms each spring. Late summer brings cherry-sized plums, although production is erratic from year to year. Depending on your site, pruning may be needed to keep these sprawling shrubs from forming overgrown thickets. Requires cross-pollination for fruit production.

Clove currant
(*Ribes odoratum*, Zones 4–8)
This Midwest native begins the season with 2in. long, yellow trumpets of fragrant blossoms. Mid summer brings large, tangy, black-colored currants that ripen over a period of weeks. Clove currant is a tough, spreading shrub that laughs off cold, heat, drought, and pests, including deer.

THE CLOVE CURRANT *ripens from mid to late summer. Most varieties produce blue-black fruit although some are yellow-orange.*

Black raspberry
(*Rubus occidentalis*, Zones 2–6)
Very tasty even if it's not particularly attractive. Prune the thorny canes annually to remove those that fruited the previous year, then thin young canes to six per clump, and shorten sideshoots to 12in. Black raspberries are drier and richer in flavor than the more familiar red raspberries—and, of course, black.

Juneberry
(*Amelanchier spp.*, Zones 3–8)
Native in every state of the U.S. Although resembling blueberries, juneberries possess their own unique flavor, which combines the sweetness and richness of sweet cherries along with a hint of almond. These large shrubs or small trees are often grown as ornamentals for their showy, white or pinkish blossoms of spring, their fiery fall leaf color, and their neat growth habit.

Elderberry
(*Sambucus canadensis*, Zones 2–9)
Decorative, large shrub that explodes with flat-topped clusters of small, white blossoms in late spring or early summer. Clusters of small, blue-black berries, good for pies and jams, appear in summer. Keep the shrub youthful with periodic removal of old stems at ground level.

American persimmon
(*Diospyros virginiana*, Zone 4–8)
Grows to become a large, care-free tree with foliage that looks fresh and healthy all summer long. The soft, orange fruits taste like dried apricots that have been soaked in water, dipped in honey, and given a dash of spice. For the tastiest fruit, plant named varieties such as 'Szukis', 'Mohler', 'Garretson', or 'Wabash'.

Pawpaw
(*Asimina triloba*, Zones 4–8)
Medium-sized, native tree with tropical aspirations: large, lush

AMERICAN PERSIMMONS *ripen in fall; the fruit is ready to harvest only when it becomes extremely soft.*

leaves; botanical 'roots' in the custard-apple family; and fruits that look like mangos. Yet the plant is very cold hardy. The creamy, white flesh resembles banana along with flavor hints of mango, pineapple, and avocado. The only care needed is to prune away root suckers; few insects or diseases bother it. Pawpaw needs cross-pollination.

HARVEST THE LARGE, OVAL PAWPAW *fruits when they begin to soften, but before they fall from the tree.*

mid fall

Chilly nights remind us that it's time to prepare the garden for the coming cold weather. Where crops have finished for the season, remove debris and add it to the compost pile. Garden hoses should be drained, collected, and stored in a shed or garage.

The harvest of late vegetables now replaces the summer crops, with stout leeks, fat cabbage, and chunky carrots, beets, and other root crops ready to be gathered. There are still apples, pears, and quinces to be picked and enjoyed or stored away; remember to keep an eye on all your stored produce, looking out for rotting specimens and removing them quickly.

All tender plants should be protected or moved back under cover before the first frosts strike, which usually occurs before the end of mid fall, except in very mild regions. The weather is unpredictable at this time of year—one week you may have a glorious Indian summer and the next you may experience chilly rain and frost. Best be prepared for anything.

vegetables | GENERAL ADVICE

ALL REGIONS

Clear up the vegetable garden | Remove spent stems and debris to avoid harboring pests and diseases, and to expose slugs and other pests to the birds and the changeable weather conditions of fall.

Sow cover crops | There is still time to sow cover crops, including winter rye, crimson clover, and vetches. These establish in fall, survive the winter, and are ready to be cut and plowed into the soil early next spring.

Prepare beds for spring | Incorporate well-rotted bulky organic matter such as farmyard manure or garden compost into the soil so it will be ready for spring sowings when the soil is warm enough.

Extend the harvest | The cropping season for many vegetables can be extended for a few more weeks by covering them with floating row covers.

MILD-WINTER REGIONS ONLY

Sow and transplant fall crops | A sowing of many cool-season crops such as turnip, lettuce, mustard, spinach, and radish can be made now for winter harvest.

MANY VEGETABLES, *particularly cool-season crops such as cabbage, broccoli, lettuce, peas, and spinach, thrive in fall, as nighttime temperatures begin to cool. Additionally, many pests are less prevalent during this time of year.*

vegetables | WHAT TO DO NOW

ONION FAMILY

Garlic

Plant garlic cloves

In all regions, garlic can be planted now, and in mild-winter regions planting can continue until early to mid winter. Be sure the soil is well drained, otherwise bulbs may rot. On heavy ground that could become waterlogged over winter, plant on a mounded ridge or in a raised bed.

PLANT EACH GARLIC CLOVE (top) in the ground with its pointed tip up and set about 1in. below the surface. Space cloves 4in. apart, in rows 9–12in. apart.

DIG UP LEEKS AS REQUIRED (above), trying to avoid scattering soil over the remaining plants. Leeks are difficult to clean, and the cleaner they are in the garden, the simpler their preparation will be once they are brought into the kitchen.

The largest, outer cloves will develop into the largest bulbs, so plant these in your garden and use the smaller cloves for cooking.

Space cloves 4–6in. apart within the row, to provide sufficient space for bulbs to form. Depending on the variety and your region, garlic matures in 180–270 days after planting.

Leek

Harvest leeks as they are needed, lifting the roots gently with a garden fork.

Onion and shallot

Check stored crops

Look at stored onions and shallots often and remove any rotting bulbs before they have a chance to infect the rest.

Finish planting onion sets

In mild-winter regions, there is still time to plant fall onion sets for an early crop next summer.

CABBAGE FAMILY

General

When preparing the soil for any cabbage-family crop, work the ground deeply, incorporating plenty of well-rotted organic matter. Digging in fall gives the soil time to consolidate over winter. Check the soil pH; the ideal range for brassicas is 6–7.5. If the pH is too low, you may need to apply lime, which will help to deter clubroot.

Plant cabbage-family crops on different ground each year; avoid returning to the same piece of ground for at least two years. Crop rotation minimizes the buildup of soil-borne diseases and pests and prevents the soil there from becoming starved of nutrients (see also page 25).

BRUSSELS SPROUTS *should be harvested when they are about the size of a walnut. Snap them off or remove with a sharp knife and pick only firm sprouts. Start from the bottom and work upwards.*

KALE LEAVES *will be ready to harvest in mid fall and often continue until mid spring. Remove leaves when they are still young and tender; this will encourage more to develop.*

Broccoli

Transplant winter crop

In mild-winter regions, broccoli plants can be moved to the garden for harvest in early winter.

Brussels sprouts

Stake where necessary

On exposed sites or in windy weather, this top-heavy crop may be blown over. If needed, support plants with a stake to keep them upright. Step carefully around the bases of the plants, to ensure they are firm, in case any have been loosened in the soil by windrock.

Harvest from the base up

Depending on the variety, Brussels sprouts may be ready to pick now. Start harvesting at the base of the stalk, where the sprouts are largest, and work your way up. The lower leaves can be removed as you harvest; this will make picking easier and may encourage remaining sprouts to mature.

Cabbage

Continue harvesting

Keep cutting heads as required. To produce sound, large heads of crispy leaves, cabbage need a sunny site and firm soil. If your results are disappointing, make sure you choose a better site next year.

Transplant for winter crop

In mild-winter regions, transplant cabbage seedlings to the garden for winter harvest.

Cauliflower

Protect curds and harvest

Cold weather may cause browning of the curds and leaves, although this can also be caused by boron deficiency. To prevent the curds from being discolored by a severe frost followed by a rapid thaw, or by direct sunlight, bend some of the uppermost leaves over the developing curd to protect it. Continue to harvest heads when they reach the appropriate size for the variety.

Colorful cauliflower

If you would like a change from pure white cauliflower, there are varieties with colorful heads: 'Graffiti' produces rich purple heads, 'Panther' has lime-green heads, and the heads of 'Cheddar' are orange.

Kale

Start harvesting

Fall kale can now be harvested. Use thinnings in salads or stir-fries. Kale is one of the hardiest of winter vegetables, and leaves will be available in mild regions throughout winter and into spring. The flavor of kale improves significantly after plants are exposed to frost.

Kohlrabi

Continue harvesting

Harvest the mature stems of kohlrabi before they become woody. They will tolerate some cold weather; in fact, their flavor is sweeter after a frost or two. In addition to the bulbs, the leaves are a good addition to stir-fries and soups.

LEGUMES

General

Remove the above-ground portion of pea and bean plants once the crop has finished. Leaving the topgrowth in place encourages the growth of weeds and provides hiding places for slugs and other pests.

Put the topgrowth on the compost pile; dig the roots into the soil as they will help enrich it with nitrogen. Remove the supports used by vining peas and pole beans and store them for next year's use.

Peas

Harvest fall peas

Pick peas from summer sowings as they reach the appropriate size, but be sure to harvest before the first hard frost.

ROOT AND STEM CROPS

General

In mild- and mid-temperate regions, many root crops, including carrots, beets, rutabaga, winter radishes, and parsnips are best left in the ground and dug as you need them. But where frozen soil prevents harvesting or threatens to damage these crops, lift and store them in a frost-free shed or basement. Use at once any roots that are damaged during digging; they should not be stored.

Carrot

Harvest as needed

Lift carrots as needed. Protect those left in the ground with a heavy layer of straw.

Celeriac

Harvest roots when large enough

Lift celeriac as needed, when the roots are between the size of an apple and a coconut. In mild regions, on light soil, celeriac can remain in the ground all winter and be harvested until early spring as required. In cooler regions and on heavier ground, where soil is prone to waterlogging, lift celeriac by late fall and store.

Parsnip

Start lifting roots

Traditionally, parsnips are not harvested until after the foliage has died back, which is a sign that the roots have begun to sweeten. A hard frost will turn the starch content of parsnips into sugars, which is why parsnips make a popular winter vegetable. They are at their sweetest during the coldest weather.

Begin to lift parsnips as required, using a fork to ease them carefully out of the ground. The roots are often extremely long and may snap off if the fork is not inserted deeply all around each plant, in order to get underneath the whole root.

A HARD FROST TURNS THE STARCH OF PARSNIPS INTO SUGARS *so leave them as long as possible in the ground, even after the foliage has died back in fall. Dig them up only when you want them.*

Rutabaga

Harvest roots as needed

After the first frost, the flavor of rutabaga improves. Harvest roots as needed, leaving the others to continue to sweeten.

Sweet potato

Finish harvesting roots

Dig all sweet potatoes before the first hard frost. A light frost often kills vines, but does not usually hurt the roots. Continued exposure to cold temperatures, however, will damage the roots. Handle them gently when digging, because the roots are easily bruised, which leads to decay in storage.

Turnip

Sow late crop

In mild-winter regions, sow turnip seeds for a winter crop.

Lettuce

Sow a late crop

In mild-winter regions, make a late sowing of lettuce seed for winter harvest. As soon as seedlings are large enough to handle, thin them to 4–12in. apart, depending on the variety.

In mid-temperate and cold-winter regions, seed can be sown in prepared soil in a cold-frame; this sowing will produce lettuce in early winter, and often beyond.

Spinach

Sow for spring

Sow spinach from now until the ground freezes, for an early spring crop. Using floating row covers in winter will hasten growth of the plants.

HARVEST WINTER SQUASH (top right) once their shells harden but before they are damaged by a hard frost, leaving a short stem attached to prevent rotting. They will keep for several months if properly cured.

ALTHOUGH RUTABAGAS (right) can be harvested now, they are quite tolerant of cold temperatures; in fact, it improves their flavor.

Winter squash and pumpkin

Continue to harvest

Once their shells harden and they have developed full color, harvest winter squash and pumpkin. Although light frosts will not injure the fruit, they should be harvested before the first hard frost. The shell is sufficiently hardened when it is not easily pierced with your thumbnail. Leave 1–3in. of stem attached to each fruit, to help prevent rot.

Cure fruit in a warm area for a week or two. Once cured, store them in a cool, dry, frost-free room.

General

Pick off any unripe fruit from peppers, tomatoes, and eggplants before it is damaged by frost and take indoors to ripen. If you have an abundance of any of these crops, consider canning or freezing some for winter use.

Clear away all topgrowth. If your crops showed signs of disease, do not add them to the compost pile. Remove and store cages, stakes, or other supports.

Tomato

Extend the harvest

If an early light frost is predicted, covering tomato plants with a sheet or floating row cover often provides sufficient protection to prevent damage to the fruit. Remove the covering in the morning when temperatures rise. Since the next frost may not happen for a week or two, this precaution is often well worth the effort to extend your tomato harvest.

Ripen fruit indoors

Harvest tomatoes before they are damaged by frost. If your vines are still loaded with fruit when frost is predicted, pick all unblemished fruit and bring it indoors to ripen. Fruit that has begun to turn red usually ripens quickly in warm temperatures indoors. Tomatoes do not need light to ripen.

Place full-sized, green fruit in a shallow box, in a single layer, and cover with a few sheets of newspaper; the newspaper helps trap ethylene gas, which stimulates ripening. For faster ripening, place fruit in a drawer or paper bag with an apple or banana. Check the tomatoes frequently and use them as they turn red.

Asparagus

Cut down ferns

Cut asparagus foliage down to the base as soon as it turns completely yellow. Remove weeds, preferably by hand; hoeing can be difficult because the plants are shallow rooted, and the roots are easily damaged. Once all the weeds have been cleared, apply a layer of organic mulch, to help prevent more weeds from appearing.

Prepare new beds

If you intend to plant asparagus next spring, start preparing the bed now. This is a long-lived crop, which can remain productive for 20 years or more, so make sure you do the job properly. Dig the soil deeply, thoroughly working in plenty of well-rotted organic matter. If the drainage needs improving, dig in some grit; asparagus will not thrive in waterlogged soil. On heavy, clay soils, asparagus will do better in a raised bed.

Globe artichoke

Mulch crowns

In mild regions, where globe artichoke are grown as perennials, apply a mulch of straw or leafmold over their root area if you have not already done so.

ASPARAGUS FOLIAGE (top) turns completely yellow in fall—when this happens, cut it down to the base. By then it will have done its essential job of building up the plant's food reserves for future crops.

fruit | WHAT TO DO NOW

General

Winter sunscald can cause serious injury to fruit trees, usually on their south or southwest side. Bark can absorb a great deal of heat on a sunny, winter day and, when followed by a dramatic drop in temperature at night, cells may rupture and die, resulting in the bark's splitting. This makes trees more susceptible to diseases and insect pests that can enter through the wounded bark. Protect fruit trees from sunscald by wrapping trunks with commercial tree wrap or by painting the trunk on their south and southwest sides with white latex paint.

Mice, rabbits, and voles often nibble on the bark of young fruit trees and may completely girdle the tree, destroying the vascular tissue and causing it to die. Prevent this damage by removing vegetation and mulch that provide protection for these animals next to the trunk and by installing a metal or plastic collar or cage of hardware cloth that extends 1–2ft. higher than the anticipated height of snowfall.

If you are planning to add new fruit trees to your kitchen garden next year, it is a good idea to prepare the soil thoroughly well in advance of planting. Have your soil tested and incorporate recommended additions into the soil so that the pH and fertility are optimal for the trees. By the time you are ready to plant, the soil will be in good shape to give the trees a good start.

Apples and pears

Continue harvesting

Pick apples and pears as they are ready. Harvest time varies greatly depending on variety.

To test if an apple or pear is ready to pick, place your hand under the fruit and lift it gently rather than pulling it: If it is ready for picking, the fruit stalk will separate from the tree quite easily.

DEPENDING ON THE VARIETY *and your location, apples are ready to harvest from mid summer to late fall. Planting several trees with different harvest seasons assures a continued supply of fresh fruit.*

Order new trees

Order new stock from specialist fruit nurseries for delivery during the dormant season. Take advantage of local apple festivals to help you choose your varieties; these often include tasting sessions, and there will be experts to advise you and often specialist suppliers to consult. Check on pollination groups before completing your order to make sure you have compatible varieties, and select a rootstock that is appropriate for the circumstances in your garden and region.

Inspect stored fruits

Check over fruits in storage frequently, removing any rotting fruit immediately so it does not have time to infect adjacent stored fruit.

Keep an eye out for damage by mice, as these often move into sheds and garages at the onset of fall, and will enjoy nibbling your stored fruit.

Prune out dead wood

Cut out dead, dying, or diseased shoots as soon as they are observed.

Collect windfalls and leaves

Pick up all fallen fruit, as well as dried fruit left on the tree, as it may harbor disease.

Removing the fruit promptly helps prevent the infection from being carried over the winter. Rake leaves beneath apple and pear trees, to reduce overwintering diseases and insects.

Figs

Protect outdoor trees

In mid-temperate and mild-winter regions, protect wall-trained trees during winter, to ensure the survival of the embryonic figs. These fruits need to remain on the tree all winter in order to develop fully and ripen next year. A double layer of floating row cover may be sufficient,

ONE GOOD INDICATION OF RIPENESS *is when healthy apples begin to fall from the tree. Be sure to collect windfalls, to prevent diseases and insects from overwintering and reinfecting next year's crop.*

but in cooler gardens insulate the tree by using plastic netting to hold a loose layer of straw or dry leaves in place around the plant.

Move potted trees indoors

Move figs that are growing in containers back into an unheated greenhouse, enclosed porch, basement, or garage for the winter.

Peaches and nectarines

Control peach leaf curl

Rake all fallen leaves from beneath peach and nectarine trees and burn or destroy them. If peach leaf curl was a problem on your trees this year, consult your local extension agent for fungicide recommendations.

Plums

Deal with broken branches

When trees carry a heavy crop, it is not uncommon for branches to break under the weight of the fruit, and you might find you have a broken branch to deal with now. Cut the branch off cleanly.

Quinces

Finish harvesting fruit

Pick any remaining quinces before the first frost. The fruit stores well and will continue to ripen after it is picked.

SOFT FRUIT

Blackberries

Prune out old canes

Remove one-year-old blackberry canes once they have fruited. Then bundle the new canes for winter or train them along the supporting wires, using strips of cloth or pieces of pantyhose.

Weed and mulch

Remove weeds from blackberry rows and spread a mulch such as leafmold or compost around plants. Keep the mulch several inches away from the base of canes.

Black currants

Plant new stock

Plant container-grown black currants from now until late spring. After planting, cut all the stems back to one or two buds above ground level, to encourage basal shoots. Allow 6ft. of space for individual bushes. The varieties 'Consort', 'Crusader', 'Coronet', and 'Koska' are resistant to white pine blister rust (see page 54).

Blueberries

Weed and mulch beds

Remove weeds, ideally by hand so that surface roots are not injured, and cover the soil with a 2–3in. layer of an organic mulch such as pine needles, leafmold, wood chips, or well-rotted garden compost.

REMOVE WEEDS THEN MULCH *around blueberries and other bush fruit, to help retain moisture and moderate soil temperatures over winter. Keep the mulch away from the crown, to avoid rot.*

PROPAGATING CRANBERRIES

While the soil is still warm and moist, dig up an established clump of cranberries and gently pry it apart with two garden forks held back to back. Discard the woodier center and replant the outer, younger divisions.

If you don't want to disturb your plant, remove rooted sections carefully from the parent, potting them into a bed or pot of soil-based potting mix for acid-loving plants, topped with grit. Water in well.

Cranberries and lingonberries

Continue to harvest

Pick cranberries and lingonberries as they ripen. It takes at least three years after planting before you will enjoy a significant harvest of lingonberries. Both lingonberries and cranberries will keep in good condition in the refrigerator for several weeks.

Prune plants

Trim plants after harvesting. Every two or three years, thin them to aid air flow and optimize fruit ripening.

Raspberries

Prune everbearing raspberries

If you are willing to sacrifice a summer harvest, you can cut all the canes of everbearing raspberries back to the ground anytime after a hard frost until early spring, before the buds break. Although you will miss the summer fruit, your fall crop will be much larger and disease and insect problems will be minimized.

Order new stock

Make sure you buy certified stock from a reputable supplier so that you start off with disease-free canes.

Strawberries

Care for newly planted beds

If there is a dry spell, water newly planted strawberries carefully, to help encourage root growth before the ground freezes.

VINE FRUIT

Grapes

Pick remaining fruit

Finish harvesting any remaining grapes now. For most types of grapes, clip off entire clusters. Muscadine grapes, however, should be picked individually. Store fresh grapes in the refrigerator or preserve them as jams and jellies.

HARVEST GRAPES *after they develop the appropriate color for the variety, and the white bloom becomes more pronounced. Another indication of ripeness is the seed color—it changes from green to brown.*

| How to store homegrown fruit

Although most fruits freeze well and many can also be dried or made into preserves, this limits their use thereafter because they are no longer in their fresh state. By choosing varieties that have an extended storage life, you can continue to eat these fruits raw and so benefit from their maximum vitamin content.

Apples, pears, and quinces are the best crops for fresh storage. Some varieties are best when eaten immediately, fresh from the tree, while others can be stored successfully for only short periods. But provided you have the right varieties and a suitable storage area—such as a cool garage or basement –you can often enjoy these crops fresh for several months after they have been harvested.

Other storage methods

Freezing

Many fruits such as raspberries, strawberries, and blueberries freeze very well, and can be defrosted for use without cooking. Lay such fruits on a shallow tray so they are not

EARLY APPLES (above) are at their best when eaten within a few days of picking, while some of the later varieties can last for months if stored well.

THIS ORCHARD RACK has sliding drawers to allow easy access for checking stored crops. They are spaced to provide good air circulation.

A SELECTION OF FRUITS WITH LONG STORAGE PERIODS

APPLES	TYPE	SEASON OF USE
'Cortland'	Dual-purpose	Mid fall to mid winter
'Melrose'	Dual-purpose	Mid fall to late winter
'Mutsu'	Dessert	Late fall to late winter
'Northern Spy'	Cooking	Late fall to early spring
'Rome'	Cooking	Early winter to early spring
'Suncrisp'	Dual-purpose	Mid fall to early spring

PEARS	TYPE	SEASON OF USE
'Aurora'	Dessert	Early fall to early winter
'D'Anjou'	Dessert	Late fall to early spring
'El Dorado'	Dual-purpose	Mid fall to late winter
'Kieffer'	Cooking	Late fall to mid winter
'Moonglow'	Dual-purpose	Early fall to mid winter
'Winter Nellis'	Dual-purpose	Late fall to late winter

touching, and freeze them; once frozen, bag them up.

Other fruits, such as peaches, nectarines, and plums, can be frozen raw, for later use with or without cooking them (adding a bit of lemon juice helps reduce browning), while others such as apples and pears are often frozen in their cooked state.

Preserves

The majority of fruits make excellent jams and jellies. If you are taking advantage of a bountiful harvest, don't wait until the fruits are overripe because this can impair their ability to set. This is controlled by the levels of pectin present; fruits with a naturally high pectin content, such as apples, set very readily and can be added to low-pectin fruits, such as strawberries, to improve their setting ability. Alternatively, fruit pectin—as powder or liquid— can be purchased to add to jelly and jam recipes to assure proper set.

Drying

Dried fruits can be used in cakes, breads, or similar foodstuffs, or be eaten on their own as a naturally sweet snack. To dry fruits, you can use an oven on its lowest setting, leaving the door slightly ajar. However, a food dehydrator, with slatted trays and a fan that circulates warm air over them, is the ideal piece of equipment.

PLUMS *have a moderate level of natural pectin in them so this type of jam or jelly is relatively easy to set.*

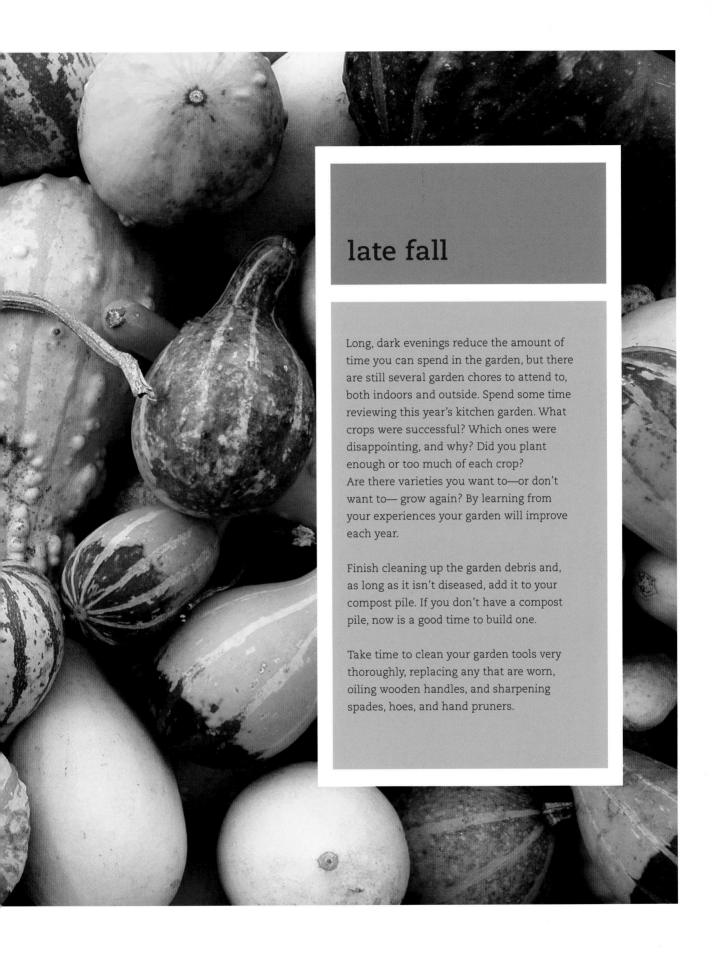

late fall

Long, dark evenings reduce the amount of time you can spend in the garden, but there are still several garden chores to attend to, both indoors and outside. Spend some time reviewing this year's kitchen garden. What crops were successful? Which ones were disappointing, and why? Did you plant enough or too much of each crop?
Are there varieties you want to—or don't want to— grow again? By learning from your experiences your garden will improve each year.

Finish cleaning up the garden debris and, as long as it isn't diseased, add it to your compost pile. If you don't have a compost pile, now is a good time to build one.

Take time to clean your garden tools very thoroughly, replacing any that are worn, oiling wooden handles, and sharpening spades, hoes, and hand pruners.

vegetables | GENERAL ADVICE

Make your own compost | Use your garden waste and crop remains to make compost—an invaluable soil conditioner whatever type of soil you have. Buy or build two compost bins: one to fill while the contents of the other is rotting. Bins should have a capacity of not less than 1 cu. yd.

Add a mix of organic waste from the garden and kitchen to the bin. About a third of the waste should be soft green, nitrogen-rich material such as kitchen waste and lawn clippings; the rest should be strawlike or woody, carbon-rich material, such as spent crops. Do not add perennial weeds to the mix, since they may simply grow there. Keep adding waste until the bin is full, and watering the contents if it looks dry, then leave it to rot. Turn the pile with a garden fork regularly, to make sure all parts of it are decomposed by the organisms in the pile. When you have filled one bin, tip its contents into a second, empty bin as a way of turning the pile.

Have your soil tested | Fall is a good time to have your soil tested because you have the opportunity to amend your soil, as recommended by the test results, well before it's time for spring planting.

Continue to work soil | Turn the soil in areas of the vegetable garden as they become vacant.

GREEN CABBAGE *(right) is best eaten when freshly harvested, but some, if mature, can be lifted in fall for storage.*

WORM COMPOST

In small gardens where there is not much room for a compost pile, worm composting is another option. Worm bins consist of an upper chamber where worms feed on waste, and a lower sump where liquid collects. The liquid contains plant nutrients and is watered onto growing crops. Eventually the upper chamber fills with compost, which is added to the garden. The worms are recovered for the next batch. Even if quite small, these bins usefully recycle waste. Both bins and worms can be bought as kits from specialist suppliers.

vegetables | WHAT TO DO NOW

ONION FAMILY

Garlic

Finish planting cloves

In mild areas and in free-draining soils, continue planting garlic cloves. If your soil is heavy, consider planting garlic in a raised bed.

Check new plantings

For the first month or so after planting, regularly check the crop for signs of bird or animal damage; push back any uprooted bulbs before they dry out. As garlic is shallow rooting, it dislikes competition so weed the soil regularly—taking care not to damage the bulbs.

Leek

Lift some plants before bad weather strikes

If your soil is likely to freeze soon, dig up a supply of leeks and heel them in to a shallow trench in a patch of light soil near the kitchen. They will keep perfectly well there, and you will always have some plants at hand if the soil freezes solid and prevents you from digging in the garden.

HARDY WINTER CABBAGE *in milder regions can be left where it is growing and harvested only when it is needed for the kitchen. Be sure to select a variety that is tolerant of cold weather.*

THE LEEK IS A VERSATILE AND USEFUL VEGETABLE *that's easy to grow in the right soil conditions. Grown for its stemlike rolled leaves, it can be harvested over an extended period in fall and winter.*

CABBAGE FAMILY

Brussels sprouts

Remove yellowed leaves

Take off old, yellow leaves from Brussels sprouts plants as you pick the crop. Be sure to harvest spouts from the bottom up as soon as they are full size and firm. Also remove old, lower leaves where sprouts have been harvested, to make further picking easier. Retain healthy, green leaves as these are required for continued growth; they also help to protect the developing sprouts.

Cabbage

Harvest as required

Except in very cold regions, hardy winter cabbage such as 'January King', 'Roulette', and 'Brunswick' can be left where they are growing for harvesting as they are needed through mid-winter. Round-headed, fall-maturing varieties, on the other hand, are best cut this month

'BLOWN' SPROUTS

Instead of developing tight, firm buttons, Brussels sprouts plants sometimes form loose, leafy, open-centered sprouts that are known as 'blown' sprouts. These are especially common lower down the stems. A major cause is loose soil; all cabbage-family plants need to be very thoroughly firmed in. On windy sites, the roots can be loosened in the soil by windrock, and firming soil around the plant bases occasionally will help give the stalks more support. Poor nutrition is another contributing factor, so grow sprouts in rich, fertile soil and give regular applications of balanced fertilizer. Avoid nitrogen-only fertilizers; although sprouts are heavy feeders, an excess of nitrogen can encourage blown sprouts. Modern hybrid varieties are less likely to produce blown sprouts than some older types.

REMOVE YELLOWING LEAVES (top) from Brussels sprouts plants and compost them. Tamp down soil around any plants with roots that have worked loose because of windrock.

YOUNG, TENDER KALE LEAVES (above) are delicious in salads or cooked briefly with oil and garlic. Because only a few leaves are cut at a time, kale really earns its keep in the vegetable garden.

and stored in boxes of straw in a cool, well-ventilated shed or garage. Fall cabbage varieties that are good for storage include 'Premium Late Flat Dutch', 'Storage No. 4', and 'Mammoth Red Rock'.

Cauliflower

Protect curds from frost damage

In mild regions, where cauliflower is still growing in the garden, bend a couple of outer leaves over the top of cauliflower curds, breaking the stems of the leaves but not snapping them through completely. This prevents discoloration and helps minimize frost damage. Floating row covers can also be used to provide protection and to extend the harvest season.

Harvest heads

Harvest cauliflower heads when they have reached full size for the variety, but the curds are still tight and smooth. Cauliflower will tolerate some cold weather without damage, but it is not as hardy as other cabbage-family crops.

Kale

Harvest young leaves

Kale is completely frost hardy, and young leaves can be picked and enjoyed right through fall, and in mild regions until mid spring. Harvest all types while the leaves are still young and tender; older leaves quickly become tough and bitter.

Harvest the crop as required, because kale is best fresh and will keep in the refrigerator for only a few days.

Kohlrabi

Harvest stems

The flavor of kohlrabi sweetens after a couple of frosts so harvest as needed. Kohlrabi is one of the easiest of the cabbage-family crops to grow; both green and purple varieties are available. Try it grated in coleslaws or added to stir-fries. Its crunchy texture and mild flavor are sure to please.

ROOT AND STEM CROPS

Carrot

Protect roots
Carrots retain their flavor best if they are left in the soil and harvested as needed. A heavy layer of straw mulch will protect the crop so that it can be harvested into winter. In many mid-temperate and mild-winter regions, it is possible to harvest carrots through winter until early spring.

In cold-winter regions and where soil is very heavy, dig up and store your carrots, otherwise they will be difficult to harvest or they may rot. Carefully lift the carrots using a garden fork, then cut off the leafy tops, leaving about 1in. of growth above the root. Store them in slightly moistened sand in a cool basement or garage. Alternatively, place carrots in a plastic bag in the refrigerator, where they will keep for a couple weeks.

IN COLD-WINTER REGIONS, *where the ground will soon be frozen, carefully lift mature carrots. They can be stored in the refrigerator for about 2 weeks or buried in moist sand for winter use.*

Celeriac

Harvest as required
Celeriac can be left in the ground over winter in mild- and mid-temperate regions, but like carrots the rows are best covered with an insulating layer of straw or similar material to make lifting of the crop easier.

Remove the thick skin from the harvested bulbs and either grate the white flesh for use raw in salads, or dice and cook it. Place the prepared vegetable in cold water with a squirt of lemon juice added, to keep the flesh white; otherwise it will turn brown when exposed to air.

Parsnip

Harvest as needed
Continue to lift roots for use as needed. Leave remaining roots for harvest throughout winter, but draw 2–3in. of soil over the tops of roots, for added protection.

Look out for canker
Parsnip canker causes brown or orange, sunken lesions on the roots, particularly at the shoulders. It is a soil-borne fungal disease for which there is no cure, and is worst on heavy, poorly drained soils and in wet weather. Early sown crops and very large roots are particularly prone to the disease.

If parsnips are badly affected by canker, lift the crop, remove the damaged portion, and use them as quickly as possible. Improve soil drainage for next year and grow parsnips in a different place. Choose resistant varieties such as 'Andover', 'Gladiator', and 'Javelin', and sow them in mid or late spring rather than the early spring.

Potato

Check stored potatoes
Make sure stored potatoes are not exposed to light, which turns them green and toxic; always fold over the sacks tightly after removing potatoes for use. If you come across any rotten potatoes, or notice an unpleasant smell, tip the tubers out of their sack and go through them carefully, removing any rotting or wet specimens. Allow the rest to dry off, then replace them in thick paper bags. Never store potatoes in plastic bags as these hold condensation and encourage rotting.

A WELL-GROWN, WELL-TENDED CELERIAC *is quite a sight and can easily rival a coconut in size. When harvesting, ease the roots out of the ground with a fork and trim off the foliage and fine roots.*

Radish

Harvest winter radish

This hardy, often black-skinned root is much hardier than summer radish. It also forms larger roots, which can be thinly sliced or grated for salads or stir-fries. Harvest roots as needed.

Rutabaga

Protect roots from cold

Rutabaga are hardy and will store well in the soil, but as their shoulders are above ground level they will benefit in very cold weather from a dry straw or similar mulch.

LEAFY GREENS

General

There is no need for the salad season to have ended yet. Chicory and endive, hardy winter lettuce, mustard, arugula, corn salad, winter purslane, and cress can all keep you supplied with a steady supply of fresh greens through the fall and winter months.

Chard

Continue harvesting

In mild-winter regions, chard can be grown nearly year-round. Continue to harvest the outer leaves for use; this will encourage the growth of new leaves.

Chard can be eaten raw in salads or be cooked, alone or in soups and stir-fries. It is an excellent source of vitamins A and C, iron, potassium, and dietary fiber.

Chicory

Blanch chicons

Force witloof chicory by covering the roots to exclude light and raising the temperature. Lift the roots now and plant them in deep boxes of moist potting soil or sand (see page 190). Place in a reasonably warm shed. After several weeks, plump, pointed, white chicons will have been produced. Keep them completely dark, to reduce their bitter taste.

Blanch endive

In mild regions, harvest broad-leaved Batavian endives from now until mid winter, as these are more hardy than the curly-leaved types. Blanch to reduce bitterness, either by gathering the leaves together and tying them, or by covering the center of the plant with a large, lightweight plate. Make sure the leaves are dry before blanching, to reduce the chance of rotting.

WITLOOF, OR BELGIAN, CHICORY *can be forced to develop chicons such as these. Although this can be done outdoors, without having to dig up the roots, better results are often achieved by forcing indoors.*

Lettuce

Harvest fall varieties

In regions where hardy varieties continue to grow outdoors, harvest lettuce as needed. To extend the harvest season, cover plants with a floating row cover. In colder regions, lettuce growing in cold-frames and under plastic tunnels can also be harvested now. At this time of year, watch out for botrytis (gray mold) and downy mildew; where these are a problem, thin plants to increase air circulation. Slugs may also be a nuisance.

Mustard

Harvest leaves as needed

In mild climates, mustard can be grown year-round. In cooler regions, it grows well in cold-frames, providing fresh greens throughout the winter months. Begin harvesting leaves from plants sown earlier in fall as needed. Pick the outer leaves first, to allow new leaves to continue to develop at the center.

BOTH RED AND GREEN VARIETIES *of mustard tolerate frost and will add pungent flavor to fall salads.*

Spinach

Sow spinach for spring

For an early spring crop, continue sowing spinach seed until the ground freezes. Sow seed thinly in rows spaced 12–18in. apart.

CUCURBITS

Winter squash and pumpkin

Check stored fruits

Ensure pumpkins and squash are stored in a dry, well-ventilated, cool place; ideally the temperature should be kept near 50°F. Store them in a single layer and ensure they are not touching. Properly cured and stored, winter squash will keep for several months. Use pumpkins first, as these do not store as long as most winter squash. At the first sign of rotting, remove the fruits, cut away the damaged parts, and use the rest immediately.

FRUITING CROPS AND CORN

Tomato

Check fruit ripening indoors

Gradually ripen geeen tomatoes over several weeks indoors, but remove promptly any tomatoes showing signs of rotting or that have become wrinkled and withered. If you have large quantities of green tomatoes at the end of the growing season, consider using some of them in their unripe condition. Battered and fried, they make a delicious side dish that is a southern tradition, or they can be made into chutney or relish.

PERENNIAL VEGETABLES

General

Cut back the foliage of asparagus and rhubarb if you have not already done so. Remove weeds, taking care not to injure shallow roots, and cover the roots with an organic mulch after the soil freezes.

SOW SPROUTING SEEDS

At this time of year and through the winter and early spring, fresh salad vegetables are scarce, but nothing could be easier than growing sprouting seeds to fill the gap. These quick-growing crops are packed with vitamins and flavor.

Special seed sprouters are available, but no special equipment is necessary—just a reasonably large jar—a quart canning jar is ideal. Find a clean piece of muslin or cheese cloth and cut out a circle that will fit over the top of the jar and overlap the edge. Rinse the seeds and soak them in clean water in the jar for a few hours; fix the circle of cloth over the top of the jar with a rubber band or canning jar rim and drain off the water. From then on, rinse and drain the seeds twice a day. Keep the jar in a warm place; if you like blanched seed sprouts, keep the jar in the dark, otherwise grow them in the light. Try both ways —the sprouts have a slightly different flavor.

Once the seeds have sprouted sufficiently, they are ready to eat, usually within 2–7 days. Alfalfa, mung beans, fenugreek, adzuki beans, broccoli, cress, peas, lentil, mustard, onion, radish, and arugula are just a few of the seeds that can be grown in this way.

CHARD LOOKS AS GOOD AS IT TASTES and is remarkably easy to grow, even tolerating some neglect. It is a useful, late fall vegetable, and in mild regions can often be grown throughout winter.

| How to store vegetables

Most vegetable growers would love to be able to provide fresh produce straight from the vegetable garden every week of the year, but even the best organized and largest of gardens would be hard pressed to achieve this. The majority of crops are produced in summer and early fall. A few can be harvested through the winter in milder regions, and even less during early spring, a time traditionally referred too as the 'hungry gap.'

Fortunately many crops can successfully be stored for use through the leaner winter and spring months. There are several methods of storage, some very simple, others requiring more preparation. Whichever method you use, select only sound, undamaged produce for storage.

LEEKS (above) have a big advantage: They can be harvested over a long period, from fall to winter, remaining 'stored' in the ground.

ALLOW POTATOES TO DRY (right) after harvesting before bagging them up in a paper or burlap sack or wooden boxes.

Storage methods

In the ground

This is often the best, and certainly the easiest, method of storing many vegetables—just leave them where they are growing. In mild-winter and mid-temperate regions, root crops such as parsnips, carrots, rutabaga, and turnips, brassicas such as winter cabbage and Brussels sprouts, and hardy crops such as leeks can often be left where they are and harvested as required. However, they are more prone to weather and pest damage, and in some areas may be inaccessible because they are frozen into the ground during cold weather.

In boxes or sacks

Use sturdy wooden boxes if possible. In a cool but frost-free shed or garage, put a layer of slightly moist sand or straw in the base of the box, lay the vegetables on top so they are not touching and cover them with more sand or straw.

Potatoes store well in burlap or strong paper sacks (not plastic, which will encourage rotting). Be sure to keep them in the dark.

On the shelf

In a cool, frost-free shed, garage, or basement, set up a system of slatted wooden shelves, which will allow a good flow of air around produce and encourage it to last throughout the winter months. Produce such as mature pumpkins and winter squash, winter cabbage, onions, garlic, and shallots will all keep well in such a storage environment.

When produce is stored for a long time on shelves, it can start to rot underneath, where the wooden slats press against it. Hanging the produce

STORED VEGETABLES AND FRUIT *will start to deteriorate once the weather starts to warm up, so finish them off quickly before they start to shrivel or sprout.*

in nets or stringing up onion-family members in ropes or braids gets around this problem.

In the kitchen

Many fresh vegetables in optimum condition after harvesting are best frozen as they deteriorate quickly (for example, peas, beans, asparagus, and corn). Freezing is relatively simple, although many vegetables need to be blanched in boiling water before they are frozen. Freezing vegetables on trays before they are placed in plastic bags makes it easier to remove the amount you want when it's time to use them.

Other vegetables can be canned either whole or processed into sauces, juices, relishes, pickles, or chutneys. Yet another option is to dry vegetables using a warm oven or a food dehydrator.

MAKE PICCALILLI *and other pickles, chutneys, and relishes with vegetables that deteriorate quickly once harvested.*

fruit | GENERAL ADVICE

Plant trees | Although container-grown fruit trees can be planted year-round, bareroot trees must be planted while the tree is dormant. This is often done in late winter or early spring, but fall or early winter planting of fruit trees has some advantages, particularly in mild-winter regions.

The major advantage to fall planting is providing more time for the tree roots to become established before the above-ground growth begins the following spring. But in cold regions, spring planting is usually preferred because fall-planted trees are more susceptible to damage by rodents, deer, and extreme low temperatures.

For planting fruit trees in fall, follow the same procedures as outlined for early spring on page 50.

Guard against rabbits | Rabbits will eat the bark from the base of young trees during the hungry days of fall and winter, and they can easily kill a tree by stripping off a complete circle of bark. Use tree guards to keep rabbits away. There are various protective products available including plastic spiral guards that wrap round the trunk and extend as the tree grows, and wire or plastic mesh guards that encircle the tree.

MANY VARIETIES OF PEARS *that were picked and stored in the past months are ready to enjoy. Be sure to inspect stored fruit regularly. Late varieties such as 'Winer Nellis' are now ready for harvesting.*

fruit | WHAT TO DO NOW

TREE FRUIT

Apples and pears

Complete harvest
Finish picking any remaining apples and pears and store the fruit, or eat it right away if it is not a long-keeping variety. Also, pick up and dispose of fallen apples, and pick off and burn any mummified fruit that is clinging to the trees because, if left, it can spread diseases to next year's garden.

Clear up fallen leaves
Rake up leaves infected with scab, then remove them; they should not be left lying under the trees. Good hygiene will help to keep the disease under control in future years.

Get ready for new trees
Prepare suitable sites for planting new trees. Test the soil pH and adjust it if necessary—a pH of 6–7 is ideal for most fruit trees.

Apples and pears are good cool-climate fruit because they tolerate low winter temperatures, and there are varieties that suit most sites and soils. In fact, the choice is so great that it is sensible to consult a local specialist nursery or grower who can recommend varieties that are suitable for your local conditions and that will be able to pollinate each other.

The ideal position for an apple or pear tree is a sunny, sheltered site, well away from any frost pockets. Poorly drained or shallow soils should be improved or avoided.

Plant and prune trees to train as cordons
Cordons are popular tree forms for small gardens, because they fit almost anywhere. In mild-winter and mid-temperate regions now is a good time to plant a tree to train as a cordon: a feathered maiden (a branched, one-year-old tree) is the best tree to select, because it

PLANT AN OBLIQUE CORDON *angled at 30–45 degrees, to encourage a system of fruit spurs to develop along its trunk.*
Tie the leader to a cane, fixed to each support wire with sturdy ties.

will start cropping earlier than a maiden whip (a one-year-old tree without branches).

If the feathered maiden is wispy with poor branching, lightly prune the leader to encourage more sideshoots and fruiting spurs below; otherwise the leader should be left untouched. Cut shoots longer than 4in. back to two or three buds.

If a maiden whip has been purchased, shorten the leader by about two thirds to a healthy bud after planting, to encourage sideshoots to develop. Thereafter, follow the same procedure as for a feathered maiden.

Prune established cordons
Although the majority of pruning takes place in summer, after a few years it may be necessary to thin out overcrowded spur systems between now and the end of winter. Prune as little as possible in the dormant season, though, as winter pruning stimulates vegetative growth.

Occasionally, wispy growth develops on cordons after summer pruning. This is usually because the pruning has been carried out too early, before the plant has started to slow down for dormancy. If this happens, prune back the growth to one bud now.

Plant and prune trees to train as espaliers

Plant against a warm, sunny wall or fence or on open ground. Establish a framework of horizontal wires 18in. apart, starting from 18in. above ground level.

After planting a maiden whip, cut it back to 18in. above the ground, to encourage buds to break just beneath the cut. Attach the central trunk to a vertical cane tied to the wires. (In cold-winter regions, wait to plant until early spring.)

Plant trees to train as fans

If buying a feathered maiden, make sure that it has a good pair of sideshoots growing at 14–18in. above the ground. Prepare the soil for trees planted against a wall particularly thoroughly, incorporating plenty of organic matter, to retain soil moisture. (In cold-winter regions, wait to plant until early spring.)

Plant trees to train to a central leader

After planting a maiden whip, prune it back to 30in. above ground. After planting a branched tree, select three or four branches at 24–28in. above the ground to form the first tier and remove all others. Leave the retained branches unpruned unless they are spindly, in which case cut each tip at a downward-facing bud. Shorten the leader to 5in. (about five buds) above the chosen branches. (In cold-winter regions, wait to plant until early spring.)

Apricots

Prepare a site for new trees

If you can grow a peach in your garden, then you should be able to succeed with an apricot as they require similar growing conditions—a warm, sheltered site in full sun. Although tolerant of a wide range of soils, apricots prefer well-drained soils and they will struggle in shallow conditions. Dig plenty of well-rotted organic manure into soils before planting. Popular varieties include 'Tilton', 'Sungold', and 'Moorpark'. Prepare the planting site now so it will be ready in early spring while the tree is still dormant.

PLANTING AN ESPALIER

1 CHOOSE A WARM, SUNNY SPOT *on which to transform a young tree into a superb decorative feature, using a method that is both highly ornamental and efficient.*

2 DIG THE PLANTING HOLE *large enough to accommodate the tree's roots. Sprinkle over slow-release fertilizer or mix it in with the removed soil. Place the tree in the hole.*

3 TRAIN THE HORIZONTAL BRANCHES *along the supporting wires, tying at regular intervals. Backfill the hole and water thoroughly.*

Cherries

Prepare a site for new trees

Both sweet cherries (*Prunus avium*) and sour cherries (*P. cerasus*) prefer to be grown in a site in full sun. While cherries are fairly tolerant of both acid and alkaline soils, they do need good drainage. Cherry tree roots are naturally very shallow, and so any waterlogging will cause them to rot or to succumb to water-borne root diseases. Both types flower in early spring—sweet cherries first and sour cherries shortly thereafter—so they are both subject to frost damage. If possible avoid sites with southern or southwestern exposures, which can promote earlier blooming.

Good varieties of sweet cherries include 'Stella', 'Kristin', and 'Windsor'; 'Montmorency' and 'Morello' are popular sour cherries. Prepare the site now even if you are not going to plant until early spring, so it will be ready before trees begin growth.

Figs

Protect trees from cold weather

If you have not already done so, bring figs growing in containers into a protected area for the winter. An unheated garage, porch, or basement is ideal.

Protect outdoor-grown figs from cold temperatures by covering the base of plants with a heavy mulch or mounding loose soil up around the lower portion of the plant. For greater winter protection, insulate trees with loose straw or dried leaves secured with plastic netting.

Peaches and nectarines

Prepare a planting site for new trees

Peaches and nectarines require a soil that is well drained but contains plenty of well-rotted humus, to help retain moisture. Peach trees will struggle in light, shallow soils, so any underlying compacted soil must be broken up and plenty of well-rotted organic matter incorporated into the soil before planting.

Early spring blossoms can easily be damaged by cold, so do not plant these trees in a frost pocket. Prepare the planting site now even if you don't plan to plant until early spring. Take a soil sample and add the suggested amendments now so the soil can settle properly before the growing season gets under way.

SITE SELECTION FOR FRUIT TREES

Select a site in full sun, or at least 6 hours of sun per day, with deep, well-drained soil, and have your soil tested. While the pH and fertility can be adjusted according to your test results, poorly drained sites should be avoided. Most fruit trees prefer a fertile soil with a pH of 6.0–7.5.

Avoid low-lying spots, where frost tends to settle, or areas where air circulation is limited, such as next to a fence row or wooded area. Trees planted in such a location are more subject to damage from late spring frosts, which can kill blossoms. Ideally, select a site that is higher with good air circulation.

Fruit trees often double as ornamental specimens, so can be given a prominent location in the landscape. If space is limited, consider a restricted form such as an espalier or fan; and dwarf fruit trees often grow well in containers.

Prepare your site the season prior to planting, removing weeds and grass in a circle, 4ft. in diameter. Work amendments into soil to a depth of 12–18in., so they are incorporated into the area where roots will develop.

Plums

Prepare planting site for new trees

Plant plum trees in a sunny spot with well-drained soil—waterlogged soils are not suitable. Add well-rotted, bulky organic matter such as manure to sandy or shallow soils before planting.

Plums are one of the earliest fruit trees to flower in the fruit garden. While the plants themselves are often extremely hardy, the flowers can easily be killed by frosts. It is therefore essential to position your trees out of frost pockets or windy sites. Prepare the planting site now even if you don't plan to plant until early spring.

Protect trees in pots

Plums can also be grown in containers, but make sure the pots are of sufficient size to prevent the potting soil from drying out in summer, and to provide some insulation from cold in the winter. If your container can be moved, consider overwintering your dormant plum in an unheated garage or sink the pot into loose soil and cover it with mulch. This will help prevent frequent freezing and thawing of the soil, which can damage roots.

Quinces

Prepare planting site for new trees

Add plenty of organic matter to light or shallow soils before planting quinces, which can be done now or in early spring. They are best grown in soil that is relatively moist throughout the summer, yet well drained to avoid waterlogging in winter. Mulch the trees thoroughly after they have been planted.

Quinces need a long growing season to ripen well and can be trained as fans or as freestanding trees. Avoid frost pockets, as quinces flower early and the flowers will be damaged by frost. Freestanding specimens will attain a height and spread of 12–20ft. at maturity, depending on the rootstock, location, and soil type.

SOFT FRUIT

General

Most bush fruit (including blackberries; black, red, and white currants; blueberries; and raspberries) can be planted now or in early spring in most regions; however, the selection of varieties in many nurseries may not be as great now as in spring. In mild climates, they can be planted throughout the dormant season as long as the ground is not frozen. Follow the procedures provided for early spring planting (see pages 54–58). If you are planning a spring planting, now is an excellent time to prepare the bed.

Blackberries

Train established blackberries

If you have not already done so, remove canes that produced fruit this year and select the strongest new stems, which will produce next year's crop. Tie these stems to support wires, using soft twine or cloth strips.

Black currants

Prune established bushes

Cut back black currants when dormant—from now until late winter. Plants produce fruit on the young wood, mainly from one- or two-year-old stems, and it is important to bear this in mind when pruning.

AFTER REMOVING *last year's fruiting canes, select the strongest first-year blackberry canes and secure them to support wires using soft twine or lengths of cloth. Space them to maximize air circulation.*

Up to and including the fourth year after planting, remove weak, wispy shoots, retaining a basic structure of 6–10 healthier shoots. After year four, cut out about one third of the older wood at the base, using a pair of loppers or a pruning saw. This will encourage and make room for younger, healthy wood. Also remove weak shoots and low ones leaning towards the ground.

Blueberries

Mulch beds for winter

If you haven't done so already, mulch blueberries with organic mulch such as pine needles, wood chips, or well-rotted garden compost, to provide shallow roots with protection from sudden changes in temperature.

Cranberries and lingonberries

Plant now or later

In mild regions, cranberries can be planted now or in early spring; in cold-winter regions, they are best planted in spring. Lingonberries can be planted during the dormant season, from now to early spring, as long as the

BLUEBERRIES BENEFIT *from an acidic mulch such as peat moss or pine needles, which not only prevent moisture loss and weed growth but also help maintain the preferred soil pH of 4.5–5.0.*

CONTAINER-GROWN STRAWBERRIES, *such as this strawberry pot, require winter protection in most regions. Bring containers into a well-ventilated porch or garage, where it is not likely to freeze.*

ground is not frozen. Be sure to work plenty of peat moss or other acidic amendment into the soil for these acid-loving plants. Mulch to protect shallow roots over winter.

Mulch and prune established plants

Maintain a 2in. layer of an organic mulch on established beds; pine needles, well-rotted compost, leafmold, or wood chips are ideal. If stems of cranberries become crowded, cut them back anytime from now until early spring. For established lingonberry beds, cut back a portion of the bed each year to 1in. above ground level. This will provide a continuous renewal of the planting.

Strawberries

Mulch beds

Once plants have gone completely dormant, mulch new and established plantings with a heavy layer of straw to protect them from low-temperature damage. Unprotected plants are subject to frost heaving from soil—plants are pushed out of the soil as a result of alternate freezing and thawing. Do not apply the mulch too early or it will encourage rot.

Protect container-grown strawberries

Strawberries that are grown in containers will need protection from winter temperatures. If possible, bring the pots into an unheated porch or garage for the winter. Alternatively, sink the pot into the soil and cover plants with mulch.

VINE FRUIT

Grapes

Prepare a planting site

Now is a good time to prepare the planting site for grape vines, even though in most regions they are best planted in early spring. The soil will have time to settle before you are ready to plant. Test the soil and add the necessary amendments. Grapes prefer a pH of 6.2–7.0, and they need a well-drained soil supplemented with organic matter. Start thinking about which varieties you will want to grow. Base your selection on usage: dessert, raisins, jams and jellies, or wine; season; disease and pest resistance; and adaptability to your region.

| Grow your own pear varieties

Despite their delicate aromas and their buttery rich flavors, pears are less popular than apples. Therefore, there are likely to be fewer pear trees growing nearby, and this is important when selecting a tree as it will need pollinating from another pear variety. Keep in mind that pears often give lower yields than apples and that the blossom is more sensitive to frost because it opens earlier in the season.

With the exception of a few cooking varieties such as 'Kieffer', pears do not store nearly so well as apples. They remain in peak condition for eating for a very short time, so must be looked over regularly if they are not to become overripe and oversoft.

HARVEST PEARS (above) just before they are fully ripened. They should be firm and swollen, with a subtle color change to their skin.

A GLUT OF PEARS (right) will need to be stored carefully. Spread them out evenly and ensure they do not touch each other.

Dessert varieties

'D'Anjou'
(pick mid fall, store until early spring) A nearly round pear with smooth, juicy flesh. Its skin remains green even when it is fully ripe. This dual-purpose pear can be eaten fresh or used in baking. It is an exceptionally good keeper.

'Bartlett'
(pick late summer to early fall, store until late fall) The large fruit of 'Bartlett' has sweet, tender, white flesh that is very juicy; this pear is exceptionally good for both fresh eating and canning. The fruit (below) is highly aromatic.

'Concorde'
(pick early fall, store until late fall) A fine, compact hybrid (of 'Conference' and 'Doyenné du Comice') bearing heavy yields of medium to large fruit with a long, tapered neck. The flavor is vanilla sweet and the texture juicy and firm.

'Conference'
(pick early fall, store until late fall) This is a popular commercial variety due to its reliable, heavy crops. The greenish fruit is distinctive with an elongated shape. It is self-fertile and will also bear 'parthenocarpic' fruits without being pollinated at all.

'Doyenné du Comice' ('Comice')
(pick mid fall, store until early winter) Plant 'Doyenné du Comice' for its outstanding flavor and perfumed aroma. The fruit (below) is green with a red blush. Trees bear their fruit inconsistently.

'Highland'
(pick mid fall, store until mid winter) The fruit of 'Highland' is large, typically pear shaped, and yellow with a light russeting. It has a smooth, melting texture and sweet flavor, which improves after a month of suitable storage.

'Seckle'
(pick early fall, store until late fall) 'Seckle' fruit are often referred to as sugar pears or honey pears. The small fruit (below) is highly prized for its very sweet and juicy flesh; it is perfect for a small snack or garnish. Trees are productive and resistant to fireblight.

Cooking varieties

'Bosc'
(pick mid fall, store until early winter) An elegantly shaped variety with a russeted skin, firm texture, and spicy–sweet flavor; 'Bosc' fruit (below) has an exceptionally high sugar content. These pears hold their shape when cooked.

'Gorham'
(pick early fall, store until mid fall) Dual-purpose pear that ripens early. The fruit is golden-yellow with light russeting and has a sweet, musky flavor. 'Gorham' is an excellent variety for canning.

'Kieffer'
(pick mid fall, store until late winter) The fruit of this old American variety is rather hard and coarse, but it stores exceptionally well and is very good for canning, cooking, or making preserves. The tree is very resistant to disease.

'Winter Nellis'
(pick mid to late fall, store until late winter) This late-season variety of pear is best for baking, although it is tasty fresh if you like a firm-fleshed, richly flavored pear. The fruit is relatively small, rounded, and green with light russeting. It has excellent storage characteristics.

early winter

Order your seeds and plants as soon as you can. The earlier you can order, the better—you will be more sure of getting the varieties you want, as popular or new varieties often sell out quickly. This is the time to get ready for the busy sowing season ahead, cleaning flats, potting benches, and cold-frames, making sure heat mats are in good working order, and if necessary buying new flats, pots, and seed-starting mix.

There is always garden clean up to be done when the weather allows. There is no point in trying to work frozen soil, and walking on heavy, very wet soil will ruin its structure. There are usually some bright, dry days in early winter when working outside is a tonic, with the air just crisp enough for you to enjoy the warm glow that hard exercise brings.

vegetables | GENERAL ADVICE

Get ready for spring | Turn over vacant ground, spread manure, check the pH and add lime if required, and make sure the soil is in the best condition possible for an early start on next year's garden.

Conduct an inventory | Assess the crops that you grew this year, noting varieties that performed well and those that did not. Also determine whether you had enough or too much of any crop. This information will come in handy as you order next year's seeds.

Order seeds | Draw up plans for next year's vegetable garden, and order seeds. Bear in mind that mail-order suppliers generally have a significantly wider selection of varieties and often offer savings over retail outlets. When seed arrives, store it in cool, dark, dry conditions until you are ready to use it.

Use winter crops | Continue to harvest winter vegetables from the garden and eat those in storage, discarding anything rotten.

Turn compost | Empty compost bins, mix the contents, and refill them. This will help to speed up decomposition and give a better end product.

IT'S NOT TOO SOON *to be drawing up plans for next year's garden and ordering new seeds. If you have leftover seeds from last year, store them in a cool, dry location.*

vegetables | WHAT TO DO NOW

Leek

Continue to harvest
Harvest leeks as needed from the garden. To protect the remaining leeks, cover them with a thick layer of straw.

Prepare the planting site
Leeks do best in a sunny site on most well-drained soils that don't become waterlogged in winter. Dig the planting site for next spring now and leave it rough in clods so that winter frosts can help to break the soil down to fine crumbs. For light, sandy soil, it's important to add plenty of well-rotted organic matter to produce a good crop.

Onion and shallot

Check stored crop
Look over stored onions and shallots frequently for any sign of rot. Remove infected bulbs immediately, before the rot spreads to others.

Weed and thin overwintering onions
If you planted onions in the fall for a spring crop, keep them free of weeds and, if you have not done so already, thin them to 2–4in. apart, depending on the variety. Use the thinnings as green onions.

CABBAGE FAMILY

General

Although harvesting season is over in most cold-winter regions, mild-winter and some mid-temperate regions may still be enjoying freshly harvested winter varieties from this family. Continue to harvest as needed. Keep remaining crops well weeded.

Broccoli

Harvest sideshoots
In mild regions, broccoli may continue to produce sideshoots into winter. Harvest these as needed.

Brussels sprouts

Continue to pick sprouts
Harvest sprouts as required, when they are large enough, starting from the lowest sprouts and working upwards.

Remove yellowed leaves
Pick off yellowing leaves, to prevent the spread of fungal diseases in the sprout patch.

Refirm and stake plants
Firm soil around the base of sprout stalks, to prevent rocking of the roots. Stake plants in exposed sites.

HARVEST BRUSSELS SPROUTS *by twisting them from the stem. Begin picking from the bottom and move upward. Remove the leaves below the sprouts that you are picking for better access.*

| Grow your own root crops

Root crops provide some of our most useful staple vegetables. They are invaluable in winter, when they serve as the basis of many hearty soups and casseroles. Packed with comforting carbohydrates, root crops are ideal vegetables to enjoy on cold days. Many varieties are completely hardy and, in most regions, can be pulled straight from the ground all winter, or a supply can be lifted in fall and kept in storage in a shed or under a pile of loose soil near the kitchen door. However, roots are not just winter fare; they are also delicious when pulled young and tender. With a little careful planning and staggered sowings, gardeners in many regions can have fresh roots available for harvest year-round.

BEETS AND CARROTS (above) intended for storage are best lifted by gently easing them up with a fork, to avoid damaging the roots.

CARROTS ARE READY FOR HARVESTING (right) 12–16 weeks after sowing. Young carrots can be pulled up carefully by hand.

Beet

The roots may be round or long, and are usually deep red, but golden yellow varieties such as 'Badger Gold' are also available. Harvest them from the mini 'baby beet' stage until they are the size of a tennis ball for the most succulent, tender roots. Mature roots can be stored through the winter months.

'Chioggia'
A very early, Italian, heirloom variety (below) with slightly flattened, globe-shaped roots that display attractive concentric circles of alternating red and white when sliced.

'Detroit Dark Red'
An early variety with smooth skin (below), very dark red flesh, and sweet flavor. Excellent for fresh eating or canning.

Carrot

If you choose the right varieties, in many regions you can harvest carrots from late spring to the following early spring. Carrots store well over winter and come in a range of colors, from red to yellow to purple.

'Atomic Red'
These 9in. long roots are coral-red and best enjoyed cooked, which improves the flavor.

'Bolero'
Produces heavy crops of uniform, thick, slightly tapered roots 7–8in. long (above). Excellent for sowing in fall for a winter storage crop.

'Parmex'
Round-rooted carrot ideal for shallow soils and containers (below). It has good uniformity and core color.

'Purple Haze'
Sweetly flavored roots are purple skinned with orange interiors. Roots are tapered, 7–8in. long.

Parsnip

Parsnips are extremely hardy and can be left in the ground over winter for harvesting as needed. They grow best in well-drained soils, ideally ones that are light and sandy. The seeds are very slow to germinate.

'Andover'
A very productive, sweet-flavored variety. Roots are cylindrical with rounded crowns.

'Javelin'
Wedge-shaped, smooth-skinned, canker-resistant variety with 8in. long, tasty roots (below).

'Lancer'
Smooth-skinned, canker-resistant parsnip. Produces uniform, long, slender roots with very sweet flavor.

Rutabaga and turnip

Good rutabaga include 'Helenor' (below) and 'Laurentian'; both produce uniform roots with flavor that sweetens after exposure to frost. 'Purple Top White Globe' and 'Tokyo Cross' are high-yielding turnips.

Cabbage

Sow seed indoors

In very mild regions, cabbage seed can be sown indoors for later transplanting into the garden.

Harvest mature heads

Cut mature heads of winter cabbage as needed. Draw soil up around the base of plants left in the garden, to provide some protection from wind and cold.

Cauliflower

Protect curds

In mild-winter regions, continue to protect the curds of winter-maturing cauliflower from discoloration, by breaking a leaf over the top of the plant.

Kale

Continue harvesting

Kale is ready to pick 50–65 days after sowing. Remove leaves from the plants as needed, once they reach 6in. long, taking a few of the outer leaves from each plant, or harvesting entire plants to provide better spacing for the ones remaining. In addition to being one of the most cold-tolerant crops, kale is an excellent source of vitamins A and C. It is also rich in fiber.

KALE IS ONE OF THE HARDIEST VEGETABLES *and in milder regions it provides a constant supply of fresh greens throughout winter.*

ROOT AND STEM CROPS

General

In mild spells, lift a supply of roots and either heel them into a shallow trench near the kitchen, loosely covering them with light soil, or store them in boxes of damp sand, soil, or straw in a shed. Continue to inspect stored crops and remove any that show signs of rot.

Celeriac

Protect plants

In mid-temperate and mild-winter regions, where celeriac may still be in the garden, protect the plants from really cold periods with a heavy layer of straw mulch, if this has not already been done.

Radish

Continue to harvest

In mild-winter and mid-temperate regions, where they are still in the ground, harvest winter radishes as needed. 'China Rose' and 'Long Black Spanish' are excellent varieties for winter use.

IT IS TIME TO START EATING TURNIPS *and any other stored root vegetables before they begin to deteriorate in storage.*

General

In mild climates, leafy salad crops such as corn salad (also called mache or lamb's lettuce), spinach, sorrel, claytonia (also called miner's lettuce), mizuna, pak choi, and arugula will be available for harvest throughout the winter. In colder regions, many winter greens can be grown in a cold-frame or unheated greenhouse.

If you don't have the facility or climate to grow greens outdoors in winter, you can grow fresh sprouts indoors. Most sprouting seeds take less than a week to produce a crop. Keep sowing a range of different seeds (see page 227) so that you always have a ready supply for salads and sandwiches.

Chicory

Continue forcing
Keep forcing witloof chicory to produce chicons for winter salads (see page 190).

Mustard

Harvest leaves as needed
In mild-winter regions, harvest mustard as needed to add fresh, spicy flavor to salads and stir-fries. If plants are crowded, thin them to stand about 12in. apart and use the thinnings in salads.

Harvest outer leaves first so the plant continues to produce new leaves from the center. In cooler regions, mustard can be grown in a cold-frame. Cold weather improves the flavor.

Spinach

Protect crops and harvest as needed
Although, in mild-winter regions, spinach often produces leaves all winter without any special treatment, the leaves are more tender if they have some protection. Either use a polytunnel (polyethylene supported with hoops) or cover your row with a floating row cover. Be sure to secure the base of the covering. Harvest entire plants when they reach full size for the variety, or cut just the outer leaves and allow the plant to continue to grow.

Winter squash and pumpkin

Check stored crop
Examine stored pumpkins and squash frequently and remove any that show signs of rot or that are becoming soft. Pumpkins do not usually last as long in storage as winter squash, so use them first. Keep your stored winter squash in a cool room, just above 50°F, with good ventilation. A high humidity (70–80 percent) will keep the squash from shriveling. With good storage conditions, acorn squash should keep for 1–2 months; other types such as butternut, hubbard, and turban squash can remain in good condition for 3–4 months.

General

Check stored tomatoes and peppers regularly and remove any that show signs of rot before it spreads to other fruit.

Asparagus

In mild-winter regions, asparagus can be planted from now until late winter as long as the ground is not frozen. Add a generous amount of manure or well-rotted compost to the soil and work it in prior to planting. Dig 6in. deep furrows and set the crowns into it, carefully spreading the roots. Crowns should be spaced 12in. apart in each direction. Place 3in. of soil over the crowns and water well.

Rhubarb

Prepare bed
In mid-temperate and cold-winter regions, prepare a site for rhubarb that will be planted in spring. Select a site that is in full sun with well-drained soil. Because it is a perennial crop, place rhubarb in a separate area outside the vegetable garden or at one end of the garden.

fruit | GENERAL ADVICE

Buy new plants | In mild regions, you can plant fruit trees and shrubs now until early spring. If the soil is too wet for planting, heel in the new plants until conditions improve. Keep the plants in a frost-free place and ensure the roots don't dry out, particularly if they are bare root.

Apply dormant spray | Use a dormant spray on fruit trees, to control pests and diseases that overwinter on the bark and branches. Lime-sulfur is an effective dormant fungicide and horticultural oil targets overwintering insects and mites. Always follow the label instructions.

THE PRINCIPALS OF PRUNING

Because dormant pruning stimulates growth, give vigorous trees only a light trim, to avoid an excessive reaction. Alternatively, instead of pruning, train branches downwards towards a horizontal position, to encourage fruiting instead of vigorous growth. Only trees lacking in vigor should be pruned hard, to stimulate more growth. Research shows that trees recover better when wounds are left unpainted. The paint can sometimes seal in infections and can also inhibit the tree's natural ability to callus over the pruning cuts.

When to prune: Pruning can be done while the tree is dormant or while it is growing; but the results of pruning at different times are dramatic. Dormant pruning tends to stimulate growth, while pruning during the growing season suppresses growth. For this reason, most pruning of restricted forms of apples and pears is done in summer so that their growth is limited. Summer pruning can also help to prevent biennial fruiting (fruiting every two years).

Dormant pruning is frequently done with central-leader trained apple and pear trees, when it is easy to see the shape of the tree because it is leafless. In mild-winter regions, dormant pruning can begin now and continue through winter. In mid-temperate and cold-winter regions, pruning should wait until late winter or early spring, to avoid winter injury. Prune apples and pears first, as they are less prone to winter damage, and early-blooming trees such as cherries last.

Tools

Hand pruners (pruning shears): These should be used for thinning out fruiting spurs and cutting branches no thicker

than ¾in. in diameter. A good-quality pair with sharp blades is essential; keep blades clean and well sharpened. Bypass pruners are the best type, as they make a clean cut. Avoid anvil pruners, as these tend to crush the branch.

Pruning saws: On branches that are too thick for hand pruners, use a pruning saw. This is long and narrow, so its blade will fit between the narrow angles made by branches. Bow saws should be used only to cut up large pieces of wood, once they have been removed from the tree.

Extended saw: Sometimes called a pole saw or long-armed

saw, the extended saw is useful for cutting branches above head height. It is far safer to prune from the ground and therefore an extended saw is a better option than climbing a ladder and using a shorter saw. Always wear head and eye protection when using this tool.

Loppers: These are useful for chopping up prunings once they have been removed from the tree, and they can be helpful when actually pruning, particularly with cane fruit such as raspberries and blackberries. However, they don't make as clean a cut as a pruning saw. Never use loppers from a ladder as they require two hands to operate.

Ladders: Sometimes ladders are needed to reach high branches. Stepladders are best, because they are easiest to get in close to the tree and among the branches. Only use ladders on level ground and make sure that the legs are fully extended. Never overstretch or lean out too far over the sides. Very large fruit trees will need to be pruned by a professional tree surgeon. Don't risk it yourself.

Basic safety

Using a pair of thick protective gloves is particularly important when pruning thorny plants such as gooseberries. Gloves will also reduce the risk of cutting your hand with pruners or a pruning saw. Wear eye protection to prevent sawdust from blowing into your eyes or a sharp branch scratching them.

General guidelines

Although each tree should be treated individually when it comes to pruning, there are some general guidelines that should be followed.

Remove long, heavy branches in stages to avoid tearing the bark with their weight.

If pruning a branch back to the trunk, leave a small collar, because this will help the tree to callus over the wound.

When cutting back, always check that a replacement branch is growing in the required direction and that it is at least one third the width of the branch that has been removed.

Make pruning cuts at an angle just above a bud—never through a bud. Slant the cut downwards from ¼in. above the bud, sloping away from the bud. Where there are opposite buds, make a flat cut at a similar distance above the buds, (that is ¼in.) A long stub left between the cut and the bud may cause the branch to die back, increasing the risk of disease.

Maximize crops

Once you understand how your tree produces its fruit, you can then prune it to maximize potential yields (see page 274). Peaches and sour cherries, for example, bear fruit mainly on wood from the preceding year, so on such tip bearers you must ensure that plenty of new shoots are retained for next year's crop. Sweet cherries, however, develop their fruit on a series of spurs built up over the last two or three years, so a system of spur pruning is necessary.

Summer-fruiting raspberries bear fruit on canes produced the previous year, whereas fall-fruiting ones form fruit on the current season's growth.

Grape vines bear fruit on shoots produced in the current year. Prune them annually in winter, to encourage new, healthy canes, and avoid using water shoots (canes coming directly off the central trunk) because they will contain far fewer clusters of grapes. Instead, try to select canes coming off the spurs of the trunk, for optimum fruit production.

fruit | WHAT TO DO NOW

General

Remove diseased or crossing branches when they are noticed. Further dormant pruning of fruit trees should be done now only in mild-winter regions. Wait until late winter or early spring in other regions, to prevent damage from cold weather and drying winds.

Apples and pears

Remove cankers

Cankers on branches are often caused by fireblight infection and can cause the branch above the canker to die; they also provide bacteria a place to overwinter. Remove the cankers by cutting back the branch 12–18in. below the lowest canker, cutting back into healthy wood. Remove the prunings and disinfect the pruning tool between cuts to prevent the spread of disease.

Check stored apples

Make regular inspections of your apples, checking them carefully for any sign of disease or discoloration, such as bitter pit, which may show up as small, sunken, dark brown spots on stored fruit. Use up affected fruit quickly, cutting out the pitted areas. Make a note to apply a controlled-release fertilizer in spring to the trees that have produced affected fruit, and to ensure they do not run short of water next season. Mulching is beneficial, too, as it helps to conserve soil moisture.

Clear up fallen leaves

If you have not already done so, pick up fallen leaves from below fruit trees. If the trees were affected with diseases such as scab, remove the collected leaves from your yard rather than putting them on the compost pile. This will help to prevent the disease from being carried over to the following season.

APPLES AND PEARS *are often affected by cankers, caused by fireblight or black rot, which can serve as a source of infection the following spring. Remove such cankers promptly.*

SPUR THINNING

Mature cordons and espaliers benefit from their spurs being thinned every two or three years in winter, when their shape can be seen better because the leaves have fallen. Where the swollen, short sideshoots are crowded, remove the older spurs in favor of the younger wood, to encourage new growth to replace the old spurs.

Dormant pruning

Do this now only for mild-winter regions. For cold-winter and mid-temperate regions, wait until late winter for dormant pruning.

Prune cordon-trained trees where necessary
(mild-winter regions only)

Thin out congested spurs to stimulate growth (see box, left) and help to rejuvenate the apple or pear tree. Don't carry out major pruning of restricted forms in winter, as this will stimulate excess growth; the main pruning is carried out in summer.

Carry out formative pruning of espaliers
(mild-winter regions only)

Cut back the central stem to a healthy bud 18in. above the highest established tier (at the height of the next tier wire). This will encourage buds to break below the cut; these will form the next tier. Repeat this process each year until the desired number of tiers have been created on your apple or pear espalier.

Carry out formative pruning of fans
(mild-winter regions only)

Tip prune the branches that have developed by removing about one third of the new growth, ideally to an upward-facing bud.

Prune established fans *(mild-winter regions only)*

When they are the desired length, prune the main branches on apple and pear trees and thin the spur system (see box, left). If the fan is predominantly a tip bearer (see page 250), use a form of replacement pruning, whereby some of the older fruiting branches are removed to create space for younger shoots.

Prune established central leaders
(mild-winter regions only)

Once established, prune a central-leader trained tree to keep the upper branches shorter, in order to maintain the pyramid shape and to allow sunlight to reach the lower tiers of the tree.

On the top tiers, cut back the older branches every two or three years, to ensure shorter branches and a regular supply of cropping wood each year. On the lower tiers, remove some of the older branches, to make space for

WHEN FORMING A CENTRAL-LEADER TREE *(top) cut overly long branches back to a downward-facing bud in winter; otherwise leave them unpruned and tie down the branches as they grow.*

TO MAINTAIN THE VIGOR OF A MATURE CENTRAL-LEADER TREE *(above), renew the cropping wood from time to time by removing older branches and training new growth in their place.*

new ones, and tie them down if there is space. Remove completely or cut back other branches to three or four buds, to encourage fruiting spurs to form.

Train trees as open-center (bush) forms
(mild-winter regions only)

An apple or pear tree trained with a short trunk and open center is another method of growing apples and pears. Not only do they look attractive but their open structure also allows for good air circulation. To do this, you need to create a basic structure of about four strong branches that will form the open shape and regularly bear fruiting sideshoots and spurs.

For an apple tree on a dwarf rootstock and any pear tree planted in fall as an unbranched whip, prune back to 26–30in. Thereafter, follow the same procedure as for a two-year-old feathered maiden (young, branched tree). If a feathered maiden was planted in fall, remove the leader, cutting back to three or four good strong branches above ground level (and above the graft union). These branches should ideally form a wide angle with the trunk. They will become the primary branches of the tree and will form part of its permanent structure. Remove any other branches from the trunk. Cut back any vigorous branches by one half to an outward-facing bud and shorten less vigorous ones by two thirds.

By the following winter, the three or four branches chosen the previous winter should have developed a few sideshoots of their own. Select two or three equally spaced sideshoots from each of these branches; you should avoid those growing into the center of the tree. Cut back the selected sideshoots by one third and shorten any other shoots to three or four buds, to encourage them to develop as fruiting spurs. Prune back the main branches by one third, and remove any new shoots that have formed lower down the trunk.

By the third winter after planting, the tree should have a well-established framework of branches. Continue to extend the network of branches by tip pruning new, well-spaced sideshoots by one third. Reduce other sideshoots

to short spurs of three or four buds or remove them completely. Also cut out branches that are crossing or growing into the center and remove any branches that are diseased or damaged.

Prune established open-center (bush) forms
(mild-winter regions only)
Continue to keep the center of apple or pear trees open by removing branches growing into the center, with a pruning saw. Lightly prune vigorous trees; those that are making poor growth can be pruned harder. Cut out all diseased or dead wood.

If the tree is predominantly a spur bearer, such as 'Cox's Orange Pippin', 'Redspur Delicious', 'Jonafree', and 'Sturmer Pippin', tip back one third of the new sideshoots to three or four buds, to encourage fruit buds, and eventually spurs, to develop along their length; leave shorter sideshoots alone. On predominantly tip-bearing apple or pear trees, remove any dense or crossing branches; leave unpruned any remaining sideshoots or new growth, to avoid removing potential fruits that form in the tips. Tip-bearing apple varieties include 'Richard',

REMOVE CROWDED AND CROSSING BRANCHES *on established open-center trees in winter or early spring. Aim to keep the center of the tree open, to allow for good air circulation and therefore healthy growth.*

FRUIT BUDS ARE FAT *as they contain not only next year's leaves but also the flower buds. When pruning an apple or pear tree, it is important to distinguish these fruit buds from vegetative buds, which are smaller and thinner.*

WHEN PRUNING BACK LARGE BRANCHES *leave an angular cut and try not to damage surrounding bark. Clean cuts using sharp tools should heal quickly.*

'Rome Beauty', 'Florina', 'Irish Peach', 'Tydeman's Red', and 'Orin'. Only a few pear varieties are tip bearers— 'Jargonelle' and 'Josephine de Malines' being among the best known.

Remove some of the older branch framework on an apple or pear open-center form, to make way for new, younger shoots. Also cut away all water shoots growing directly from the trunk flush with the trunk. Do this before they spoil the look of the tree.

Training and pruning a standard open-center tree (mild-winter regions only)

Standard and half-standard trees are essentially bush trees but on taller stems, so that the branches start at a different height. The training and pruning methods are the same (see page 249).

Rejuvenate neglected trees (mild-winter regions only)

If you live in a mild-winter region, you can restore an old or neglected tree to its former glory any time during winter. In cooler regions, you should wait until late winter or early spring. The technique, however, is the same.

BEFORE STARTING TO RENOVATE A TREE *(top), study it carefully when it is dormant and you can see its branch structure. Usually, this is a tangle of twiggy branches. Then thin out the crown (above) and remove dead, diseased, and crossing branches. Never cut out more than a quarter of the branches in one growing season.*

DEALING WITH OLD TREES

There are a number of reasons why apple and pear trees benefit from rejuvenation. Congested canopies cause poor air circulation, which can potentially encourage a buildup of pests and diseases: They also create shade, which reduces the light levels necessary for fruit-bud initiation and ripening and therefore causes low yields. Furthermore, fruit that is produced is usually undersized, has poor color, and rarely tastes good because the tree hasn't been able to produce adequate sugars. With proper pruning (see below), these trees can resume a productive life and they often contribute significant beauty to the landscape.

Oversized, congested apple trees often dominate older gardens, and the question of whether they are worth restoring is often an issue confronting the owner. An oversized tree in a small garden can certainly be a problem, with it casting too much shade or its roots absorbing too much moisture and nutrients at the expense of the rest of the garden. Mature trees will never be as fruitful as young trees—most apple and pear trees are most productive for the first 8–20 years. However, they can still continue to give large, healthy crops for considerably longer if looked after properly. This means that the trees must be pruned and fertilized regularly and pests and diseases must be attended to. Old trees can also create an invaluable habitat for wildlife, and they can make attractive features with their old, gnarled trunks. Climbing plants such as roses and clematis can be trained up into them, to compensate for any lack of bloom.

If the decision is made to remove an apple tree completely, it may be worth consulting a fruit expert to discover whether the variety is rare—many old varieties have been lost and it would be tragic to lose yet another one. One method of preserving the variety would be to save a few branches and send them off to a fruit nursery to be propagated (either by grafting or budding) onto dwarf rootstocks, which can then be replanted in the garden at a more manageable size.

REMOVE DYING BRANCHES *close to their base, where they join the main framework of the tree. Use a sharp and clean pruning saw for this pruning task and protect your hands with gloves.*

THIN OVERCROWDED STEMS *growing into the center of the tree and those that are rubbing against other stems. Such crossing stems are vulnerable to damage, and this provides a potential entry point for disease.*

REMOVE WATER SHOOTS *growing from the main trunk, below the main network of branches, as early as possible. At the same time, prune out suckers and clear competing weeds around the base of the tree.*

The restoration should be done gradually and in stages over a few years (see box, above). Otherwise, making lots of large cuts and removing all the large limbs will stress the tree, causing it to overcompensate the following year by sending out an excess of branches.

That said, apple and pear trees are resilient and can deal with far more pruning than other trees. Dispense with hand pruners and use only a pruning saw. Tree restoration requires big decisions and usually big cuts. Snipping away with hand pruners will just encourage more vigorous growth to develop.

Once the leaves have fallen off the tree and you can see its framework, assess the tree from the ground, looking at the overall shape. Identify the original shape of the tree—was it supposed to be open centered or have a central leader? Which branches are making the tree look unbalanced or lose its shape? If the tree is too high for picking the fruit or for spraying, decide how to cut branches back to lower limbs. Are any of the large branches dead or diseased?

Once the main limbs have been identified, use a stepladder to get in close to the tree and begin to saw out

ONCE APPLES HAVE BEEN HARVESTED *for the season, it is important to remove any fruit remaining on the tree to prevent overwintering sites for diseases and pests. Rake leaves and collect and destroy fallen fruit from the ground below the tree as well.*

selected branches. Always cut back to another branch. Don't leave large stubs, because these will die back and can cause problems with diseases. When in the canopy of the tree it will be easier to identify crossing branches that have been rubbing against each other and causing damage to the bark. Remove these initially, as well as dead and diseased branches such as those riddled with canker. Cut out large branches in many sections, making undercuts to prevent the bark from tearing.

Over a period of several years, prune most branches lower down close to the crown of the tree. A useful rule of thumb is to remove no more than a quarter of the branches in one pruning season. Don't make the mistake of cutting back all the tips on the growth—a bit like hedge trimming—because the tree will regenerate from these cuts, making it top-heavy, which will cause shading and poor fruiting. Keep getting down from the ladder to

reassess the tree, which will look very different from the ground than from up close when you are on a ladder.

Peaches and nectarines

Move container-grown trees under cover
If this has not already been done, move container-grown trees to a protected area, such as a garage or an unheated porch, without delay.

Quinces

Carry out formative pruning
(mild-winter regions only)
Quinces bear their flowers singly at the tips of one-year-old stems and to a lesser extent on short fruiting spurs.

If you live in a mild-winter region, formative pruning can be carried out now. Aim to create a system of well-spaced branches on a clear stem, as for apples (see page 249).

The erratic growth of quinces means that you'll occasionally have to remove wayward stems as they're produced, but it is better to sacrifice an inappropriate shoot in the initial stages of training rather than trying to remedy the situation once the tree's framework is otherwise well established.

Prune established quinces *(mild-winter regions only)*
Established pruning simply consists of removing dead, diseased, and damaged growth, along with thinning out congested or unproductive stems. Remove any suckers as soon as they develop at the bottom of the trunk.

SOFT FRUIT

General

Gooseberries, red and white currants, and black currants can all be propagated by hardwood cuttings now. Prepare a site for the cuttings—either a trench lined with sharp sand in the open garden or deep pots of sandy soil, which are then placed in a cold-frame. Insert cuttings, each 8in. long, with two thirds of their length below the soil and firm them in well. Once roots form, grow plants in a partly shaded area for a year before planting them in their final position in the garden.

Gooseberries

Prune established bushes
Shorten last summer's new shoots back to one or two buds and prune back the branch leaders by one quarter.

Raspberries

Prune fall-fruiting varieties
Cut all the canes, which will have fruited, back to ground level between now and late winter. Although this pruning will eliminate a summer crop, it will encourage a much heavier fall crop. It may also reduce disease and pest problems. (To prune for both summer and fall crops, see box on page 255.)

Red and white currants

Prune established bushes
Red and white currants should be pruned in exactly the same way as gooseberries (see left).

VINE FRUIT

General

Pruning of grapes and kiwi can be done now until late winter in mild-winter regions. It is best to wait until late winter to prune in colder regions, to avoid injury from cold temperatures and drying winter winds.

FALL-FRUITING RASPBERRIES *(top) fruit on the current season's canes, so all this year's canes can be cut to ground level between now and late winter. New canes will grow in spring.*

PRUNE RED AND WHITE CURRANT SIDESHOOTS *(bottom) back to two buds in winter, to keep the plant compact and to ensure that growth is concentrated in the spurs.*

EXTENDING THE RASPBERRY SEASON

Fall raspberries bear most of their fruit on the current year's canes, but they can be forced to crop like summer varieties by careful pruning. This allows a single fall variety to yield both summer and fall crops, thereby extending the season in minimum space, and so this is a particularly useful technique for small gardens. Good fall-fruiting varieties include 'Fall Bliss', 'Fall Gold', 'Heritage', 'Caroline', 'Anne', and 'Polana.'

Instead of cutting all the canes down to the ground by late winter, remove the fruited, upper section on a few of them. Because the lower section of these canes did not bear the fruit in the previous fall, they will produce fruiting shoots in spring—much as summer varieties do. Once harvested, cut these canes back to soil level.

Grapes

Prune cordon vines *(mild-winter regions only)*

On vines that were planted last fall, cut back the leader by about one third. Shorten any lower growth back to one or two buds. On established cordons, cut the leader back to one bud above the top wire and shorten the other shoots to two buds. Thin congested spurs.

Prune Kniffen-system trained vines *(mild-winter regions only)*

Continue to replace and tie in the fruiting arms, selecting new ones that are strong and vigorous (see page 277). Select a renewal spur as close to the trunk as possible for each of the four arms of the grape vine. Remove all other growth, including any stems arising from the roots or lower portion of the trunk. Shorten the fruiting canes to about six buds for young vines and to 10–12 fruiting buds on vigorous, well-established vines.

Kiwi

Prune established plants

On kiwi vines, pruning can be quite drastic each year once a framework of branches has been established. Because they have a tendency to bleed sap if pruned in spring, it is best to prune kiwi vines while they are dormant. Remove tangled, congested branches as well as those that are weak, diseased, or dead. Select one-year-

IN MILD WINTER REGIONS, *remove unwanted branches from the trunk and main lateral branches of grapes (top), with clean, sharp hand pruners. For other regions, wait until late winter or early spring.*

TO GROW GRAPES *using the two-arm Kniffen system (above), tie the main stem to a sturdy pole to train it upward until it can support itself. Later, lateral branches will be selected as the arms.*

old shoots along the main stem that haven't fruited, retaining one of these every 10–12in. Remove the other shoots, to prevent crowding. Cut back the new shoots, to about 6in. long.

mid winter

The weather is usually at its coldest now, and it is a good idea to check tender fruit such as figs regularly to ensure that the protection you have provided is still doing its job.

If you haven't ordered your seeds yet, there is still time, but don't wait much longer or you may find that the varieties you want are no longer available. For gardeners in mild-winter regions, some crops can now be sown indoors, and a few can be sown in the garden in very mild regions. If you have leftover seeds from previous seasons, you can test their viability by placing ten seeds between wet paper towels. Keep the towels moist, and check the seeds after several days to see if they show signs of germination.

This is a great time for tackling a project such as building a cold-frame, raised bed (see page 48), or trellis. You can find plans online or at your library. Start now, and your project will be ready to use when you need it.

vegetables | GENERAL ADVICE

ALL REGIONS

Continue clearing the vegetable plot | Clear away crop debris and weeds and incorporate manure or other organic matter into the soil where appropriate. Work out your rotation plan (see box, right) so that you know where manure and lime should and should not be incorporated.

Keep off wet soil | No matter how eager you are to prepare the soil for spring, do not work on very wet soil. Trampling over it when it is sodden will destroy the soil structure. If your soil is poorly drained, work in as much organic matter as possible, to improve it, as soon as conditions allow. Consider whether constructing raised beds might be worthwhile.

Sanitize flats and pots | If you plan to reuse flats and pots for starting your seeds, be sure to wash them thoroughly, to prevent diseases. Disinfect your old containers using a solution of one part bleach to ten parts water.

MILD-WINTER REGIONS ONLY

Sow early crops indoors | Lettuce, cabbage, and broccoli can be sown indoors for early spring crops. A greenhouse or cold-frame provide an ideal environment, but a sunny window supplemented with artificial lights can give satisfactory results. Adjust lights as the plants grow, keeping them 4–6in. above the tops of plants.

Prepare for early plantings | After digging, cover areas of the soil with clear plastic where you want to make early sowings. This will keep the soil dry and help it to warm up, encouraging early plant growth. In mild regions, peas can be sown as soon as the soil can be worked.

KEEP CROPS ON THE MOVE

Moving crops to different areas of the vegetable garden is important in order to avoid the buildup of soil-borne diseases. It also helps to ensure that heavy feeders such as brassicas do not deplete the soil of nutrients. You need to plan ahead where each crop will be planted, so you know whether to add manure to the soil or not.

There are several different schemes for crop rotation, but a simple one is a three-year rotation, dividing the vegetable garden into three equal-sized beds, and grouping crops into roots, brassicas (cabbage family), and everything else. In year one, grow roots in bed one; do not add lime or manure to the soil but add a balanced fertilizer in spring. Grow brassicas in bed two, digging in manure or compost in fall and adding lime (depending on soil pH) in spring. In bed three, add balanced fertilizer in spring and grow all the other crops such as beans, peas, leafy greens, and fruiting crops. The following year, move the roots to bed two, the brassicas to bed three, and everything else to bed one; the year after that, move roots to bed three, brassicas to bed one and everything else to bed two. Your crops have now been fully rotated around the plot. Then repeat this cycle.

PARSNIPS can be harvested and stored for use throughout the winter. If there is a hard frost, the ground will freeze and they will be difficult to harvest, so make sure you have enough in storage during cold spells.

vegetables | WHAT TO DO NOW

ONION FAMILY

Leek

Sow indoors

To start a crop that will mature from late summer to fall, sow leeks in a flat from now until late winter in a heated greenhouse or on a bright windowsill supplemented with lights. Prick out the seedlings into cell packs or space them 2in. apart in a flat, and continue growing them indoors before hardening them off in a cold-frame, for planting out in spring.

Onion and shallot

Sow onions indoors

For large onions, sow seed indoors under lights, or in a heated greenhouse.

CABBAGE FAMILY

General

In mild regions, keep cutting cabbage, cauliflower, sprouting broccoli and kale, and picking Brussels sprouts.

Broccoli

Sow seed indoors

In mild-winter regions, sow broccoli indoors for transplanting into the garden after hardening off seedlings in late winter or early spring.

Cabbage

Sow seed indoors

In mild-winter regions, sow cabbage seed indoors for transplanting outdoors after hardening off seedlings.

CUT OFF EACH CABBAGE (top) close to the ground, with a sharp knife. If it is not to be used immediately, remove some of the outer leaves, then store the cabbage in a straw-lined box in a cool, dry place.

SOWING IN CELL PACKS (above) means that seedlings do not need transplanting until they have outgrown their individual cell, but you must thin them, to leave only one plant per cell.

LEGUMES

Peas

Sow outdoors

In mild-winter regions, peas can be sown outdoors in the garden as soon as the soil can be worked.

Follow the planting procedure on page 41.
Provide a trellis for vining types of peas.

ROOT AND STEM CROPS

General

In many areas, root vegetables can stay in the ground all winter. Insulating crop rows with a heavy straw or similar mulching material will help protect the roots. In colder regions, where soils are frozen through much of the winter, it is advisable to lift the majority of the crop and keep it in storage.

Potato

Choose potato varieties

Decide which potato varieties you are going to plant, so that you can order the desired tubers from a reliable source. Always purchase certified, disease-free potatoes. Characteristics to consider when selecting your varieties include disease resistance, earliness, flavor, color (both skin and flesh), kitchen use, and suitability for storage. (See Grow your own potatoes, page 272.)

LEAFY GREENS

Chicory

Continue to force plants

Keep forcing witloof chicory in boxes of compost in a warm place, for winter salads (see page 190) or braising. Ensure all light is excluded, to keep the chicons white and to reduce their bitter flavor.

Lettuce

Sow indoors or outdoors

In mild-winter regions, lettuce can be sown indoors or in a cold-frame for transplanting into the garden in late winter. Be sure to open cold frames on warm days, to allow excess heat to escape. Other options to provide extra protection from cold for growing lettuce include constructing a temporary hoop house—suspending clear

THE COLD-FRAME ADVANTAGE

Cold-frames are simple structures that can extend the garden season on both ends by protecting crops from strong winds and elevating both day and night temperatures. They are also very useful for starting early crops from seed, which will be transplanted into the garden, and for hardening off crops that were started indoors.

You can purchase a ready-made cold-frame or build one yourself. A simple cold-frame consists of a box—constructed of wood, cinder blocks, or even bales of straw—with a back that is several inches higher than the front. This angle allows rain to drain off the top. An old window makes an ideal top, although a frame covered with clear plastic or fiberglass works well too. Site your cold-frame so it faces south, to get maximum exposure to the sun. During very cold weather, you can cover the cold-frame at night with a heavy blanket for insulation. And don't forget to raise the top on warm, sunny days, to allow excess heat to escape.

IN MOST MILD- AND MID-TEMPERATE REGIONS, *lettuce and mustard that was sown in a cold frame in fall can be harvested throughout winter. Plant different types to provide variety.*

plastic or row-covering material over a frame—or simply covering plants with a floating row cover. In the mildest regions, lettuce can be sown directly in the garden.

Read the sowing instructions on the seed package, because some varieties of lettuce require light for germination and should not be covered. To harden off lettuce for transplanting, move indoor-grown seedlings to a cold-frame or other protected area and reduce water for 2–3 days prior to transplanting.

fruit | GENERAL ADVICE

Apply dormant spray | Apply dormant sprays to fruit trees and shrubs, to kill overwintering pests and diseases. Follow the directions on the label carefully and spray only when the temperature is within the appropriate range.

Fertilize fruit trees and shrubs | Apply a topdressing of a balanced fertilizer to all established fruit, as recommended by your soil test. If you haven't tested your soil, do so now so you will have results before spring.

Plant new stock | In mild-winter regions, purchase and plant dormant fruit trees and shrubs in soil that has been well prepared in advance.

Check stored fruit | Continue to make regular visits to any places where fruit has been stored. Check to be sure that the temperature is appropriate and that the environment is dry, and keep an eye out for mice. Remove rotten or diseased pieces of fruit before the rot spreads; feed them to garden birds.

SNOW COVER *is a good insulator for fruit tree roots, reducing rapid fluctuations of soil temperatures, which can cause damage. It also prevents soil from drying out over winter.*

fruit | WHAT TO DO NOW

TREE FRUIT

General

Ensure tree stakes and ties are firm and sound. Loosen ties if they are too tight around the tree trunk before they constrict growth or damage the bark. And to help insulate roots, use a generous amount of well-rotted garden compost or manure to mulch around fruit plants. Keep the mulch away from the trunk, to discourage mice from feeding on the bark.

Apples and pears

Collect shoots for grafting in spring

If you have a fruit tree that you want to propagate, whip-and-tongue grafting is a good way to do it. On a dry day, cut some shoots 9in. long from the tree you want to propagate. Store them in a plastic bag in the bottom of a refrigerator, to ensure they remain dormant.

Buy a suitable rootstock from a specialist fruit nursery and plant this out now, so it is ready to be grafted with the stored grafting shoots in spring.

COLLECT GRAFTING SHOOTS *from young and healthy hardwood stems that you wish to propagate by whip-and-tongue grafting (see page 77). Bundle them together and then store until spring.*

REMOVE AFFECTED BRANCHES *as soon as cankers are observed, to prevent disease spread. Cankers show as depresssions and cracks within the branches on apple and pear trees..*

Prune out canker

Continue to prune out disease cankers from apple and pear trees, making the cut well below the canker. Destroy all affected wood. Disinfect pruning tools after each cut, to avoid spreading the disease.

Peaches and nectarines

Control peach leaf curl

If your trees suffered from peach leaf curl last year, apply a suitable dormant fungicide, such as lime-sulfur, now or in late winter, before buds swell. As with all pesticides, follow the label instructions carefully.

SOFT FRUIT

General

In mild regions, unless there are freezing conditions, you can prune currants and gooseberries now if they were not already pruned in early winter; if there is a severe cold spell, wait until the weather is a bit warmer.

In mid-temperate and cold-winter regions, delay pruning until late winter or early spring, to avoid injury from cold temperatures and drying winds.

Use some of the prunings from currants and gooseberries to increase your stock by hardwood cuttings. Make each cutting 10in. long, cutting just below a bud at the base of the stem and just above a bud at the top.

Insert the cuttings in a trench or in large pot of sandy soil and leave until next fall, when they should have rooted.

Raspberries

Prune canes

If this has not already been done, cut out all canes that have fruited. Remove all canes from fall-fruiting varieties down to ground level, while on summer-fruiting varieties prune out only those canes that bore fruit last summer; these can be identified because they are a darker brown than the new canes.

Strawberries

Sow alpine strawberries

Start off seed of alpine strawberries in pots or flats of moist seed starter mix indoors under lights or in a heated greenhouse. Ideally, the temperature should be kept at 60–70°F. Seeds often take 3–4 weeks to germinate.

When they have several leaves, transplant the seedlings into individual pots or set them 3in. apart in a deep flat. They can be planted outdoors after all danger of frost has passed and the weather has settled. The small, sweet, aromatic fruits will be produced in summer; they are not as juicy as large-fruited strawberries but have a very special flavor of their own.

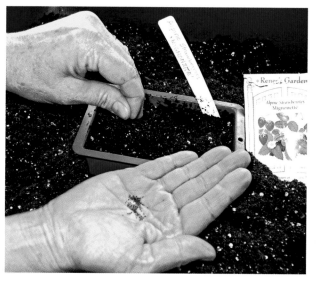

SOW ALPINE STRAWBERRY SEEDS *indoors now for a delicious summer crop. Keep the growing mix moist and have patience—the seeds may take 3–4 weeks to germinate.*

late winter

No matter how bad the weather, there is still a distinct note of optimism this month: the worst of the winter is behind you, and spring is right around the corner. Yet sometimes the hardest thing to do at this time of year is to control your impatience. After a long winter it seems as though spring may never arrive, but the shortest day is long past, and the lighter evenings are now really noticeable.

It is a mistake to do too much too early, however, because winter can still have a few unpleasant tricks in store. Cold spells this season are common, sometimes with the temperature not rising above freezing for days at a time. But there may yet be vegetables to harvest from the garden, with winter brassicas and roots shrugging off the harsh weather. You should still be enjoying your stored harvests, too, though it pays to use these up quickly before they deteriorate too much.

vegetables | GENERAL ADVICE

ALL REGIONS

Order seeds | If you haven't done so already, order your vegetable seeds now.

Check supplies | Be sure you have all the supplies and tools you need, including pots, flats, seed starter mix, lights, and heat mats, if you are planning to start your plants indoors.

Turn under cover crops | As soon as weather and soil conditions allow, cut cover crops with a string trimmer, mower, or hand pruners. Wait a week or so, then work their remains into the soil.

MID-TEMPERATE REGIONS ONLY

Sow early crops indoors | Start broccoli, cabbage, Brussels sprouts, and leeks indoors so they are ready for transplanting to the garden in spring.

MILD-WINTER REGIONS ONLY

Sow tender crops indoors | Start eggplants and peppers indoors under lights, so they are ready to transplant outdoors when the weather warms.

Transplant brassicas | In most mild regions, broccoli, cabbage, and other brassica crops that were started indoors can now be transplanted into the garden, after they have been gradually hardened off.

Sow seed outdoors | Several cool-season vegetables can be sown directly into the garden for early crops including: carrots, lettuce, turnips, radish, spinach, and peas.

PURPLE CAULIFLOWER *and other brassica crops can be transplanted to the garden in mild regions, after they have been hardened off.*

vegetables | WHAT TO DO NOW

Leek

Continue harvesting

Keep on pulling leeks, making sure you use them up before the plants begin to grow again in spring. Once they resume growth they produce a flower stem, which forms a firm, dense core in the center of the leek; these are still edible, but their quality is not as good.

Onion and shallot

Plant shallots

In mild-winter regions, plant shallots in well-drained soil, setting the bulbs 9in. apart in rows 12in. apart, with their stem side uppermost.

Plant onions

In mild-winter regions, onion sets or plants can be planted, spacing the sets or plants 3–4in. apart in rows 10–12in. apart. Be sure to work plenty of well-composted organic material into the soil before planting.

Thin overwintered onions

Onions that were sown in late summer can be thinned to their final spacing, 3–4in. apart, or slightly wider if you want to encourage larger bulbs.

CABBAGE FAMILY

Broccoli

Sow seed indoors

In mid-temperate regions, sow broccoli indoors or in a coldframe for transplanting into the garden from early to mid spring. 'Blue Wind', 'Nutri-Bud', and 'Flash' are some early season varieties.

LEEKS SHOULD BE HARVESTED (top) *before they start to bolt in the warmer spring weather, when they have developed a solid flowering stem in the center of the plant.*

PURPLE-SPROUTING BROCCOLI (above) *produces many small florets rather than one large central head. Green-sprouting varieties are also available. Frequent cutting will encourage the production of more florets.*

Transplant to the garden

In mild-winter regions, move broccoli plants that were started indoors or in cold-frames to the garden, when they are about 4–6in. tall and after they have been thoroughly hardened off. Space plants 18–24in. apart in the row and allow 2ft. between rows. Water the plants thoroughly with a diluted liquid fertilizer. Use floating row covers to prevent pest damage.

Brussels sprouts

Sow seed indoors

In mid-temperate regions, sow Brussels sprouts indoors now, for a summer harvest.

In many mild-winter and mid-temperate locations, however, Brussels sprouts grow better when planted in summer for fall harvest, because the quality of sprouts improves as the weather cools.

Cabbage

Sow summer varieties

In mid-temperate regions, sow cabbage indoors in flats or cell packs or in cold-frames for later transplanting into the garden in spring. Good early varieties include 'Farao', 'Invento', and 'Red Express'.

Transplant to the garden

In mild-winter regions, move cabbage plants from indoors or cold-frames to the garden. Space plants 12–18in. apart, depending on the variety.

LEGUMES

Peas

Sow outdoors

In mild-winter regions, continue to sow peas directly in the garden where they will grow. For variety, include garden peas (also called English peas) such as 'Strike' (an early variety), 'Feisty', or 'Caselode'; snap peas such as 'Sugar Ann' or 'Super Sugar Snap'; and snow peas such as 'Snow Sweet' and 'Oregon Giant'. Garden peas are shelled before eating, both snap peas and snow peas are edible-podded types.

ROOT AND STEM CROPS

Beet

Sow outdoors

In mild-winter regions, make the first sowing of beet in the garden as soon as the soil can be worked. Be warned, however—the seed does not germinate well at temperatures below 45°F.

Sow beet seed 1in. deep in rows 12in. apart, spacing seeds about a thumb's width apart. The large, corky-textured seed is easy to handle but can be slow to germinate (see box, below). When they are large enough to handle, thin seedlings if necessary to 2–3in. apart. For a steady supply of young beets, make small successive plantings at three-week intervals.

BEET SEED

For many beet varieties, each corky 'seed' is in fact a cluster of seeds, which produces several seedlings. These seedlings will need thinning shortly after germination if the remaining seedlings are to have room to develop into healthy plants. However, modern varieties such as 'Alvro Mono' and 'Moneta' are 'monogerm,' which means that only one seedling is produced, saving the trouble of thinning them out so early in the growing process.

Carrot

Sow an early crop

In mild-winter regions, for an early carrot crop sow carrots in the garden where they will grow as soon as the soil can be worked. In mid-temperate regions, sow carrots in a cold-frame or unheated greenhouse, to harvest during late spring.

Parsnips

Continue harvesting

Keep lifting parsnips that have been left in the ground. Once they start into growth again in early spring, their roots become flabby and unappetizing, so make sure you have used the crop before this happens.

Potato

Start to sprout seed potatoes

Buy certified seed potatoes that are free from viruses. Start them into growth by sprouting, or 'chitting', them 4–6 weeks before planting. Set the tubers on end, in egg cartons or seed flats, and place in good light in a cool room. Usually most of the eyes are at one end of the tuber (known as the rose end), and this end should be exposed to light. The advantage of chitting potato tubers is that it gets them into early growth, ready for the season ahead; each tuber will develop sturdy, green shoots, to give them a head start when planted out.

Plant seed potatoes

In mild-winter regions, plant potatoes in the garden. Sprout the tubers first (see left) or plant them without chitting, either whole or cut in pieces, each with 2–3 eyes (buds). Plant them in loose, well-drained soil, spacing them 12in. apart in rows 24–30in. apart.

Mound soil around plants

When the first shoots emerge from your newly planted potatoes, use a hoe to mound soil up and over them, to produce a rounded ridge. Be careful to avoid breaking the fragile shoots.

Radish

Sow seed outdoors

In mild-winter regions, sow early varieties directly in the garden as soon as the soil can be worked. Sow seed thinly and cover the seed with ½in. of soil. Thin seedlings to at least 1in. apart as soon as they can be easily handled.

TAKE CARE WHEN DIGGING UP PARSNIPS *as canker can develop in any roots damaged when adjacent ones are dug up. Some varieties such as 'Lancer', 'Javelin', and 'Gladiator' have good resistance to canker.*

WHEN CHITTING POTATOES, *it can take several weeks for them to sprout, after which they will be ready for planting. When planting chitted potatoes, take care not to damage any of the delicate, new shoots.*

RADISH VARIETIES

Radishes are an easy-to-grow, cool-season crop that contributes zesty flavor to salads and raw vegetable plates. Daikon radishes (also called Oriental radishes) make flavorful additions to stir-fries. Radishes can be sown directly in the garden in spring or fall (and, in mild regions, late winter); depending on the variety, they are ready to harvest in as few as 21 days. Their rapid growth makes them useful for marking rows of slower-to-germinate crops such as parsnip and carrot. They are also easy to fit into the spaces between slower-growing plants such as Brussels sprouts or cabbage. The radishes can be harvested before the slower-growing plants need the additional space.

Many radish varieties are available with different shapes (from round to elongated), sizes, colors, and flavors. Popular selections include: 'Amethyst' (above right), which sports bright purple skin and white flesh; 'Ping Pong', which produces uniform, round, all-white roots; 'D'Avignon' (right), an elongated type with 3–4in. red roots with white tips; and 'Nero Tondo', a black-skinned selection that has crisp, white flesh with a very spicy-hot flavor.

THIN TURNIP SEEDLINGS *as they develop, to prevent overcrowding. It is often easiest to cut rather than pull the surplus seedlings so that remaining seedlings are not disturbed.*

Turnip

Start sowing now

In mild-winter regions, make the first sowing now, as soon as the soil can be worked. As with most root crops, turnips do not transplant well and must be sown outdoors directly where they are to grow.

Sow thinly in ½in. deep furrows, spacing rows 9–12in. apart. Thin the emerging seedlings in stages until the plants are 4–8in. apart. If necessary, use floating row covers to protect the rows from frost. It is best to sow short rows at intervals of 2–3 weeks, so that gluts are avoided and you can continually harvest the emerging young plants while the roots are most tender.

LEAFY GREENS

Lettuce

Sow seed indoors

In mid-temperate regions, sow lettuce seed indoors for transplanting to the garden in spring.

Sow or plant outdooors

In mild-winter regions, lettuce can be sown directly in the garden. If you started lettuce indoors last month, plants should be ready to transplant into the garden as soon as they have been hardened off. Space plants (or thin seedlings) 4–12in. apart, depending on the variety.

Spinach

Sow seed outdoors

In mild areas with well-drained soil, sow spinach directly in the garden. Sow seed thinly in ½in. furrows in rows 12in. apart.

FRUITING CROPS AND CORN

General

In mild-winter regions, sow eggplant, peppers, and tomatoes indoors for transplanting outside after all danger of frost has passed and the soil has warmed. Use heat mats beneath flats, to hasten germination. Once seedlings develop a true set of leaves, transplant them to individual pots or, if they were sown in cell packs, thin them leaving one seedling per cell.

In mid-temperate regions, you can sow eggplant but should wait another month before you start to sow peppers and tomatoes.

PERENNIAL VEGETABLES

Asparagus

Sow seed indoors

Although they take longer to begin cropping, asparagus can be grown from seed. Soak the seed overnight, and then sow ½in. deep into 3in. pots of seed starter mix. Keep the soil moist. 'Martha Washington' and 'Mary Washington' are long-established varieties that can be grown from seed; 'Jersey Supreme' and 'Jersey Knight' are newer, all-male hybrids (see box, right).

Prepare new beds

Turn the soil in new beds, adding well-rotted manure

ONCE TOMATO SEEDLINGS EMERGE, *move the container to a warm, well-lit spot and let the seedlings grow. Pot them up individually into 3in. pots as soon as they are large enough to handle.*

or compost. If your soil is heavy, consider making a raised bed (see page 48).

Plant crowns outdoors

In mild-winter regions, plant crowns outdoors in well-prepared beds as soon as the soil can be worked.

Globe artichoke

Sow seed indoors

In mild-winter and mid-temperate regions, sow globe artichoke seeds now. Good varieties include 'Tempo', 'Imperial Star', and 'Green Globe'.

MALE AND FEMALE ASPARAGUS

Asparagus produces male and female flowers on different plants. Male plants are more desirable: they have thicker spears, which tend to emerge earlier in the spring, and the plants are more productive and often longer lived. Another advantage of male asparagus plants is that they do not produce berries (as female plants do); these are a nuisance when they self-seed.

It is therefore a good idea always to look for all-male plants when buying asparagus crowns.

| Grow your own potatoes

Potatoes are one of our staple foods. Whether eaten with butter and parsley in spring, as salad in summer, roasted or mashed for a fall feast, or cooked as a hearty winter soup, few days go by without potatoes appearing on our plates in one form or another.

While they are readily available, and usually inexpensive to buy, it is still worthwhile growing your own. The flavor of the bland supermarket potato bears little resemblance to the wonderfully rich taste of potatoes freshly dug from the soil. Growing your own allows you to choose exactly the variety you want and to try out unusual shapes and colors to liven up the dinner table. And there is always something truly exciting about harvesting the potato crop, uncovering the cache of hidden treasures nestled beneath the soil.

WHEN HARVESTING POTATOES *(above) dig very carefully into the surrounding soil, to avoid spearing the tubers with your garden fork.*

Different varieties of potato are often recommended for different uses. Catalogs from companies selling seed potatoes will tell you whether each variety is good when mashed or roasted or made into French fries or potato salad; some varieties are good all-rounders. If you are interested in something a little out of the ordinary, try small, flavorful 'fingerlings,' or varieties with deep blue or red flesh and skins. When selecting varieties, it's best to inquire with your local extension service or garden center expert about which perform best in your locale. Don't use potatoes from the grocery store—these may or may not be suitable for growing in your area, and they may have been sprayed with a growth inhibitor to prevent sprouting.

About eight weeks after planting, you can begin to dig the first tasty 'new potatoes.' Continue to harvest as needed, being careful to avoid damaging the plant. Dig the entire crop after the tops die, but before frost.

Recommended varieties

'Huckleberry'
An excellent potato for baking, steaming, or for summer salads. It has a bright, berry red skin and light, rosy flesh.

'Russian Banana'
A fingerling type with a banana shape, yellow-tan skin, and pale yellow flesh. Delicious flavor. Its waxy texture maintains its shape when boiled. Good for storage.

'Kennebec'
This high-yielding potato bears a late crop of large, buff-skinned, white-fleshed tubers. 'Kennebec' is a good, all-purpose variety that also stores very well.

'Rose Finn Apple'
An excellent salad potato with pink-beige skin and waxy, yellow flesh. This fingerling variety is also good for roasting, boiling, and grilling.

'Red Pontiac'
A widely adapted, productive, late-season variety with a thin, red skin and white flesh. It is an all-purpose potato, and it stores very well.

'Dark Red Norland'
An early, heavy-cropping variety with a dark red skin, pure white flesh, and good flavor. Use 'Dark Red Norland' for boiling and roasting.

'Yukon Gold'
A thin-skinned, early variety that produces small- to medium-sized tubers that pack great flavor. The flesh is yellow and very moist. 'Yukon Gold' is very tasty as a new potato.

'Charlotte'
A long, oval variety producing yellow-skinned, waxy tubers with creamy yellow flesh. 'Charlotte' is excellent when eaten hot as well as when used cold in salads.

'Red Gold'
An all-purpose variety with a nutty flavor. Its skin is tan with raspberry-pink eyes, and its flesh is pale yellow. Is good mashed, baked, roasted, or fried. Excellent as a new potato.

fruit | GENERAL ADVICE

Prune fruit trees | Prune before the trees start growth in spring, beginning with the latest blooming trees and finishing with the earliest bloomers.

Plant bareroot trees | Get all bareroot fruit trees planted as soon as possible now.

Fertilize fruit | Using the rates and type recommended by your soil test, apply a topdressing of fertilizer to all fruit if this was not done in mid winter.

Check recently planted fruit | Fruit trees and bushes that have been recently planted may have been lifted by frosts, which cause the soil to expand. Tread round the root area to firm them into place again. Also check that all ties are secure and not rubbing.

FRUITING SPURS OR FRUITING TIPS?

Successful fruit pruning depends on having a basic understanding of a plant's physiology. Fruit trees—particularly apples—fall into two categories as to how they produce their flowers and therefore, after pollination, their fruit: these are spur bearers and tip bearers. Most fruit trees form both types of growth but are usually prone to producing more of one type than the other. Spur bearers, which are the most common, bear their fruit on short, stumpy shoots (the spurs), which are usually more than two years old. The fruit of the tip bearers develops on shoots that were formed in the previous season. Trees that are mainly tip bearing in habit, such as 'Orin', are unsuitable for growing as restricted forms (see page 60).

VISUAL IDENTIFICATION

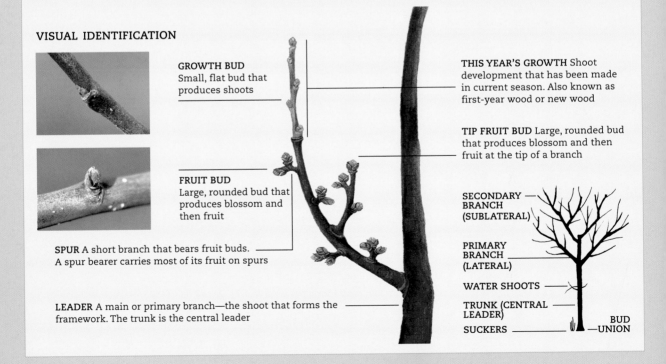

GROWTH BUD Small, flat bud that produces shoots

THIS YEAR'S GROWTH Shoot development that has been made in current season. Also known as first-year wood or new wood

TIP FRUIT BUD Large, rounded bud that produces blossom and then fruit at the tip of a branch

FRUIT BUD Large, rounded bud that produces blossom and then fruit

SECONDARY BRANCH (SUBLATERAL)

PRIMARY BRANCH (LATERAL)

SPUR A short branch that bears fruit buds. A spur bearer carries most of its fruit on spurs

WATER SHOOTS

TRUNK (CENTRAL LEADER)

LEADER A main or primary branch—the shoot that forms the framework. The trunk is the central leader

SUCKERS

BUD UNION

fruit | WHAT TO DO NOW

TREE FRUIT

General

In mild regions, dormant pruning can be done throughout winter, but in cold-winter and mid-temperate regions it is safest to wait to prune until late winter or early spring. This timing helps prevent cold-winter injury. Follow the pruning procedures provided on page 249. Remember that dormant pruning can stimulate excessive vegetative growth, so don't prune too heavily— particularly on healthy, established trees.

Most fruit trees will benefit from feeding at this time, so nutrients will be available as growth begins in spring. It is always best first to take a soil test, so that you can provide the best balance of nutrients for your specific soil and adjust the pH if necessary.

If you haven't tested your soil and think your trees are in need of feeding, a general rule of thumb is to apply ¾–1lb. of 10–10–10 per year of tree age. However, if fireblight has been a problem on pears or apples, do not apply nitrogen. Broadcast the fertilizer beneath the tree (staying well clear of the trunk) and 2–3ft. beyond the drip line. It is often helpful to apply half the fertilizer now, and half after the fruit sets, especially if your soil is sandy. And be sure to test your soil for next year.

FRUIT TREES *can be pruned from now until buds begin to swell in early spring in all regions. Remember, however, that dormant pruning stimulates vegetative growth, often at the expense of flowers and fruit.*

Apples and pears

Rejuvenate neglected trees
In mid-temperate and cold-winter regions, old, neglected trees can be restored by pruning now or in early spring. The process should be done gradually, over a few years. Follow the procedure on page 251.

Apricots

Feed trees
Apricots benefit from a topdressing of a balanced fertilizer at this time of year, followed by mulching around the rooting area with well-rotted farmyard manure or garden compost.

Protect blossoms from frost
Apricots flower very early, and their flowers may need protection against frost if their blossoms are to survive and set a good crop. Where practical, a double layer of row-covering material or a sheet spread over the tree, supported so that it does not touch the flowers, will provide some protection. Remove this during the day in mild weather, so that insects can access the flowers to pollinate them.

Figs

Repot container-grown plants

Container-grown figs usually need repotting every other year. Turn the tree carefully out of its pot and crumble away loose soil from around its rootball. Trim back very thick roots with hand pruners.

Repot with fresh soil-based potting mix, either into a pot one size larger than previously, or in the same size pot. This job must be done while the tree is dormant.

Peaches and nectarines

Protect blossoms from frost

Cover the blossoms of peaches and nectarines with a sheet or row-covering material where practical, so they are protected against frost. Remove it during the daytime in mild weather.

Spray against peach leaf curl

If peach leaf curl was a problem on your trees last year, and you applied a preventative fungicide in fall, you may benefit from a second application now, particularly if the winter was long and wet. Your extension service can recommend an appropriate fungicide. Follow the label directions carefully.

SOFT FRUIT

General

Complete the pruning of blackberries, black currants, gooseberries, red and white currants, and raspberries. Remove and destroy the pruned wood, to reduce the spread of diseases.

Hand weed around black currants, gooseberries, and red and white currants. Feed with a balanced fertilizer and mulch with well-rotted manure or compost, but keep it away from the crown of the plant.

Black currants

Weed bushes carefully

Hand weed around the base of black currant bushes. Avoid hoeing as the blade might cut through new shoots developing at the base of the plants.

Blueberries

Prune plants

Keep established plants productive by taking out a portion of the older wood; cut out two or three of the oldest stems to their base. At the same time, tip back vigorous, new shoots to a plump, healthy bud, to encourage side branching.

Take hardwood cuttings

Use prunings of one-year-old wood as hardwood cuttings. Cut them into 8in. lengths and insert into a trench of moisture-retentive but well-drained, acidic soil so that only the top 3in. is above ground.

Gooseberries

Feed with a balanced fertilizer

Apply a balanced fertilizer around the base of gooseberry bushes. Avoid feeding gooseberries with too much nitrogen, as this can encourage wispy, sappy growth, which is prone to gooseberry mildew.

Raspberries

Prune back canes

Tip back summer-fruiting raspberry canes to 6in. above their top support wire.

Strawberries

Plant strawberries in prepared beds

In mild-winter regions, strawberries can be planted now, but, in other regions, planting should wait another month or two. Beds should be weed free and the soil fortified with generous amounts of manure. Dig holes for each plant, spacing June-bearing varieties 18in. apart and everbearing ones 12in. apart in rows spaced 30in. apart.

Take particular care to spread out the roots and set the plants so that their crown rests right on the soil surface; plants set too deeply or too shallowly may not survive. Firm soil around the roots and water well.

Order plants

In mid-temperate and cold-winter regions, order plants for setting out in early to mid spring—if you haven't done so already.

PRUNING A KIWI PLANT

SHORTEN WELL-PLACED NEW SHOOTS *to 5–6in., to encourage new spurs and fruit production.*

THIN OUT SOME OF THE OLDER BRANCHES. *Removing congested growth will encourage air circulation and more productive growth.*

VINE FRUIT

Grapes

Plant new vines

Plant bareroot vines as soon as the soil can be worked. (In cold-winter regions, you will have to wait until early spring.) Do not allow the roots to dry out prior to planting. If you must delay planting, protect the roots by heeling them in with moist, loose soil until you are ready to plant the grape vine.

Dig a hole that will accommodate the roots without crowding and incorporate a generous amount of well-rotted manure, compost, or sawdust into the soil. Loosen the soil in the bottom of the hole with a garden fork. Examine the roots; use hand pruners to remove any that are broken and to trim very long roots. Prune the vine back to two buds.

Set the roots in the hole, spreading them out evenly, then backfill with the amended soil. Be sure that the vine is set at the same depth it was growing previously, as indicated by a dark line on the stem. Water thoroughly.

Provide support to new vines

Grapes require sturdy supports, so if you have not constructed support posts and wires for new vines, do so now, before roots begin to grow.

Prune established vines

On established grape vines, prune vines following the procedures on page 255.

Kiwi

Feed plants

Apply a topdressing of high-potassium fertilizer now and follow it up with a more balanced feed in early spring.

Prune established vines

If not already done, prune established kiwi vines now. If pruned too late, kiwis have a tendency to bleed. Remove weak or diseased branches, thin congested growth to encourage air circulation, and shorten fruiting stems to 5–6in., to encourage fruit production.

TRAINING GRAPES: THE FOUR-ARM KNIFFEN SYSTEM

The Kniffen system is a popular way to train grapes on a trellis. Secure parallel wires, at 36in. and 60in. above the ground, between two sturdy posts set 20ft. apart along the row. The year after planting, as buds begin to grow, select the strongest shoot from each vine; remove the others. Train the selected shoot upwards on a stake. When it reaches the first wire, choose two lateral branches and secure them to the wires with twine. When the main stem reaches the second wire, select and tie in two more lateral branches. These four laterals form the arms of the vine. Remove other laterals and cut back the main stem a few inches above the top wire.

| Vegetable sowing and harvesting charts

The following charts provide general information about planting and harvesting times for each of the three regions covered in this book: cold winter, mid temperate, and mild winter. Even within each region there is considerable variation in climate, as well as changing weather conditions from year to year, so the actual planting times will vary to some extent. Many local or state cooperative extension services provide planting dates calculated for precise locations within their region. Harvest times will also differ somewhat, depending on weather conditions and varieties. Within each region, crops have been listed in alphabetical order.

COLD-WINTER REGIONS

		EarlySpr	MidSpr	LateSpr	EarlySu	MidSu	LateSu	EarlyA	MidA	LateA	EarlyW	MidW	LateW
Asparagus	Plant:		•										
	Harvest:			•	•								
Beet	Sow:		•	•	•	•							
	Harvest:				•	•	•	•					
Broccoli	Sow:	•			•								
	Plant:		•	•									
	Harvest:				•	•	•	•	•				
Brussels sprouts	Sow:	•	•	•	•								
	Plant:			•									
	Harvest:					•	•	•	•				
Cabbage	Sow:	•	•		•								
	Plant:		•	•		•							
	Harvest:					•	•	•	•	•			
Carrot	Sow:		•	•	•	•							
	Harvest:				•	•	•	•					
Cauliflower	Sow:	•			•								
	Plant:		•	•		•							
	Harvest:				•				•	•			
Celeriac	Sow:	•											
	Plant:			•									
	Harvest:						•		•	•			
Chard	Sow:		•	•	•	•							
	Harvest:				•	•	•	•					
Chicory	Sow:				•	•							
	Harvest:							•					
Corn	Sow:			•	•								
	Harvest:					•	•						
Cucumber	Sow:			•	•	•							
	Plant:				•								
	Harvest:					•	•	•					
Eggplant	Sow:	•		•									
	Plant:				•	•							
	Harvest:					•	•	•					
Fava beans	Sow:		•										
	Harvest:				•	•							
Fennel	Sow:		•	•									
	Plant:			•	•								
	Harvest:						•	•					
Garlic	Plant:							•	•				
	Harvest:					•	•						
Globe artichoke not recommended													
Kale	Sow:		•	•	•	•							
	Harvest:			•	•	•	•	•	•	•			

		EarlySpr	MidSpr	LateSpr	EarlySu	MidSu	LateSu	EarlyA	MidA	LateA	EarlyW	MidW	LateW
Kohlrabi	Sow:		•	•			•	•					
	Harvest:			•	•			•	•	•			
Leek	Sow:	•	•										
	Plant:			•									
	Harvest:					•	•	•	•	•	•		
Lettuce	Sow:	•	•	•			•						•
	Plant:		•	•	•								
	Harvest:			•	•	•	•	•	•				
Lima beans	Sow:			•									
	Harvest:					•	•						
Melons	Sow:		•	•	•								
	Plant:			•	•								
	Harvest:					•	•	•					
Mustard	Sow:		•			•							
	Harvest:			•			•	•	•	•			
Okra	Sow:		•	•									
	Plant:			•	•								
	Harvest:					•	•						
Onion and shallot	Sow:	•	•	•			•						•
	Plant sets:		•	•									
	Plant seddlings:			•									
	Harvest:					•	•	•	•				
Parsnip	Sow:		•										
	Harvest:					•	•	•	•	•			
Peas	Sow:		•	•			•						
	Harvest:			•	•	•			•				
Peppers	Sow:	•	•										
	Plant:			•	•								
	Harvest:					•	•	•					
Potato	Chit:	•											
	Plant:		•	•									
	Harvest:					•	•	•	•				
Radish	Sow:		•	•	•		•	•					
	Harvest:		•	•	•	•		•	•				
Rhubarb (perennial)	Sow:		•										
	Harvest:			•	•								
Rutabaga	Sow:				•	•							
	Harvest:								•	•	•		
Snap beans	Sow:			•	•	•							
	Harvest:					•	•	•					
Spinach	Sow:		•	•	•	•	•						
	Harvest:			•	•		•	•	•				
Summer squash	Sow:			•	•	•							
	Harvest:					•	•	•					
Sweet potato	Transplant slips:			•	•								
	Harvest:								•				
Tomato	Sow:	•	•										
	Plant:			•	•								
	Harvest:					•	•	•					
Turnip	Sow:		•	•	•	•							
	Harvest:			•	•	•	•		•				
Winter squash and pumpkin	Sow:		•	•	•								
	Harvest:						•	•	•				

MID-TEMPERATE REGIONS

		EarlySpr	MidSpr	LateSpr	EarlySu	MidSu	LateSu	EarlyA	MidA	LateA	EarlyW	MidW	LateW
Asparagus	Plant:	•	•										
	Harvest:		•	•									
Beet	Sow:		•	•	•	•							
	Harvest:				•	•	•	•	•				
Broccoli	Sow:	•	•			•	•						•
	Plant:	•	•				•						
	Harvest:			•	•			•	•	•			
Brussels sprouts	Sow:	•				•							•
	Plant:	•	•			•	•						
	Harvest:				•	•	•		•	•	•		
Cabbage	Sow:	•	•			•	•						•
	Plant:	•	•										
	Harvest:			•	•			•	•	•	•		
Carrot	Sow:		•	•	•	•							
	Harvest:					•	•	•	•	•	•		
Cauliflower	Sow:	•				•							
	Plant:		•				•						
	Harvest:			•	•			•	•	•			
Celeriac	Sow:	•			•								•
	Plant:		•	•									
	Harvest:								•	•	•	•	
Chard	Sow:		•	•	•	•							
	Harvest:				•	•	•	•	•	•	•		
Chicory	Sow:			•	•	•							
	Harvest:							•	•	•			
Corn	Sow:			•	•								
	Harvest:					•	•						
Cucumber	Sow:		•	•	•								
	Plant:			•									
	Harvest:				•	•	•	•					
Eggplant	Sow:	•											•
	Plant:			•	•								
	Harvest:					•	•	•	•				
Fava beans	Sow:	•											
	Harvest:			•	•								
Fennel	Sow:	•	•	•	•	•							
	Plant:			•									
	Harvest:				•	•	•	•	•				
Garlic	Plant:								•	•	•		
	Harvest:				•	•	•						
Globe artichoke (grown as an annual)	Sow:											•	•
	Plant:			•									
	Harvest:					•		•	•				
Kale	Sow:		•			•	•	•					
	Harvest:			•	•				•	•	•	•	
Kohlrabi	Sow:		•			•	•						
	Harvest:				•					•	•		
Leek	Sow:	•	•									•	•
	Plant:		•	•									
	Harvest:						•	•	•	•	•		
Lettuce	Sow:	•	•	•		•							•
	Plant:	•	•										
	Harvest:			•	•			•	•				

		EarlySpr	MidSpr	LateSpr	EarlySu	MidSu	LateSu	EarlyA	MidA	LateA	EarlyW	MidW	LateW
Lima beans	Sow:			•	•								
	Harvest:					•	•	•					
Melons	Sow:		+	•									
	Plant:			•	•								
	Harvest:					•	•	•					
Mustard	Sow:	•	•				•						
	Harvest:			•	•			•	•	•	•		
Okra	Sow:	•		•	•								
	Plant:			•	•								
	Harvest:					•	•	•					
Onion and shallot	Sow:	•	•				•						•
	Plant sets:	•							•				
	Plant seedlings:		•	•									
	Harvest:					•	•	•	•				
Parsnip	Sow:		•	•									
	Harvest:								•	•	•	•	•
Peas	Sow:	•	•			•	•						
	Harvest:			•	•			•	•				
Peppers	Sow:	•	•										
	Plant:			•									
	Harvest:					•	•	•	•				
Potato	Chit:												•
	Plant:		•	•		•	•						
	Harvest:					•	•	•	•	•			
Radish	Sow:	•	•	•		•	•	•					
	Harvest:		•	•	•		•	•	•	•	•		
Rhubarb	Plant:	•	•										
	Harvest:		•	•									
Rutabaga	Sow:			•	•	•	•						
	Harvest:							•	•	•	•	•	
Snap beans	Sow:			•	•	•							
	Harvest:				•	•	•	•					
Spinach	Sow:	•	•				•	•	•	•			
	Harvest:		•	•	•			•	•	•			
Summer squash	Sow:		•	•	•	•							
	Harvest:				•	•	•	•					
Sweet potato	Transplant slips:			•	•								
	Harvest:							•	•				
Tomato	Sow:	•	•										
	Plant:			•	•								
	Harvest:					•	•	•	•				
Turnip	Sow:	•	•	•		•	•						
	Harvest:		•	•	•			•	•	•			
Winter squash and pumpkin	Sow:		•	•	•								
	Harvest:						•	•	•				

MILD-WINTER REGIONS

		EarlySpr	MidSpr	LateSpr	EarlySu	MidSu	LateSu	EarlyA	MidA	LateA	EarlyW	MidW	LateW
Asparagus	Plant:	•									•	•	•
	Harvest:		•	•									
Beet	Sow:						•	•	•				
	Harvest:	•							•	•	•	•	•
Broccoli	Sow:					•	•	•				•	
	Plant:								•				•
	Harvest:	•	•						•	•	•	•	
Brussels sprouts	Sow:					•	•	•				•	
	Plant:								•	•			
	Harvest:	•	•						•	•	•	•	
Cabbage	Sow:					•	•					•	•
	Plant:	•											
	Harvest:	•	•	•				•	•	•	•	•	
Carrot	Sow:	•	•	•		•	•	•	•				•
	Harvest:			•				•	•	•		•	•
Cauliflower	Sow:					•	•	•				•	•
	Plant:												
	Harvest:	•	•					•	•	•	•	•	
Celeriac	Sow:	•							•				
	Plant:		•	•									
	Harvest:	•	•						•	•	•	•	•
Chard	Sow:	•	•	•			•	•	•				•
	Harvest:		•	•	•	•			•	•		•	
Chicory	Sow:	•	•	•			•	•					
	Harvest:												
Corn	Sow:		•	•	•								
	Harvest:				•	•	•	•					
Cucumber	Sow:	•	•	•	•	•							
	Plant:		•										
	Harvest:			•	•	•	•	•					
Eggplant	Sow:	•											•
	Plant:		•	•	•	•							
	Harvest:				•	•	•		•				
Fava beans	Sow:	•							•	•			•
	Harvest:	•	•										
Fennel	Sow:	•	•										
	Plant:		•										
	Harvest:				•	•	•	•					
Garlic	Plant:								•	•	•		
	Harvest:		•	•	•								
Globe artichoke	Sow:											•	•
	Plant:	•											
	Harvest:					•							
Kale	Sow:					•	•	•					
	Harvest:							•	•	•	•	•	•
Kohlrabi	Sow:	•				•	•						
	Harvest:		•	•				•	•	•			
Leek	Sow:	•	•					•				•	•
	Plant:	•							•	•	•	•	
	Harvest:	•							•	•	•		•
Lettuce	Sow:	•						•	•			•	•
	Plant:	•											•
	Harvest:	•	•						•	•	•		•

		EarlySpr	MidSpr	LateSpr	EarlySu	MidSu	LateSu	EarlyA	MidA	LateA	EarlyW	MidW	LateW
Lima beans	Sow:		•	•	•								
	Harvest:				•	•	•	•	•				
Melons	Sow:	•	•	•									
	Plant:		•										
	Harvest:				•	•	•	•					
Mustard	Sow:	•					•	•					•
	Harvest:	•	•					•	•	•	•	•	•
Okra	Sow:	•	•	•	•								
	Plant:		•										
	Harvest:				•	•	•	•					
Onion and shallot	Sow:	•	•				•	•	•	•			
	Plant sets:	•						•	•			•	•
	seedlings:	•										•	•
	Harvest:	•	•	•	•	•							•
Parsnip	Sow:	•	•				•	•	•	•			
	Harvest:							•	•	•	•	•	•
Peas	Sow:	•					•	•				•	•
	Harvest:	•	•						•	•			
Peppers	Sow:	•											•
	Plant:		•	•	•								
	Harvest:				•	•	•	•	•				
Potato	Chit:										•	•	
	Plant:	•					•					•	•
	Harvest:			•	•					•			
Radish	Sow:	•					•	•	•			•	•
	Harvest:	•	•						•	•	•		•
Rhubarb not recommended													
Rutabaga	Sow:				•	•	•						
	Harvest:							•	•	•	•	•	•
Snap beans	Sow:		•	•	•	•	•						
	Harvest:			•	•	•	•	•	•				
Spinach	Sow:	•					•	•	•	•			•
	Harvest:	•	•						•	•			
Summer squash	Sow:		•	•	•	•	•						
	Harvest:			•	•	•	•	•	•				
Sweet potato	Transplant slips:		•	•	•								
	Harvest:					•	•	•					
Tomato	Sow:	•	•										•
	Plant:		•	•		•							
	Harvest:				•	•	•	•	•				
Turnip	Sow:	•	•				•	•	•				•
	Harvest:	•	•	•					•	•	•	•	
Winter squash and pumpkin	Sow:	•	•			•							
	Harvest:					•	•	•	•	•			

| Fruit production chart

Knowing when each crop is likely to be available, either fresh or from storage, will help you plan for the inevitable gluts and shortages. Most fruit is ready to harvest in late summer and early fall, but by freezing, canning, and preserving the surplus produce you can enjoy your bounty for much longer.

+ from storage • fresh

	EarlySp	MidSp	LateSp	EarlySu	MidSu	LateSu	EarlyA	MidA	LateA	EarlyW	MidW	LateW
Apples	+					•	•	•+	•+	+	+	+
Apricots					•	•						
Blackberries					•	•	•					
Black currants					•	•						
Blueberries				•	•	•						
Cherries				•	•	•						
Cranberries							•	•				
Figs						•	•					
Gooseberries				•	•							
Grapes							•	•	•			
Kiwi							•	•+	+			
Lingonberries							•	•				
Nectarines					•	•	•					
Peaches					•	•	•					
Pears	+					•	•	•+	+	+	+	+
Plums					•	•						
Quinces							•	•+	+	+	+	+
Raspberries				•	•	•	•					
Red currants				•	•							
Strawberries		•	•	•	•	•	•	•				
White currants				•	•							

| Dealing with pests and diseases

When a pest or disease strikes, early detection and prompt action can make all the difference. It is important to inspect plants regularly, particularly at the times you know pests and diseases are likely to occur—for example, the reddish eggs of squash bugs can often be spotted on the underside of squash leaves beginning in late spring, and potato blight can be expected in warm, wet weather in summer. Walk among your plants and look them over frequently. Do not forget to check the undersides of the leaves because this is often where a pest or disease symptom can first be spotted.

When you do identify a problem, decisions need to be made. Is the effect likely to be serious enough to warrant taking action? Sometimes a small amount of damage can be tolerated if you think it is unlikely to get much worse. At other times, however, it is vital to act swiftly— give a cluster of cabbage white butterfly eggs or tiny, newly hatched caterpillars on the underside of a cabbage leaf a week or two and they will reduce the plant to a tattered skeleton.

The next decision to be made is what type of control method you are going to use. Simple, nonchemical controls can be tried first; if these fail to overcome the problem you might then want to consider using a commercial pest or disease control product. Organic gardeners need not feel that all pest and disease control products are unsuitable for their use; increasing numbers of products are made from naturally occurring

IRON DEFICIENCY (top) causes leaves to lose their green color, particularly between the veins; it results in stunted growth and reduced yields. It is a common problem on soils with a high pH.

POWDERY MILDEW (above) affects many crops such as cucumber (seen here), squash, beans, and peas, covering plants with a fine powder that can spread quickly. Select resistant varieties whenever possible.

CABBAGE LOOPERS (top) attack cabbage and several other crops, chewing large, ragged holes in the leaves and leaving behind their telltale, greenish black excrement.

FIREBLIGHT ON APPLE (above) is a destructive bacterial disease that also affects pears. Planting resistant varieties and using minimal nitrogen fertilizer are practices that help avoid the disease.

A BEER TRAP *can be used to attract and kill slugs. Another slug control technique is laying boards between crop rows under which slugs will hide during the day. By tipping the boards, slugs can be exposed and killed.*

YOUNG FRUIT TREES *are particularly prone to damage by rabbits—they eat the bark, which can kill the tree. Trees are easily protected by a simple plastic tree guard.*

substances that break down quickly and are perfectly suitable for use in an organically cultivated garden.

Nonchemical control methods

Provided you spot problems early, the nonchemical methods can be very effective. Pinching out and destroying a shoot tip clustered with aphids; hand picking tomato horn worms or slugs; washing aphids off beans with a strong jet of plain water; and removing smut galls from corn before they break open are all useful ways of dealing with problems.

Another good approach is to put up physical barriers to protect plants from attack in the first place—floating row covers can prevent flea beetles from attacking eggplant or brassica crops, and cardboard collars placed around seedlings will prevent cutworm damage.

Chemical controls

Where other methods fail, pesticides can be used to clear pests and diseases from crops. All pesticides must be used as directed—and that means always reading the instructions and following them. Choose the least toxic

option available. Nonpersistent pesticides that break down rapidly after use are often sufficient. You should also time your treatments so that there is minimal risk to beneficial creatures—by not spraying insecticide while plants are flowering, for example.

Prevention and cure

Among the easiest ways to prevent pest and disease problems is to select resistant cultivars of the crops you grow. Barriers, such as floating row covers and bird netting, also prevent infestations.

If a pest problem is encountered and identified, insecticides may be necessary; fungicides, on the other hand, are sometimes used as a preventive measure before symptoms appear.

Biological control—using one organism to control another—is an effective way to deal with many pest problems. There are specific biological controls for a wide range of pests, including spider mites, aphids, caterpillars, slugs, and vine weevils. In addition to predatory or parasitic insects, biological controls include predatory or parasitic mites, nematodes, and bacteria.

| Vegetable pests and diseases chart

Some vegetable crops are far more prone to pest and disease problems than others, but growing all crops in the best possible conditions will help to limit the amount of damage that occurs. When using chemical controls, always take particular care to observe the minimum time between spraying and harvesting.

Pests	Symptoms	Control
Aphids	Soft-bodied insects, usually green or black, that cluster on new growth of many crops in spring and summer. Growth is weakened; aphids can also spread viral diseases.	Spray with a botanical insecticide such as pyrethrin, insecticidal soaps, or horticultural oils. Ladybeetles, both nymphs and adults, are natural predators of aphids and often provide effective control.
Asparagus beetle	Small, reddish brown, striped or spotted beetles and dark gray larvae eat asparagus foliage and stems.	Hand pick both in spring or use floating row covers from early spring through harvest.
Cabbage worms and cabbage loopers	Black and yellow cabbage worms and green cabbage loopers feed voraciously, severely damaging plants.	Hand pick caterpillars and crush eggs. Use floating row covers. Bacillus thuringiensis (Bt) and Trichogramma wasps are biological controls.
Carrot rust fly	As well as carrots, vegetables such as celery, parsnip, and parsley may also be affected. Larvae mine the roots and make them vulnerable to rot.	Rotate crops. Use floating row covers to keep adults away. Avoid handling foliage as the scent attracts flies. Grow resistant varieties.
Colorado potato beetle	Both the black-and-yellow-striped beetle and the plump, orange larvae feed on leaves of potatoes, tomatoes, eggplants, and peppers, weakening plants and reducing yields.	To prevent infestations, rotate crops and use floating row covers. Hand pick adults and remove yellow egg clusters from the underside of leaves.
Cutworm	Caterpillars live below soil, severing tops of young plants from the roots and eating holes in root crops. Affects many transplanted crops.	Search the soil near damaged plants and destroy the caterpillars. Use barrier collars around seedlings.
Flea beetle	Tiny, black beetles eat characteristic, small, round holes in the foliage of cabbage-family crops, eggplants, and other crops. The beetles jump like fleas when disturbed.	Spray heavy attacks with pyrethrins. Clear crop debris at the end of the season.
Harlequin bug	Both the larvae and the shield-shaped, red-and-black adult infest brassica crops, eggplants, and potato. They damage by sucking plant juices, causing leaves to shrivel and turn brown.	Hand pick bugs and their striped, barrel-shaped eggs. The adults overwinter on and under crop debris, so practice good sanitation and crop rotation.
Mexican bean beetle	These black-spotted, orange beetles lay masses of orange eggs that hatch into yellow-orange larvae. Both larvae and adults feed on leaves and pods, weakening and sometimes killing plants.	Remove garden debris to reduce overwintering sites. Use floating row covers. Ladybeetles are effective predators of Mexican bean beetle.
Pea weevil	Dark, ¼in. adults feed on flowers and lay eggs on pods. The larvae enter pods and feed on the seeds.	Remove plant debris after harvest; cultivate the soil at the end of the season, to kill overwintering adults.
Rabbit	Rabbits will eat a wide range of crops, especially young plants, nibbling them to ground level.	Extend fencing underground, to prevent rabbits burrowing beneath it, or use repellents.
Red spider mite	Leaves appear dry and speckled; shoot tips are spun with fine webbing; tiny, green or red-brown mites can be seen, using a hand lens.	Spray with horticultural oils or insecticidal soap, or release ladybeetles, lacewings, or predatory mites for effective biological control.
Slugs and snails	Damage a wide range of crops, especially young seedlings, eating them off at ground level or chewing large holes in leaves.	Remove weeds and debris. Beer traps and hand picking help reduce populations, and copper barriers are effective for repelling slugs and snails.
Squash bug	Grayish tan adults lay large numbers of red eggs that hatch into gray nymphs. Both nymphs and adults cause significant damage from sucking plant juices, often killing the plant.	Remove weeds and crop debris, to minimize overwintering adults. Use floating row covers on young plants until they begin to bloom.
Wireworm	The larvae of click beetles; wireworms damage root crops, especially carrots and potatoes, and eat seedlings off at ground level.	Cultivate the soil to expose the larvae to birds. Harvest potatoes and carrots as soon as they are ready as they are more susceptible in the soil.

Disease	Symptoms	Control
Anthracnose	Fungal disease particularly affecting beans and cucumber. Discolored, sunken patches appear on leaves, stems, pods, and fruit.	Grow resistant varieties. Remove affected parts of plants and get rid of badly affected plants altogether. Practice crop rotation.
Bacterial leaf spot	Affects tomatoes, peppers, and members of the brassica family. Dark brown spots with yellow halos can spread under wet conditions.	Grow resistant varieties and avoid overhead watering.
Botrytis (gray mold)	Fluffy, gray fungus on rotted and damaged plant tissues quickly spreads in cool, damp conditions. Affects many crops, especially squash, melons, and cucumbers. Also affects stored crops.	Remove all plant debris and affected parts promptly. Space plants properly, to provide good air circulation, and mulch to prevent spores from splashing from soil to leaves.
Clubroot	A serious disease of all cabbage-family plants. First signs are usually plants failing to thrive and wilting in hot weather, with swollen, distorted roots. Clubroot likes acidic soil, is long-lived, and easily spread.	Improve drainage on heavy soils and add lime to reduce acidity. Once present, start plants in pots so they have a good rootball when planted out, and earth up stems to encourage new roots to form. Rotate crops.
Corn smut	Most common in hot summers. Some kernels become hugely swollen and deformed and turn gray then burst, to release black, powdery spores.	Pick off affected ears before the spores are released. Destroy infected plant debris and grow corn in a different area next year.
Damping off	Young seedlings collapse at soil level where stems have rotted. Common in seed flats and encouraged by overcrowded conditions.	Sow thinly using sterile growing mix and clean pots and flats; give plenty of light and good ventilation. Avoid overwatering seedlings.
Downy mildew	Causes discolored patches on leaves with fungal growth on the underside. Common on spinach and lettuce, but can affect many crops.	Remove affected foliage. Increase air circulation and keep foliage dry by watering crops from below (drip irrigation or soaker hoses are ideal) rather than using overhead sprinklers.
Early blight	The first symptom of this fungus that attacks tomatoes, peppers, eggplants, and potatoes is spots on older leaves. The spots develop a bulls-eye pattern of concentric rings and eventually leaves shrivel and turn brown. Fruit develops sunken leathery spots.	The fungus is worst in humid conditions, so grow plants at the correct spacing and remove weeds. Stake or cage plants and use mulch, to minimize contact of leaves and fruit with soil. The fungus can be spread by seed, so purchase seed from a reliable source. Rotate crops.
Fusarium wilt	There are many strains of this soil-borne fungus that attack a wide range of crops including asparagus, tomatoes, peas, and cabbage. The first symptom is wilting of plants in hot weather; affected plants usually collapse or shrivel and die once their vascular tissue becomes blocked by the fungus.	Grow resistant varieties. If your plants do become infected you should consider moving the garden to a new location next year, because the fungus remains in the soil for many years, or else grow your plants in containers.
Late blight	Affects potatoes and tomatoes and occurs in warm, humid weather. Leaves rapidly yellow and wilt. Topgrowth soon collapses completely. Potato tubers and tomatoes develop sunken, brown patches of rot.	Plant resistant varieties. Regular sprays of copper fungicide protect crops but won't control blight once present. When found on potatoes, remove and destroy all topgrowth, to prevent the spores from washing down to the tubers.
Onion white rot	White fungal growth at the bulb's base and yellow, wilting leaves. Spores persist in the soil for years.	Destroy affected plants (do not compost) and grow onions in another area in the future.
Parsnip canker	Brown, sunken areas appear on the roots, especially the shoulders. Parsnip canker often begins at a site of injury.	Avoid damaging the tops of roots by cultivation or hoeing. Improve drainage in heavy soils. Avoid very early sowings. Grow resistant varieties.
Potato scab	Tubers develop scabby patches and need thicker peeling; they may not store well. Rutabaga and turnips can be affected. Thrives in alkaline soil.	Do not lime the soil for potatoes and improve light soils with organic matter. Keep plants moist during dry spells. Grow resistant varieties.
Powdery mildew	White, powdery growth on foliage; many plants are susceptible; squash, melons, and cucumbers are often badly affected. Severe infections weaken growth and reduce yield.	Remove affected growth and plant debris. Keep the soil moist, but do not splash water on the foliage.
Viruses	Many crops affected, particularly potatoes and cucurbits. Distorts, marks, and curls foliage. Plants are often severely weakened or killed.	Control sap-sucking pests such as aphids, which spread viruses. Destroy (do not compost) affected plants as soon as they are seen.

| Fruit pests and diseases chart

Listed below are some of the common problems that can affect fruit crops. Some pests and diseases are specific to particular crops while others are more general. Early detection gives the best chance of successful treatment, so inspect plants regularly. Prompt action can often avoid the need to use chemical controls altogether.

Pests	Symptoms	Control
Aphids	Small, soft-bodied insects that feed on shoot tips and leave weakened growth; they can transmit viruses.	Spray with pyrethrins, insecticidal soaps, or horticultural oils. Ladybeetles are natural predators of aphids and can reduce populations to tolerable levels.
Birds	Birds eat many fruits, particularly cherries, blueberries, raspberries, and strawberries. They also peck fruit buds in winter.	Erect taut netting over vulnerable crops in late winter (at bud stage) or as soon as the fruits begin to show color. A fruit cage gives best results.
Codling moth	Larvae tunnel into the center of apples and pears to feed on the core. The tunneling also encourages secondary rotting, so damaged fruits won't store.	Scrape overwintering cocoons from the bark in early spring and spray with horticultural oil. Apply protective sprays of kaolin clay. Erect codling moth traps in late spring, to catch male moths, and apply a botanical insecticide in early and mid summer, before larvae tunnel into fruits.
Japanese beetles	These shiny, green-and-copper beetles feed on the foliage of many fruit crops, particularly grapes. The beetles emerge in late spring or early summer, and persist for about a month.	Hand pick and destroy beetles. Protective applications of kaolin clay help reduce damage.
Mealybug	Figs and grapes are most at risk. White, fluffy insects can be seen in and around leaf axils and midribs. Leaves are covered in a clear, sticky residue, which attracts black, sooty mold.	Spray plants with insecticidal soaps or horticultural oils. Ladybeetles provide excellent control.
Peach tree borer	In additon to peach, this borer attacks nectarine, cherry, plum, and apricot trees, tunneling into the trunk, usually near the soil line, often where the trunk has been wounded.	Prevent borer attacks by covering the base of trees with a protective wrap prior to egg laying, which occurs in summer. Destroy individual borers with a knife or wire inserted into the hole.
Pear psylla	Both adult and nymph feed on the sap of pear leaves, weakening plants and spreading disease.	Spray early in the season with horticultural oil, and protect trees with kaolin clay.
Plum curculio	This weevil attacks most tree fruit, leaving crescent-shaped scars on the fruit surface; the larvae feed on the interior of the fruit, sometimes causing premature fruit drop.	In spring, shake branches over a light-colored sheet, to dislodge adults. Repeat over the course of several weeks. Collect and destroy fruit that drops prematurely. Protect trees with kaolin clay.
Rabbit	Especially damaging to newly planted trees. The outer layer of bark is eaten away, weakening growth. Trees can die if stripping is severe.	Erect rabbit-proof fencing around multiple fruit trees or use spiral guards on individual trees.
Red spider mite	Mainly affects apples and plums, especially in hot, dry summers. Leaves are flecked and mottled with tiny mites on the undersides.	Spray affected plants with horticultural oil or insecticidal soap. Ladybeetles and predatory mites can provide effective control.
San Jose scale	These small, sucking insect infest a wide range of fruit crops, damaging twigs, stems, and fruit and weakening trees. The adult female is gray and scaly; the tiny nymphs grow from yellow to white to black before maturing to gray.	Apply a horticultural oil in late winter or early spring.
Shothole borers	Fruit tree branches become peppered with tiny holes where larvae have tunneled into and fed on the wood. They emerge as adult beetles.	More likely to affect trees that are already weak, so address problems such as lack of pruning or inadequate nutrition. Prune out affected growth.
Tarnished plant bug	Adults and nymphs suck juices from fruit flowers especially apples, peaches, and strawberries. Affected fruit is often small and deformed.	Clean up plant debris and eliminate weeds, to reduce overwintering sites. Cover strawberries with floating row covers before bloom. Spray heavily infested plants with pyrethrin.
Wasps	The high sugar content and odor of ripening fruit attracts wasps, which damage the fruit.	Hang traps in trees and harvest crops as soon as they ripen; don't leave windfalls on the ground.

Disease	Symptoms	Control
Apple scab	This fungal disease causes olive-green to brown spots on leaves and fruit. Leaves drop early and spots on fruit become corky. Trees are weakened and fruit is often small and deformed.	Plant resistant varieties. Fungicides may be necessary for susceptible trees; consult your local extension service for recommendations. Rake leaves and collect fallen fruit in fall.
Bacterial spot	Occurs on peaches, nectarines, apricots, and cherries. Irregular spots appear on leaves and the infected tissue may drop out and leaves may fall prematurely. Spots may cover large areas of the fruit, becoming pitted and cracked, and making the fruit prone to other infection.	Plant resistant varieties. Healthy trees are less susceptible, so maintain vigor and prune to provide adequate air circulation.
Black knot	This fungal disease causes irregular, black swellings on cherry and plum branches, which increase in size each year. Trees are weakened and infected branches eventually die.	Grow resistant varieties and avoid planting near infected trees. Prune out infected branches when trees are dormant.
Botrytis (gray mold)	Fungus most prevalent on soft fruit such as strawberries; is encouraged by high humidity. Fruit and other soft tissues develop a fuzzy, gray covering and then decay.	Space plants appropriately, to encourage air circulation, and water from below rather than overhead. Remove affected plant parts promptly.
Brown rot	Affects all stone fruit. May attack flowers, spurs, and shoots, but is usually first noticed when fruit develops a brown spot that enlarges quickly. A mass of fungal spores may cover fruit. Infected fruit often shrivels and clings to the tree.	Remove affected fruit from the tree and ground and prune out cankered twigs. A regular preventive fungicide program may be required; consult your local extension service for recommendations.
Crown gall	This bacterial disease causes large, woody swellings near the base of the plant or on roots, canes, or branches. It is particularly common on cane fruit such as blackberries and raspberries. Plants may become stunted or produce dry, seedy fruit.	Purchase certified, disease-free stock. Avoid wounding plants and remove affected plants or branches promptly, to prevent the spread of the disease.
Downy mildew	Common on grapes. Irregular, yellow patches on upper leaf surfaces have downy, gray growth on the undersides. Can result in early leaf drop.	Plant resistant varieties. Apply lime-sulfur spray in early spring and prune plants, to increase air circulation. Water from below, not overhead. Remove affected leaves as soon as noticed.
Fireblight	Apple, pear, and quince are susceptible to this bacterial disease. Flowers wilt and die, then the dieback progresses down the stems, giving branches the appearance of having been scorched by fire. Bacterial ooze can sometimes be seen, along with discoloration under bark.	Plant resistant varieties. Avoid high-nitrogen fertilizers. Prune out affected growth well back into healthy tissue, destroying prunings and sterilizing tools after use.
Peach leaf curl	This fungal disease affects peaches, nectarines, and apricots, causing new leaves to display thickened, distorted, and puckered growth. Infected leaves drop prematurely, weakening the tree and reducing yields.	If infection is limited, remove infected leaves as soon as they are noticed. Applications of copper or lime-sulfur fungicides in late fall and winter are effective controls. Follow the label instructions carefully.
Phytophthora	All tree and shrub fruits are at risk, especially on waterlogged soils. Plants weaken and die. Root cores, often stained orange, emit a sour smell.	There is no control for this fungus, so affected plants must be discarded. Improve drainage and avoid replanting on affected soils.
Powdery mildew	Leaves develop a milky white covering, which eventually yellows and dries out the foliage. The skin of affected fruit often cracks.	Plants suffering from drought stress are more susceptible, so keep well mulched and watered. Spray with sulfur or grow resistant varieties.
Replant disease	Most fruit trees are vulnerable when planted on a site previously supporting the same crop. Trees are weak and fail to put on new growth.	Various soil factors are to blame, including fungi and nematodes. Avoid planting the same crop on old sites.
Rust	Attacks most cane fruit, apples, plums, and pears. Orange pustules on leaves in early summer turn brown. Leaves fall early, reducing plant vigor.	Remove and destroy affected leaves promptly and protect with copper-based fungicide on soft fruit (black currant, gooseberry, and raspberry). Grow resistant varieties.
Virus	Stunting, distortion, blistering, or yellowing of foliage are common with viral diseases and yield is often reduced.	Dispose of affected plants. Control virus-spreading pests and purchase certified virus-free stock.

| Resources

The following list of books, organizations, and websites provide information on a variety of topics that will help your kitchen garden grow.

BOOKS

Vegetables and herbs

75 Exciting Vegetables for Your Garden by Jack Staub. Gibbs Smith, 2005.

All New Square Foot Gardening: Grow More in Less Space! by Mel Bartholomew. Cool Springs Press, 2006.

Burpee: The Complete Vegetable & Herb Gardener: A Guide to Growing Your Garden Organically by Karan Davis Cutler. Macmillan, 1997.

Gardening with Heirloom Seeds: Tried-and-True Flowers, Fruits, and Vegetables for a New Generation by Lynn Coulter. University of North Carolina Press, 2006.

Gourmet Vegetables: Smart Tips and Tasty Picks for Gardeners and Gourmet Cooks edited by Anne Raver. Brooklyn Botanic Garden, 2002.

Growing Vegetables West of the Cascades: The Complete Guide to Organic Gardening by Steve Solomon. Sasquatch Books, 2007.

Heirloom Vegetable Gardening by William Woys Weaver. Henry Holt & Co., 1997.

Salad Gardens: Gourmet Greens and Beyond edited by Karen Davis Cutler. Brooklyn Botanic Garden, 1995.

Seed to Seed: Seed Saving and Growing Techniques for Vegetable Gardeners by Suzanne Ashworth and Kent Whealy. Seed Savers Exchange, 2002.

The Family Kitchen Garden: How to Plant, Grow and Cook Together by Karen Liebreich, Jutta Wagner, and Annette Wendland. Timber Press, 2009.

The Herb Gardener: A Guide for All Seasons by Susan McClure. Storey Publishing, 1997.

The Vegetable Gardener's Bible by Edward C. Smith. Storey Publishing, 2009.

Fruit

75 Remarkable Fruits for Your Garden by Jack Staub. Gibbs Smith, 2008.

Blueberries, Cranberries, and Other Vacciniums by Jennifer Trehane. Timber Press, 2009.

Fruits and Berries for the Home Garden by Lewis Hill. Storey Publishing, 1992.

Landscaping with Fruit: Strawberry Ground Covers, Blueberry Hedges, Grape Arbors, and 39 Other Luscious Fruits to Make Your Yard an Edible Paradise by Lee Reich. Storey Publishing, 2009.

The Berry Grower's Handbook by Barbara L. Bowling. Timber Press, 2005.

The Grape Grower: A Guide to Organic Viticulture by Lon Rombough. Chelsea Green, 2002.

Uncommon Fruits for Every Garden by Lee Reich. Timber Press, 2004.

Techniques, practices, and problem solving

McGee & Stuckey's Bountiful Container: Create Container Gardens of Vegetables, Herbs, Fruits, and Edible Flowers by Rose Marie Nichols McGee and Maggie Stuckey. Workman Publishing, 2002.

Natural Insect Control: The Ecological Gardener's Guide to Foiling Pests edited by Warren Schultz. Brooklyn Botanic Garden, 1994.

Rodale's Vegetable Garden Problem Solver by Fern Marshall Bradley. Rodale Books, 2007.

Root Cellaring: Natural Cold Storage of Fruits & Vegetables by Nancy Bubel. Storey Publishing, 1991.

The Complete Garden Compost Guide by Barbara Pleasant and Deborah L. Martin. Storey Publishing, 2008.

The Veggie Gardener's Answer Book: Solutions to Every Problem You'll Ever Face, Answers to Every Question You'll Ever Ask by Barbara W. Ellis. Storey Press, 2008.

ORGANIZATIONS

American Horticultural Society
7931 East Boulevard Drive
Alexandria, VA 22308
(703) 768-5700
www.ahs.org

City Farmer's
Urban Agriculture Notes
City Farmer—Canada's Office
of Urban Agriculture
Box 74567, Kitsilano RPO
Vancouver, B.C. V6K 4P4 Canada
(604) 685-5832
www.cityfarmer.org

Herb Society of America
9019 Kirtland Chardon Road
Kirtland, OH 44094
(440) 256-0514
www.herbsociety.org

National Gardening Association
1100 Dorset Street
South Burlington, VT 05403
(802) 863-5251
www.garden.org/home

Seed Savers Exchange
3094 North Winn Road
Decorah, IA 52101
(563) 382-5990
www.seedsavers.org

WEBSITES

Apple Journal
www.applejournal.com/index.htm

Avant-Gardening:
Creative Organic Gardening
www.avant-gardening.com

Backyard Fruit Growers
www.sas.upenn.edu/~dailey/
byfg.html\

Container Vegetable Gardening
http://ohioline.osu.edu/
hyg-fact/1000/1647.html

Cornell Guide
to Growing Fruit at Home
www.gardening.cornell.edu/fruit/
homefruit.html

Growing Herbs in the Home Garden
www.wvu.edu/~agexten/hortcult/
herbs/ne208hrb.htm

Growing Small Fruits
in the Home Garden
http://cru.cahe.wsu.edu/
CEPublications/eb1640/eb1640.html

Harvest to Table
www.harvestwizard.com/

Home Orchard Society
www.homeorchardsociety.org/

Kitchen Gardeners International
http://kitchengardeners.org/

Mid-Atlantic Regional Fruit Loop
www.caf.wvu.edu/Kearneysville/
fruitloop.html

Midwest Fruit Explorers
www.midfex.org/

National Climatic Data Center
Freeze/Frost Maps
www.ncdc.noaa.gov/oa/climate/
freezefrost/frostfreemaps.html

National Gardening Association
Food Gardening Guide
www.garden.org/foodguide/browse

North American Fruit Explorers
www.nafex.org/

Old Farmer's Almanac Frost Chart
for United States
www.almanac.com/content/
frost-chart-united-states#chart

Orange Pippin
www.orangepippin.com/

The California Backyard Orchard
http://homeorchard.ucdavis.edu/

Vegetable Varieties for Gardeners
A Citizen Science Program from
the Department of Horticulture,
Cornell University
http://vegvariety.cce.cornell.edu/

| Glossary

Annual A plant that completes its entire life cycle in a single growing season.

Anther Portion of the stamen (male part of the flower) that produces pollen.

Balanced fertilizer A fertilizer containing equal percentages of nitrogen, phosphorus, and potassium.

Band sowing Sowing in a wide row. Instead of planting in a single file, seed is planted within the band, leaving the appropriate space between seeds in each direction (also called wide row sowing).

Bare root A tree or shrub lifted from the open ground for sale during the dormant season, with its roots bare of soil.

Basal cluster The lower cluster of leaves on a branch or stem of a plant.

Biennial bearing When fruit is borne every two years instead of each year.

Biological control A method of controlling pests using predators or parasites instead of chemicals.

Blanching Covering a plant to exclude light, to prevent it from turning green; often done with cauliflower and chicory.

Bleeding The loss of sap from plant tissues after damage or pruning.

Bolting The premature production of flowers and seed which, in the case of lettuce, for example, makes the leaves taste bitter.

Botanical pesticide A product derived from plants, such as pyrethrum or sabadilla, which is used to control pests on garden plants.

Botrytis Fungal disease most commonly seen as gray mold, usually attacking decaying or damaged parts of a plant.

Bramble Any shrubby member of the genus Rubus, such as blackberry and raspberry.

Bud A protrusion on a stem containing embryonic leaves and/or flowers. Fruit buds contain flowers and they often differ in shape from vegetative buds.

Budding Grafting using a vegetative bud as the scion.

Cane Straight stem of certain fruit such as raspberries and blackberries.

Catch crop A fast-maturing crop for growing between the harvesting of one crop and the growing of the next.

Chilling injury Damage to plants or crops resulting from exposure to cold—but not freezing—temperatures.

Chilling requirement A period of cold needed by certain plants to break their dormancy.

Clay Small particles of soil with a diameter of less than 0.002 mm.

Cloche A low glass or plastic covering used to protect young plants from adverse weather conditions early or late in the season. *See also* Hot cap.

Cold frame An unheated outdoor enclosure for starting plants from seed or cuttings, acclimatizing young (often tender) plants to outdoor conditions, or growing crops beyond their normal growing season.

Collar A circle of cardboard, plastic, copper, or other material that is placed around a plant as a barrier to protect it from pests such as cutworms and slugs.

Complete fertilizer A fertilizer that contains nitrogen, phosphorus, and potassium. It may also include micronutrients.

Cool-season crop Plants that thrive in cooler temperatures but tend to bolt (go to seed) in warm temperatures. They are typically grown in spring, planted before the last frost, or in fall. In mild-winter regions, cool-season crops are often grown through winter.

Cordon A tree or bush trained against a support to form a single rod or stem. U-shaped cordons have two stems. The stems of oblique cordons are set at an angle.

Cover crop A crop grown on garden soil to prevent erosion. It is often cut and turned into the soil, to add nutrients and organic matter. It may be grown between crop rows or between cropping seasons. *See also* Green manure.

Crop rotation Growing annual vegetables in a different site each season, primarily to prevent the buildup of pests and diseases and to maintain nutrients in the soil.

Cross-pollination The transfer of pollen between two separate plants of the same species.

Cultivar A word derived from the contraction of 'cultivated variety' to specify that a variety arose in cultivation rather than in the wild. In this book, 'variety' and 'cultivar' are used interchangeably.

Cuttings Vegetative portions (stems, roots, leaves) that are removed from a plant for use in propagating new plants. Plants reproduced from cuttings will be genetically identical to the parent plant.

Damping off A disease caused by any of several fungi that destroys emerging seedlings by rotting the stems at soil level.

Day-neutral plant A plant that will produce flowers regardless of the day length.

Determinate growth Growth that is limited, usually by the opening of a terminal flower that arrests the growth of the stem—for example, determinate tomatoes.

Dieback The death of tissue at the tips of stems or ends of branches, usually as the result of disease or low temperatures.

Downy mildew Fungal disease causing discoloring and blotches on the upper leaf surface, most commonly on young plants and those grown with poor air circulation.

Drill Groove or furrow for planting seed.

Drip irrigation An efficient watering system that uses a series of pipes, tubing, and emitters, to deliver water, and sometimes fertilizer, slowly and directly to the root area of the plant. Little water is lost to evaporation or runoff. Also called trickle irrigation.

Earthing up Drawing up soil around a plant, for example potatoes, to prevent the tubers from turning green but also to help anchor some crops in the ground and prevent them from rocking in the wind.

Ericaceous potting mix Lime-free potting medium with a pH below 7, suitable for plants such as blueberries that require acidic soil.

Espalier A fruit tree or bush trained against a support with an upright trunk, from which horizontal lateral branches arise, to create a tiered effect.

Eye Dormant bud from which a new shoot will grow under favorable conditions.

F1 hybrid First-generation plants or seeds that have been bred under strict conditions from specific parental lines to create a crop that is uniform and possesses distinct, desirable characteristics. Seeds gathered from F1 hybrids will not come true, so you will need to buy fresh stock each year.

Family tree A fruit tree in which several different varieties have been grafted on to the same rootstock. It is useful in a small garden where two or more varieties are required for pollination, but there is space for only one tree.

Fan A fruit tree or bush trained against a support, with branches splayed out to form a fan shape.

Feathered maiden A young fruit tree, usually in its first year after grafting, with branches along its length. Each branch is sometimes referred to as a feather. *See also* Maiden whip.

Festooning The practice of training fruit tree branches horizontally in order to increase the yields of fruit.

Filament Portion of the stamen (male part of the flower) that supports the anther.

Forcing The practice of accelerating plant growth and fruit production by manipulating the growing environment.

Freestanding A fruit bush or tree grown without any support such as a stake or fence.

Frost heaving The uplifting of a plant from the soil caused by alternating freezing and thawing of soil moisture. Exposed roots are often damaged by wind, sun, and low temperatures.

Frost pocket A low spot in the terrain where cold air tends to settle.

Gall An irregular growth, typically caused by a disease, insect, or mite.

Germination The active growth of the embryo of a seed, beginning the life of a new plant.

Grafting Method of propagation whereby a vegetative portion (bud or stem) of one plant (the scion) is joined to the roots of another (the rootstock) to become a single plant. Is common with fruit trees.

Green manure A crop grown in soil for the purpose of cutting it down and turning it under, to add organic matter to the soil. *See also* Cover crop.

Hardening off The process of acclimatizing plants raised in a greenhouse or indoors to outdoor conditions by gradual exposure to lower temperatures.

Hardwood cutting A vegetative method of plant propagation using woody stems.

Heading back Pruning cut that removes the end of a branch or stem, reducing its length.

Heeling in Planting in a temporary location, for example when soil conditions aren't suitable for the permanent planting of a fruit tree or when crops such as leeks are lifted before freezing weather and brought to a position nearer the house.

Horticultural oil A pesticide—derived from highly refined petroleum or from plants—that is used to smother pests such as aphids, scales, and mites.

Hot cap Cone, usually made of plastic or heavy waxed paper, to protect a young plant from cold temperatures.

Humus The dark substance that represents the end result of organic matter decomposition; the organic content of soil that helps provide plant nutrients and improves soil structure.

Indeterminate growth Growth that has the potential to continue until disease or environmental conditions kill the plant. Indeterminate tomatoes, for example, often continue to grow and produce fruit until they are killed by frost.

Insecticidal soap A pesticide that contains a mild soap solution that kills insects with which it comes into contact. It is not selective, so its use should be targeted to prevent injury to beneficial insects.

Intercropping Growing a fast-maturing crop between slower-growing ones.

King fruit The fruit at the center of a cluster.

Larva The immature stage of certain insects including moths (such as cabbage worms and loopers), beetles, and flies.

Lateral A stem or branch arising from a main stem or leader. See also Sublateral.

Leader A primary branch from which lateral branches are produced. Central leaders form the main stem or trunk at the center of the plant.

Loam Soil that is made up of sand, silt, and clay as well as significant amounts of humus, that is usually fertile, well drained, and easy to work.

Maiden whip A young fruit tree, usually in its first year after grafting, without branches. See also Feathered maiden.

Mulch A covering over the soil, often of well-rotted compost, manure, straw, leafmold, or wood chips. Its many advantages include conserving moisture by reducing evaporation; moderating soil temperatures both in summer and winter; blocking out weeds; preventing soil crusting and compaction; and reducing erosion. As organic mulches decompose, they also improve soil structure. Black plastic and gravel mulches can also be used but won't improve the soil structure.

Nematodes Very small (often microscopic) animals that can cause diseases in plants (and animals). Beneficial nematodes feed on plant pests and can be employed as a biological control.

Nymph Immature stage of certain insects such as aphids and scales.

Organic matter Material derived from something that was once living, either animal or plant, in any stage of decomposition. It is added to soil to improve structure, and it may contribute nutrients.

Offset Young plant attached to the parent, which can be separated and grown on.

Ovary Portion of the flower that, if fertilized, eventually develops the fruit and seeds.

pH A scale that is used to measure acidity and alkalinity of soil. The scale ranges from zero (acid) to 14 (alkaline), with pH7 being neutral. Most soil is between pH4 and pH9.

Perennial A plant that lives for several years.

Pinching Removal of the growing tip by nipping it off with finger and thumb, encouraging the growth of sideshoots.

Pips Apple or pear seeds

Pistil The female portion of a flower consisting of the stigma, style, and ovary.

Pollen Grains that contain the male sex cells.

Pollination The transfer of pollen from the anther to the stigma, which, if successful, leads to flower fertilization and fruit set.

Polytunnel A structure made of polyethylene that is supported by a frame, to provide plants with protection from cold and wind.

Powdery mildew Fungal disease creating a powderlike, white to grayish white cover on the leaf surface.

Puddling in The practice of applying a heavy soaking of water at the time of transplanting seedlings.

Pupa The stage of development of certain insects between the larva and adult stages.

Red spider mite Tiny, sap-sucking, web-forming mites often found in hot, dry conditions.

Rootstock The lower part of a grafted fruit tree or bush onto which the scion, or top part, is joined. The type of rootstock chosen controls the vigor of the tree or bush.

Runners Surface-running stems that grow from a parent plant (such as a strawberry). Runners bear young plants at the end, which root into the soil.

Sand A coarse soil particle with a diameter of between 0.05–2 mm.

Scion The above-ground part of a grafted fruit tree or bush, which is joined to the rootstock.

Self fertile (or self fruitful) A plant that is able to pollinate its own flowers.

Self infertile (or self sterile) A plant that is unable to pollinate its own flowers and depends on the presence of another tree of the same or closely related species nearby.

Sidedressing Application of fertilizer either around individual plants or along a row of plants, usually during the growing season.

Sideshoot A stem that arises frm teh side of a main branch.

Silt A soil particle that is larger than clay but smaller than sand, ranging from 0.002 mm to 0.05 mm in diameter.

Slow-release fertilizer A fertilizer formulated to release nutrients over an extended period.

Soaker hose A hose with pinprick holes that allow moisture to seep out of the full length of the hose, for irrigation.

Softwood cuttings A method of vegetative plant propagation using young and soft, unripened growth.

Soil crusting This occurs when the soil surface dries out and forms a layer that resists water penetration.

Spot sow Technique for planting seed directly in the garden by placing several (usually three) seeds together in one spot (station) in the row with the appropriate crop spacing between each station. Once the seeds germinate, they are thinned to a single plant per station. This is commonly done with larger seeds.

Spur A short branch or network of branches of a fruit tree, bush, or vine. Spurs bear an abundance of fruit buds and therefore carry the flowers and fruit.

Spur thinning Pruning to thin out a congested system of fruit spurs. This encourages good air flow around the fruit, deterring pest and disease attack and encouraging even ripening and fruit size.

Stamen The male portion of a flower consisting of the anther and the filament.

Standard A fruit tree or bush grown on an upright, leafless trunk.

Station sow *see* Spot sow.

Stigma The portion of the pistil (female part of a flower) that receives the pollen. *See also* Pollination.

Stone fruit Trees or shrubs belonging to the cherry family, including peaches, nectarines, and plums.

Straw A material commonly used for mulching vegetables, consisting of the stems of a grain crop that are cut after the grain has been harvested.

Strig A cluster or string of currants.

Style Portion of the pistil (female part of the flower) that supports the stigma.

Sublateral A sideshoot originating from a lateral branch.

Successional sowing Making sowings at regular intervals, to ensure a continuous fresh supply of the crop.

Sucker Any shoot that arises directly from the root or rootstock of a woody plant.

Tendrils Slender modified leaves or stems that are produced by certain vining plants, such as peas and grapes, for attaching to a support.

Thinning Removing some seedlings or plants to ensure that those left are evenly spaced with enough room to grow and access adequate light and nutrients. Also refers to removing some flower or fruit buds, to improve the size and quality of the fruit that is left.

Tilth The condition of soil with respect to cultivation. Friability.

Tip layering A method of plant propagation in which tips of stems are made to root while still attached to the main plant.

Topdressing Fertilizer applied to the soil after planting.

Transplanting Moving a seedling or plant from one place to another—for example, from a small to a larger pot or to outside into the garden.

Trickle irrigation see Drip irrigation.

True leaves The first set of leaves on a seedling, after the appearance of the seed leaves.

Variety *see* Cultivar.

Virus A submicroscopic causal agent of plant diseases (also animal diseases).

Warm-season crop A crop that thrives in warm weather but is sensitive to cold. Such crops are generally planted after all danger of frost has passed.

Water shoot Young branch that arises directly from a bare stem or trunk of a fruit tree.

Weed Any plant that is growing where it isn't wanted.

Wide row sowing see Band sowing.

Sources

SEEDS AND PLANTS

W. Atlee Burpee & Company
300 Park Drive
Warminster, PA 18974
(800) 888-1447
www.burpee.com

Baker Creek Heirloom Seeds
2278 Baker Creek Road
Mansfield, MO 65704
(417) 924-8917
www.rareseeds.com

Indiana Berry & Plant Company
2811 US 31
Plymouth, IN 46563
(800) 295-2226
www.inberry.com

Johnny's Selected Seeds
955 Benton Avenue
Winslow, ME 04901-2601
(877) 564-6697
www.johnnyseeds.com

Miller Nurseries
5060 West Lake Road
Canandaigua, NY 14424-8904
(800) 836-9630
www.millernurseries.com

Nourse Farms
41 River Road
South Deerfield, MA 01373
(413) 665-2658
www.noursefarms.com

Raintree Nursery
391 Butts Road
Morton, WA 98356
(800) 391-8892
www.raintreenursery.com

Renee's Garden
6060A Graham Hill Road
Felton, CA 95018
(888) 880-7228
www.reneesgarden.com

Southern Exposure Seed Exchange
P.O. Box 460
Mineral, VA 23117
(540) 894-9480
www.southernexposure.com

Stark Bro's Nursery
P.O. Box 1800
Louisiana, MO 63353
www.starkbros.com

Territorial Seed Company
P.O. Box 158
Cottage Grove, OR 97424
(800) 626-0866
www.territorialseed.com/

The Cook's Garden
P.O. Box C5030
Warminster, PA 18974
www.cooksgarden.com/

Tomato Growers Supply Company
P.O. Box 60015
Fort Meyers, FL 33906
(888) 478-7333
www.tomatogrowers.com

GARDEN SUPPLIES AND TOOLS

Clean Air Gardening
2266 Monitor Street
Dallas, TX 75207
(214) 819-9500
www.cleanairgardening.com

Gardeners Supply Company
128 Intervale Road
Burlington, VT 05401
(800) 427-3363
www.gardeners.com

Gardens Alive!
5100 Schenly Place
Lawrenceburg, IN 47025
(513) 354-1482
www.gardensalive.com

Lee Valley Tools
P.O. Box 1780
Ogdensburg, NY 13669-6780
(800) 871.8158
www.leevalley.com

A.M. Leonard Inc.
241 Fox Drive
Piqua, Ohio 45356-0816
(800) 543-8955
www.amleo.com

Planet Natural
1612 Gold Avenue
Bozeman, MT 59715
(800) 289-6656
www.planetnatural.com

Index

Page numbers in *italics*:
indicate a caption to its picture
or a picture on its own.
Page numbers in **bold**:
indicate a boxed entry.

Photographic Acknowledgments

Key: a above, b below, c centre l left, r right

AHS 16, 30r, 33, 105a, 203ar & br, 226, 275, 299

ARS-USDA Bob Nichols 201b; Jerry A Payne 196; Keith Weller 198, 230

Bonnie Plants 206, 261

Bugwood.org Charles Averre 286bl; David Cappaert 286ar; Howard F Schwartz 191b, 286al; University of Georgia Plant Pathology Archive 286br

California Pear Advisory Board 237

Clive Simms 200r

Fotolia AlcelVision 225b; Anne Kitzman 11a; b.neeser 122; Birgit Kutzera bc; Canoneer 183l; cherie 244r; contrastwerkstatt 194a; eAlisa 172b; Edsweb 43a; Elena Elisseeva 182a; Elena Moiseeva 183r, 195, 199r; Eric Pothier 186; Foto sapiens 204-5; fotosav 108; Florin Capilnean 150; Hamiza Bakirci bl; Hazel Proudlove 165; Henryk Dybka bl; Inta Eihmane 117; Ionescu Bogdan 194b; Kerioak 228a; klikk 80; lamaka 147a; Lezh 189a, 272; Maria Brzostowska 222a; Mario cr; Monkey Business 229b; Nano 163; onepony 134a; Pavel Bernshtam 100a; PJGCC 223a; ril 68l; Robyn Mackenzie 149al; Rudolf Ullrich 166a; Simon@naffarts.co.uk 188; Sir Henry 148; Stephen Vickers 260b; Stocksnapper XXcc; superfood 135br, 167b; Swetlana Wall 134b; tadamee 135cl; Thomas Oswald 236b; Ukr_photographer 182b, Xiaodong Ye 152a

Forrest and Kim Starr 30r, 138, 145, 172a, 240

GAP Photos Carole Drake/Sir Harold Hillier Gardens 175ar; Fiona Lea 235l; Friedrich Strauss 15b, 211; Graham Strong 192r; John Glover 200l; Rice/Buckland 99l, 125a, 228b

Garden Collection Nicola Stocken Tomkins 111

Gardener's Supply 95a, 216b

iStockphoto Dleonis 9

Jerry Pavia 32

Johnny's Selected Seeds 141l, 149a, 210a, 243ac, al, bl, 270a & c

KiwiBerry Organics 201a

Laurie Evans 39, 45, 69, 92, 113, 259

Lee Reich 133l, 158b, 202b, 203l

Marianne Majerus Garden Images Marianne Majerus 184-5; Marianne Majerus/Joanna Crane 106-7; Marianne Majerus/Helen Pitel 160-1; 264-5

Mark Winwood 60b, 199l

Monrovia Nurseries 152b, 159l

National Garden Bureau 91

Octopus Publishing Group Jane Sebire 8, 18 all, 25, 31l, 40 all, 43b, 47, 48b, 49, 70, 86, 87, 88b, 90, 109, 118l, 119a, 121a, 139 all, 140l, 141r, 144r, 164bl & r, 169a & b, 171, 173a, 174b, 177, 178, 179, 181, 187, 189b, 191a, 207a, 208r, 220l & r, 222b; 223; Stephen Robson 2, 11b, 12, 15a, 23, 28, 29a, 60b, 62-3, 67r, 72, 75bl, 82-3, 94b, 96, 104, 105b, 112, 115, 157, 170, 174a, 175 al, ac, bl & br, 180, 190a & b, 223b, 225, 238-9, 256-7; Torie Chugg 17, 20, 21a & c, 24r, 26, 27, 29, 31, 51, 52, 55, 58, 59b, 75, 77, 78, 93, 97, 98a, 99r, 100b, 101, 102, 128, 129, 130, 131, 132, 151, 153r, 154, 156, 197b & c, 214b, 231, 232, 232, 233r, 246-252, 254-5, 262r, 263a, 277, 287

Photolibrary/Garden Picture Library Christopher Gallagher 53; David C Phillips 98b; Gary K Smith 48a; Howard Rice 30l; Juliette Wade 123br; Linda Burgess 229a; Michael Howes 68r; Stephen Hamilton 73b

Renee's Garden 224

RHS Collection 41bl & br, 123ar, 273cr & bc; Harry Smith Collection 123cl;

Herbarium 217c

Rick Wetherbee 149bs

Rita Pelczar 67l, 214a, 230b

Shutterstock 7716430100 146; 8781118005 173b; 79; Alex Kuzovlev 13; Andrew Chambers 21b; Anna Chelnokova 65; Anobis 36-7; Anthony Pham 212; Ariy 166b; ason 93r; Bochkarev Photography 74; chudoba 10; David Scheuber 94a; Denis and Yulia Pogostins 88a; Dewitt 46; Dianne Maire 236a; Dusan Zidar 73a; Elnur 133r; Evron 285; Geanina Bechea 26a; George Green 176; George Vollmy 207b; Heather Barr 218-9; Inc 242b; Ingor Normann 155; James Doss 124; Jasna 135al, 164a; Jim Mills 119r; Jirsak 76; Johanna Goodyear 71; Karin Lau 135ac; khwi 95b; Krzysztof Slusarczyk 260a; KSLight 244l; LianeM 24l, 159r; Lindsay Noechel 197a; liseykina 35; Liz Van Steenburgh 193; Maciek Baran 81; Marek Pawluczuk 85; Mark Yuill 262l; Nic Neish 118r, Nicola Keegan 89; Peter Polak 209; Pontus Edenberg 217b; Rachell Coe 103; Rimantas Abromas 216a; Robert Taylor 208; Sebastien Burel 215; sevenke 144l; Sharon Kingston 140r; ShutterVision 158a; slowfish 110, 221; Smileus 253; Stefan Fierros 114, 242a; Stephen Aaron Rees 136-7; T.W. 147br; Teodor Ostojic 167a; Tomas Smolek 153l; Tutti Frutti 213; Vera Bogaerts 6b; Veronica 135ar; vesilvio 6a; Vitelle 241

Suttons Seeds 41a & bc, 123bc

Thompson & Morgan www.thompson-morgan.com 123al

USDA-NRCS Plants Database Ted Bodner 202a

W Atlee Burpee Company 123ac, cc, cr & bl, 243al, 273 all except cr and bc